D-Tour

My Unexpected Journey to Joy through PTSD

Gregory A. Wirt

Interior Image Credit: photo of author and dog Lucy by Amy Wirt

Balboa Press books may be ordered through booksellers or by contacting:

Balboa Press
A Division of Hay House
1663 Liberty Drive
Bloomington, IN 47403
www.balboapress.com.au
1 (877) 407-4847

Print information available on the last page.

ISBN: 978-1-5043-1663-7 (sc)
ISBN: 978-1-5043-1664-4 (e)

Balboa Press rev. date: 02/05/2019

EPIGRAPH

*"You know how it is.
Sometimes we plan a trip to one place,
but something takes us to another."*

– Rumi (1207-1273)

In Memory Of

Rodger Bruce Miles (1947-1968)

My dear cousin, close friend, and practical joker; a Purple Heart veteran 'grunt' of Vietnam 1965-66; K-Company 3rd Battalion 3rd Division U.S. Marine Corp around Phu Bai, Da Nang, and Chu Lai. He survived his injuries, only to leave us too soon after returning to civilian life – all before he could celebrate his birthday for the 21st time.

Rodger Marine recruit

Stanley Keith Haas (1938-2012)

My great friend with a never-ending supply of jokes, mostly good. Stan served with the 506th Signal Troop in the Australian Army in Vietnam May 1966 to April 1967. He dealt with his injuries received there that adversely impacted his life, in his own quiet way, with never a complaint. He lived a life of service, in and out of uniform, through his successful mission of putting a smile on the face of the people he met.

Stan with wife Helga 31 Dec 2011

Marguerite Amanda Wirt (17 September 1950 – 6 May 1953)

Sweet sister – every memory a happy one.

Lawrence (Larry) Henry Bennett (20 July 1948 – 15 June 1960)

Dear friend - like a brother.

You both brought me so much happiness in the curious exploration of life in the innocence of our youth. You taught me much about love, friendship, and fun in our togetherness. The essence of your being lives on with me in wonderful memories and feelings.

The reasons for your tragic departures defies my human understanding. Inadvertently, I learned the pain of sudden separation and loss of unrealised treasures - through which then, the ability to feel compassion for all the others who also held you both so dear to them. The depth of those wounds created a scale of discernment for the contrasting joy

I could eventually recover, which I perhaps would not have been able to fully appreciate otherwise.

Indeed, you taught me a greater awareness of the preciousness of life itself in each present moment. So, in my short time with each of you, *you taught me some of life's greatest lessons*. Yes, again, *the essence of your being lives on with me in wonderful memories and feelings! Thank you!*

In Tribute

Over the years I had visited many war memorials and monuments, particularly for Vietnam Veterans – New York City, Sydney, Canberra, Melbourne, Washington D.C., Angel Fire New Mexico, Missoula, Montana – to pay tribute to my fellow women and men who gave service to our countries and to those that paid the ultimate price with their lives. A bit of a soft touch for an 'old' warrior, I am always affected by the experience. Feeling blessed for being one of the lucky ones.

Sculpture created by Deborah Coperhaven honoring Vietnam veterans Rose Park, Missoula, MT

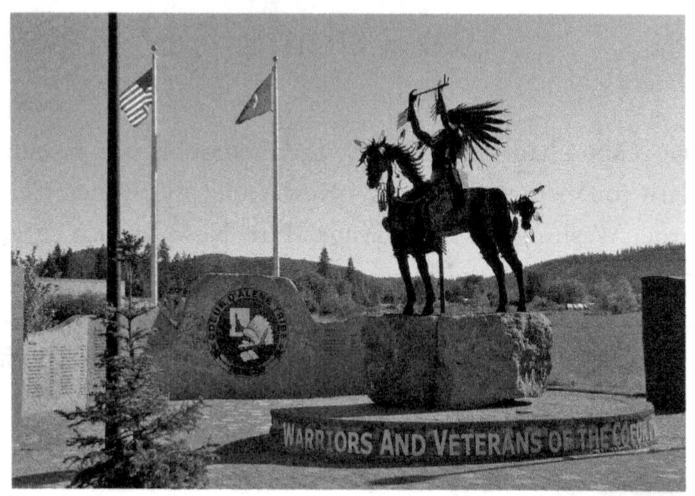

Coeur d'alene tribe monument to Vietnam vets near Post Falls, ID

Introduction

Do you ever just sit in *awe* of this world? I do. How can it be so *full of wonder* – *'devastatingly beautiful'* – yet at that very instant, if I allow myself, to be *full of wonder* at how it can be so *'devastatingly awful'*? Same words, with opposite visions viewed with the flick of a switch through my perception and focus, leaving me with very different emotions.

As a youth, I couldn't fully realise and therefore fully appreciate the amazing life I was born into. Yes, to some degree, but not totally. As I can look back with the luxury of hindsight, I was just so blessed in so many ways, despite whatever events took place. There was awesome beauty all around me. There was incredible love. Amidst it there was pain and there was joy.

This book shares some of each I have experienced, written in the hope that it might help others - to appreciate and heal their lives from whatever events and pains encountered - and to focus on joyful wellbeing.

One of my great joys as a youth, which I could appreciate even then, was the incredible assortment of delicious food that appeared in front of me daily to my delight. On the days my mother baked, the mouth-watering odours wafting through the autumn air near our home as I would approach from school would quicken my pace in anticipation of whatever awaited me.

I was always a willing test dummy for quality purposes to ensure that all was up to her usual perfection. I could just as easily deal with any rare rejects or near misses of the high standard my mother set for herself – as in all things. In reflection, I have to wonder about the motives of some of my friends who might accompany me home. Hmmm.

Hot homemade bread and a vast variety of pastries were always a favourite for me and a real crowd-pleaser. Contents and varieties varied. I loved the pumpkin pie, because I got to drink the left-over filling, and cinnamon rolls coated on top with melted brown sugar, laced with sesame seeds and/or walnuts. Oh Momma, please come back! And bring your magic with you!

This book started out something like a batch of my mother's bread. What she started off in a small bowl with a bit of yeast and water eventually grew into a massive mountain of dough in a huge stainless steel bowl, and evolved into loaves of bread and trays of rolls. Bread starts off very much as a living organism. Strangely enough, this book has felt similar for me.

On a morning in early August 2011, I awoke with a thought that I had to write this book. But it was more than that. There was a feeling within me as if 'it' already existed as an embryo within me with a purpose for being. It was as if 'it' was an entity or a spirit that demanded to be acknowledged and treated as such. 'It' just needed to be moulded into shape and manifested into a loaf of bread as such, which could be consumed. Perhaps other writers have or have had similar experiences?

'It' wouldn't leave me alone and I knew I had to act upon the demands I sensed. I contacted Balboa Press as the subsidiary of Hay House, Inc. and committed myself to making whatever message contained in the envelope within me into this project days later on August 17th. 'It' has been relentless at times in driving me to bring it out into the world, in spite of the challenges I had to face within me and many interruptions to the process. It was often delayed, but never forgotten nor did I ever want to give up.

When I finally submitted my manuscript draft to Balboa on January 6th 2019, I knew there was still work to be done, but it felt as if I had literally given birth to a seven-year-old 'something'. It was a moment and few hours and days of mixed emotions of excitement and wonder, as if sending one of my beautiful children out into the world to explore. Most of all, it was a sense of relief from the nagging within me to reach that stage. I let go now with the hope for fulfilment of my intention for being as described in the Preface. Please enjoy the journey! *May you find the awe and wonder of the beauty within you and our world and be filled with joy along the way!*

Preface

The Purpose of This Book

- *Assist others in* ***getting their life back*** *- from stress, anxiety,, depression, trauma, and PTSD*
- *Show ways to achieve* ***PEACE of MIND***
- *Share ways to manage your energy that will* ***EMPOWER YOU*** *beyond PEACE OF MIND*
- *Share a non-clinical* ***understanding of stress*** *in order to effectively manage it*
- *Share some* ***understanding of energy*** *in order to effectively manage it – the* ***key to everything***
- *Share ways to* ***attain and maintain optimum wellness*** *in your body, mind, and spirit*
- *Share ways to* ***implement effective, positive changes in your wellness and happiness***
- *Encourage you to approach healing and Life with the belief that* ***anything is possible***
- *Encourage you to* ***fall in love with Life*** *and live it to your fullest potential*
- *Provide* ***sources for further beneficial information*** *in your pursuit of wellness*

Declaration

I have written this book from the view point of *my own experiences* and my searching for solutions.

- I am not a medical practitioner or an expert in any professional field that deals with what I refer to as the 'Stress family' – i.e. tension, anxiety, depression and PTSD

- I am simply a U.S. Army veteran of the Vietnam War September 1967 to August 1969

Overview

My initial impetus for writing this book was my desire to help my fellow Vietnam veterans dealing with PTSD caused by their military service. I soon realised that PTSD and associated stress problems were far broader than that focus. They are often the subtle reason for the more obvious symptoms of health issues that surface around our bodies. Consequently, the scope of this book has expanded considerably to consider our overall wellness in an effort to restore and maintain that crucial balance of ***energy*** intertwined through our ***body, mind,*** and ***spirit***.

- Stress issues and impact have become a global epidemic
- Observers believe the numbers dealing with trauma and PTSD are probably far greater than what is officially recognised or acknowledged.
- The complexity of trauma and PTSD can often involve various members of the 'Stress family' and other aspects of our health
- I wanted to go beyond veterans to address overall ***wellbeing for everyone***

My writing of this book started some eleven years after I was diagnosed with PTSD in 2000. Over seven years has evaporated since then, with numerous interruptions to the flow. In that time, much has happened in the scientific world that contributes to the treatment of stress-related conditions. There has been an explosion of discoveries that is taking science and humanity into a new realm beyond previous belief – some not yet fully understood. That has given me greater knowledge of wellness strategies resulting in my own further healing and a greater discovery of my Self.

Anxiety, depression, trauma, Post-Traumatic Stress Disorder and other forms of stress-related conditions are having a huge impact

throughout our world. They are the underlying roots to our diseases; they are controlling our lives, affecting our health and happiness – and they are killing us!
Even though it would appear to always have been a part of human nature with our fight/flight programming, it is triggered more frequently with our *stressful* modern lifestyle, resulting in consequences we can all relate to.

🐾🐾

The intangible cost of *STRESS* to us in our relationships and health is virtually incalculable for individuals and our society as a whole. Studies in the U.S. and Australia both show increasingly detrimental effects on individual, society and business, with staggering economic costs as well, which are impossible to accurately assess. A study done over ten years ago by Australian Government Medibank estimated it cost the economy nearly $15b per year and growing. The American population of 325 million is 13x the number of Australians. Does that translate to $195b in the probably more stressful U.S.? Beyond those two environments, the '*Stress family*' and their effects are a global phenomenon as we enter 2019.

🐾🐾

We all have stress by nature. Yet many people seem to be *unaware* of the effects that stress is having on them, which has potential consequences. While it is not a problem for some people, it is at crisis point on a frequent basis for some people!

Fortunately, it is something we can learn to recognise, prevent and manage successfully, or even use its *energy* to *empower* us. It is how we deal with it that determines whether we control it or it controls us - as an individual, a community and our world.

Uncontrolled, it can be destructive, debilitating and make us more susceptible to disease. Used creatively with intention, knowledge and skill, that *energy* can be an *empowering* asset! There are many effective ways, both simple and more complex, which we can employ to prevent or conquer stressful feelings or trauma that impair our wellbeing.

- Become aware
- Recognize the symptoms
- Turn the stressful energy into positive action – employ it to our advantage
- Intentionally change our behaviour to bring those *energies* and aspects of our self into balance
- Form the habit of good health through repetition of good practices

We are all individuals with personal experiences, so it's not a case of one size fits all. My experiences aren't yours, but you can take what you want from mine, and from other sources I am providing. You may be just becoming aware of anxiety issues within yourself, or you may have been de-sensitised through trauma to the point where you've forgotten what it feels like to feel energized and truly *alive.* In any case, *now* is the time to take positive action. I fully believe you can - if that is your *intention, belief and desire.*

- I consider that 'Stress family' to be any stress-related condition: anxiety, depression, nervousness, and PTSD - often inter-connected
- It can sometimes be difficult to distinguish the differences between those conditions
- I perceive them as a complex mix of *energy* which got out of balance to debilitate me at times in my ability to function 'normally' - mentally, physically or emotionally
- I have learned a great deal about the condition, methods of treatment and about my Self
- It has been a process - I have succeeded through intention, exploration, discovery, determination, persistence, much assistance, much healing, much good fortune and *grace*

- I believe the *key* to my well-being is learning to *manage* my *energy*, thus my *stress*
- I am *still* working to be *absolutely* free of the symptoms of PTSD and stress
- I *manage* them very well for a life of *vitality* and *wellness* with *peace of mind* and an *open heart*
- I maintain my wellness balance by consistently practicing effective proven techniques
- I have kept myself ‘on-track’ for several years and keep improving my well-being
- I believe good health is achieved by focusing on *what I want to feel and be*, rather than on my past or current problems

The important aspect of my journey is the state of where I am today – *enjoying* Life’s greatest gifts - peace of mind, mental clarity, good health and happiness! ***I am so appreciative of getting my life back that I truly want to help others*** who want the same!

Breathe in/ /Breathe out/ /Breathe in/ /Breathe out/

Getting Started

Australia vs USA

Good mates indeed, the Aussies and the Yanks! Of course we all agree who has the best beaches and beer don't we? But yes, there is a conflict! Having been born and raised in the USA, and migrating to Australia in my early twenties, I have developed by default, a rather unique language of my own, some tell me.

It's a form of English of sorts, with influences of at least three countries in the use of my communication, to include the source of that crazy melting pot of words; England. All three countries claim to use English as their primary language; however both non-natives have taken some considerable licence in adapting it to their own environment. Our language is of course constantly evolving everywhere anyway.

As a self-confessed word-butcher, I have taken it into another realm. After some 47 years in Australia, I am still learning the language, oral and written. Consequently, there will be variations in spellings, meanings, and usage of words, phrases, and isms that might cause a bit of head scratching, as it has for me over most of my lifetime.

It is difficult for me, in my mutated state, to use one exclusively here at the expense of the other. This writing is a hybrid, so please beware and be prepared for any unintended misunderstanding. I hereby apologise for any confusion I may cause in the reading of this book. An Australian/American translation dictionary would be handy, *if* such did exist.

I reckon I can be excused to some extent when you consider the variety of word sources that have found their way into my vocabulary. With a rural-ish Montana upbringing, a period of military life and computer industry work world full of acronyms, and life in multicultural Australia, both city and rural, my vocabulary and use of it is understandably 'different'.

In each environment, I have to sometimes stop and think if the word or phrase has the same meaning for the expected target. Am I trying to communicate with my friends and family in the U.S. or Australia, or wherever, each with their own words or context to the same words? Is it any wonder the word-plucker in my grey matter gets confused or lost in the caldron before it can get to the tongue?

So, being a person who believes in fair play, in order to compensate for any impediment imposed on readers, I have attempted to expedite my communication in the book with the strategy of using bullets in places to short-cut drawn-out ideas in text to a more concise structure. Also in an effort to make such a publication more easily readable and digestable, I have tried to keep written structure of sentences, paragraphs and topics, short and simple when possible. Good luck in interpreting the message!

Breathe in/🐾/Breathe out/🐾/Breathe in/🐾/Breathe out/🐾

Lucy

Hi! My name is Lucy. I am a nine year old Cavoodle - a cross between a Cavalier King Charles Spaniel and a Poodle. *Purebred* of course! That makes my age over sixty in human years, but I believe I am just a feisty, fun-loving puppy. I get told I am '*beautiful*' (a lot) which makes my tail wag furiously. That always makes Greg laugh at me because he hasn't been able to work out how I can wag my tail so vigorously without it falling off when we get together. Also, how I can wee forty times in a twenty minute walk. It's a secret I want to keep to myself.

He has asked me to assist him with his book. As the best friend of man, how could I say 'no?' I am always eager to help. He believes that my ability to keep on a scent and show you the trail can be of great value.

First of all, I've been asked to mark the trail. That's with my paws, not the usual invisible trick, marking every pole, tree and bush I pass on my walks.

Greg says that one of the best ways to relax is to breathe 'consciously' for just a minute or two, several times a day. Apparently it helps to get the brain and body back into some balance of thoughts and emotions – to be 'present' or something I don't quite understand. I just pant when I feel the need. That works for me.

Anyway, he says it's important to have about a two second pause between the 'in-breath' and the 'out-breath' – helps people to be present to what they are doing and to avoid mental distractions. So I have cleverly put my front paws in the breath reminder instructions in place of the words 'pause for two seconds' – saves ink, space, and paper! Easy!

Breathe in/🐾/Breathe out/🐾/Breathe in/🐾/Breathe out/🐾

Get it? Next, let's look at your intention and priorities so that we can reconnect to the path when we start to stray a bit. Greg says he got off course at times in his life, then back on again . . . off/on etc. He calls it his 'D-Tour'. He should have just rung me!

Now, just for me to know that we both want to reach the same destination in case we get separated, let's agree to what that is. I'm going to assume that the most important objective here, is to feel good and to be healthy.

Let's call that 'feel good' feeling, 'wellness'. Wellness of our body, our mind, and our spirit, because when those aspects of our self are all in balance, we feel noticeably good or well. Even as a puppy dog, I can tell when one or more of those parts of me has a problem. When I don't feel well, I need to have a look at why and change something to get back on track. Apparently it's the same for you humans.

I've got them pretty well trained I reckon, but it's still a work in progress - daily. If only they were as clever as us animals. Perhaps I'll share some more secrets with you later, but for now I'm off to my cushion in the sun for a little lie down. Tracking and barking can get a bit tiring at times. Just follow the trail when you see my tracks. Love, Lucy.

Breathe in/🐾/Breathe out/🐾/Breathe in/🐾/Breathe out/🐾

Open Up Your Heart

"Love is the bridge between you and everything."
– Rumi (1207-1273)

Through modern science with extremely sensitive methods of measuring the energy trails in our body and mind, we are coming to a far greater understanding of humanity. 'They' have confirmed what the ancient healers and 'mystics', including Jesus and Buddha, have been saying for thousands of years – that the energy we call '*love*' is the healer of our human body, mind and spirit. They can track, observe, and record the cause and effect.

Scientists have 'discovered' an area in the heart that has the same cell structure which is the same as cells in the brain, so the heart actually has an intelligence of its own! Science has also 'proven' that the heart is not only is the centre of our 'love energy', but also an intelligence that tells the brain what it *should* do; they correspond. Is that our conscience? When they work in unison, science calls it coherence. Balanced. We *feel* good and our body then is open to healing in an optimum receptivity in that state that permeates through our entire body.

Before I could effectively be healed of my condition, several things needed to take place. One of the most important was to open up my heart. In sharing my story, I am opening up here and baring my soul beyond sensibility and reason, to give you a space to do the same in order that you can heal. As a consequence of your healing, you will also be more empowered – 'to get your life back' if that is your goal.

Opening my heart by intention could not be held open until something else was achieved first. The pain of grief and the toxins of anger towards the actions of the 'powers that be' or anyone or anything else, created an environment within me I needed to release. The anger would never go away as long as I held onto the thoughts and emotions that held me in that loop.

Acceptance and forgiveness were key steps to open my heart, freeing me to move forward –

- I had to acknowledge and accept that certain events took place conducted by many people in the case of the Vietnam story –
- that story is history; it is past and cannot be changed – I had to accept it
- it is impossible for me to know what tough considerations and decisions those in power faced in their actions – I cannot make such a judgment from my unknowing perspective
- my opinions and judgments affect my emotional, mental and spiritual balance
- forgiving all the players in their roles, including myself if I feel guilt, shame, or judgement which hold me back from giving and receiving love, is necessary for healing
- forgiving is a positive act to free negative emotions within myself, rather than making others and their actions right or wrong from my perspective
- forgiveness is amazing in restoring peace within and conserving energy wasted on hate

The magic of healing happens through the power of love and feelings of appreciation. The ultimate power of healing is when we create coherence between the heart and mind, along with a *belief* that we are already in fact whole and well – seeing one as being healed before that has actually taken place physically. Faith? It's the *believing* and *knowing* before the evidence. *Belief* is the magical power that activates healing at our cellular level throughout our body.

In saying that, I appreciate that when we are traumatised, highly stressed, emotionally hurt or shattered, it is hard to comprehend the meaning of those words, 'open your heart', much less enact it. Energy healers told me that years ago. I thought I had, but I wasn't getting past my mind. It took some time and understanding at a different level – to truly *feel* it through my heart.

It's quite natural to 'bullet-proof' our heart, consciously or unconsciously, to protect it from further hurt. Softening and breaking through that hard shell could be a process which can take some time, whether it is war-related, from a broken romance, or any painful experience. It can also happen very quickly with willingness and intention when circumstances are right. That process is another story later.

Sometimes we aren't even aware that we have shut down our heart energy into self-preservation mode. I returned from Vietnam to civilian life thinking I would be all happy and excited at being back to the life I anticipated. I didn't realise that I was actually carrying a heavy heart within me. I tried to lift my moods through alcohol and various activities, not knowing the cause of some of my depressed emotions, while some like anger were also heightened.

Many or most veterans of war zones, I believe, have experienced a similar state due to being in a place of constant vigilance for a period of time. Ambulance crews, police, hospital staff, etc. who are often or continuously facing stressful situations, danger, or trauma, also experience heightened alertness.

When we feel unsafe or insecure, an 'alert' by hormones prepares us for fight or flight, thus the coherence between the brain and the heart is disturbed. That energy is re-directed to our survival instincts, so healing and coherent heart/brain processes are put on hold.

If someone is in an elevated state of self-preservation in fight or flight survival mode, it is physically impossible to be receptive to or give the emotion of love, due to the body's biochemistry preparing the body for action. We cannot focus on love and gratitude while in that state. If we are in one of the aspects of fear - anxious, cautious, suspicious, or worried, we cannot feel the love to heal. The heart is closed down for survival. We must relax and open up, which produces the right chemistry in our body in order to do that. We come out of a war zone in such a condition. It doesn't just magically disappear with the hugs of our loved one.

If you are having trouble with feeling like your heart is in a receptive mode, try this: think of a pet or someone or something that you love - or something that you love doing. Place your focus on your heart; feel it. Put a hand over your heart. *Feel* grateful for that feeling. Thank the dog or whatever in your mind and heart for being in your life, past or present. When you reach the point of a loving feeling, dwell on it for as long as you can. Give it an image in your mind that you can easily recall to evoke the feeling again anytime.

An open heart helps you *feel* better and is scientifically proven to be physically healthier as well because of the lessened tension on the heart muscles and circulatory system.

Breathe in/❀❀/Breathe out/❀❀/Breathe in/❀❀/Breathe out/❀❀

Some simple suggestions -

- Breathe into and out of your heart centre a few times with your eyes closed
- Get out into nature and observe it – see and appreciate the beauty of it – sit in it
- Touch the earth; go barefoot (scientifically proven to benefit our well-being)
- Do or watch something funny – crazy – silly - laugh!
- Sing or play some music that you enjoy or moves you
- Watch a movie or program that is uplifting
- Play - with a child, or anyone, or an animal
- Play - or do something on your own that brings you happiness or joy
- Consider someone worse off than yourself and have a conversation with them
- Feel compassion for someone in a difficult situation
- Contemplate all the things you can be grateful for

- Feel appreciation for each of them and for life itself
- Give Lucy a hug in your mind and heart 🐾

Breathe in/🐾/Breathe out/🐾/Breathe in/🐾/Breathe out/🐾

Open Your Mind

"A man is but the product of his thoughts;
what he thinks, he becomes."
- Mahatma Gandhi (1869-1948)

The stress-related condition you might be experiencing may have been caused by just one traumatic incident. Or it may be the result of a long time thinking or 'un-thinking' behavioural pattern. My experience was some of each. Sometimes positive thinking and determination could remedy the situation in the short term to still my busy mind. When that didn't suffice, particularly with PTSD and debilitating anxiety, a transformation of both thinking and emotions was required in order to get things 'in order'.

It is a physiological condition affecting our mind and body. Trauma and PTSD are complex conditions that generally require a special way of treating them. Initially, the dawning to understand of what I was dealing with and ways to do so with counselling was effective. Eventually that reached a plateau that I wanted to cross and get beyond, to reach a level of healing from the condition that satisfied me.

I started looking outside the framework of that structure, basically counselling and anti-depressant medication. That required me opening my mind to the possibilities of what could bring results that lessened the impact of PTSD and could get me back to 'normal' overall functioning.

My thinking *should* be the captain of my 'Being' - to tame my unruly thinking and behaviour. With PTSD, the 'captain' lost control of the ship to the 'crew' – my body habits and behaviour driven by the sub-conscious. That intimate connection between the mind and the body, whicht is the glue of all effective, coherent relationships, got messy.

Albert Einstein was known for saying that we can't solve our problems by thinking about them at the same level as the problem itself. I guess he was saying we have to use a greater degree of awareness or thinking 'outside the box' in a creative way. The solution may come from 'left field'.

That requires a mind open to all possibilities and an expanded use of our imagination. He also said that the use of that human faculty was more beneficial than intelligence. In his humility as to his level of 'intelligence' he was said to possess, he attributed his achievements to his imagination and unquenchable curiosity, which he said was actually more important.

We are all in a constant state of change in varying degrees whether that is consciously or unconsciously. Correcting our disability means changes through a conscious intention to do so. That process is greatly enhanced with an 'open' mind. There are far more approaches available now than when my journey began. There are some very simple yet amazingly effective ways that bring quicker results to healing trauma and other stress-related conditions.

It is not my place to guide anyone through those processes in this book, but to make people aware of them and if possible, where to find them. I can only suggest beyond that to search with an 'open' mind.

- Do you want to set an intention of positive change?
- Are you tired of the behaviour pattern of stress/anxiety that might be holding you back from being and doing what you want?
- What is your desire or intention?
- What is it you want to become from a picture of wellness?
- Do you want to change your behaviour from patterns that are problematic for you?
- Are you prepared to do what it takes for positive change?
- Are you prepared for the consequences of change?

Be discerning as you read this book, (and every other book), but keep an open mind to the possibilities that it may hold for you. Some of it may challenge your current beliefs. Be prepared to shift your thinking in order to expand your awareness and wellness.

- Read
- Contemplate
- Decide
- Engage
- Expand
- *Enjoy!*

Breathe in/🐾/Breathe out/🐾/Breathe in/🐾/Breathe out/🐾

"What???"

Did the last two chapters lose you? Open up my mind? I thought I knew what it meant, but it was near impossible to attain and maintain at that point. You may be in that same place, at least at times. To get to a place of open-mindedness, the emotions and feelings that control us in the various states of stress need to be brought under control. I'll talk later about how we can do that. In the meantime, *try* to keep your mind in a receptive state.

Open up your heart? Again, we can travel along through life without opening up our emotional centre to receive and give love to our greatest potential, which is ultimately *'unconditional' love*. That is, loving someone or something without the expectation of being loved back or even appreciated in return. I think most parents, particularly mothers, have that innate capability and quality.

When I was in the depths of anxiety and/or depression, it was difficult for me to understand much of anything at times. It was hard enough just to think - period. Thoughts were often random, scattered, and incoherent. Sometimes it was difficult to string two thoughts together. Thoughts would get lost somewhere between the start and finish line. They would arrive at the intersection of here and there and not know which way to turn, or simply evaporate.

When I was experiencing depression and issues that created it at times in my life, I didn't realise how much I had actually closed down my heart centre. It's a natural protective measure as a result of trauma or emotional pain. It took an awakening, some effort, and healing to gradually open back up again to the extent that really enabled more extensive healing.

It often takes an intention, courage, and forgiveness to engage fully after a broken heart, but we can't live life to the fullest with a closed heart. Science has measured the energy of love with sensitive equipment. It indicates that it is the highest level of energy and emotion we can sense. Our heart is our energy centre, as if we didn't already know that. In any case, we have to open it up to receive love and for the passion to flow, which is vital to the healing process.

Just remember - thoughts are the language of the mind, and feelings are the language of the heart, so those are the pathways to healing. When they are in sync with our intentions for the greatest good, we engage a state of coherence where magic literally happens in our lives. If you have fallen 'in love', you already know that.

In technical terms, we are then in a quantum state where potentials and possibilities are unlimited, *if we allow* it to be so. That is when we feel *alive,* and excited at the unknown possibilities that lay before us. What has all that got to do with anything here? It's part of the recipe for the quicker path to wellness.

The process involved in coming into a balance of well-being is an interesting and sometimes tricky dance between the mind and heart. The long-term healing process is a fascinating interaction between those two aspects of ourselves that unlocks the chemistry within us. When that happens, it's like finding the room within the castle of your being that is filled with the love, knowingness, wisdom, peace and gratitude all waiting for you in the one place; *wholeness*! It is *within us already.*

Breathe in/🐾🐾/Breathe out/🐾🐾/Breathe in/🐾🐾/Breathe out/🐾🐾

Onto my *D-Tour*

"The right way to wholeness is made up of fateful detours and wrong turnings."
– Carl Jung (1875-1961)

Imagine you're driving along on Life's highway, and somehow you find yourself on a very different path in circumstances that are beyond your control. You suddenly reach a section of damaged road that forces to go onto a bumpy, muddy track. It is filled with potholes you now have to dodge and weave your way through. You feel bewildered and somewhat lost, wondering if the alternate path will get you to where you intended to go. You find you are not only feeling disbelief and disoriented, but disconnected, desperate, dysfunctional, debilitated, de-energized, depressed, distressed, dis-eased, dis-abled, discouraged, and dis-empowered! You . . . are on a ***D-Tour!***

"If you are going through hell, keep going."
– Sir Winston Churchill (1874-1965)

You search for answers. Somehow, you gradually come to your senses somewhat, and learn to cope enough to get by. You *dig deep* within, and start to *drag* yourself out of the *demoralising ditch* with *determination, discipline*, and a whiff of renewed faith in yourself. You eventually *discover* that perhaps the new *direction* is not the *disaster* it seemed at first. You reach a point where you no longer want to get back onto the highway you were taken from. You start to believe it is actually a blessing that helps you *develop* yourself toward a *different*, sometimes *difficult*, yet fulfilling *destiny*. You embrace the journey as a gift for the lessons you have learned, and the wonderful *discoveries* and people that you've encountered along the way. You feel happy and grateful to be on your new path with the sense of growth and greater self-empowerment with a new joy in living. There can be no going back.

That was roughly a simplified analogy to aspects of my life that took place over several years, from early 2000. I was 52 years of age at that time I became *D-Toured.*

"May you always remember that obstacles in the path are not obstacles – they ARE the path."
Jane Lotter (1952-2013)

I had felt stressed at times in my life, but I always seemed to manage. It was just 'life'. But a number of pressures presented themselves in a short space of time that took their toll on me. Rather abruptly, I was going down another track when I was diagnosed with something I knew little about; **Post-Traumatic Stress Disorder**, or **PTSD**. There had been symptoms for some time but I didn't recognise them as being part of a 'condition'. My world changed forever as I started to enter a new awareness of that complex condition and of my 'Self'.

When I realised I had emotional problems and sought help to sort them out, I really didn't think it would be a big problem or would take too long to get back on track. What I didn't realise, was that I was like the little Dutch boy in the story where he put his digit in the dike to hold back far more water from pouring out than he knew. When I pulled my finger out of my emotional wall, out came a flood of pain and grief buried deep within me to join the more obvious anger that I had suppressed for much of my life. There was no holding it back once the dam burst.

That put me on a new pathway that eventually led to healing. That had to start with letting go and holding on to take me out of the darkness. I was in for a ride I certainly wasn't expecting!

The process, over a period of more than a decade, has ultimately been a blessing of learning and healing, sometimes well-disguised within the initial emotional pain that seemed to haunt me. The overall change in myself that has taken place, started as an intention to simply get my life back on track, rather than to become another path. It has taken me through ups and downs, regression and expansion. It has truly been a journey of greater awareness and personal transformation

I didn't consciously set out to do. I could say that my experience and my learning to manage the Post-Traumatic Stress Disorder became my Path To Self-Discovery. The result has been *peacefulness* in my mind and body with *joy* as an unexpected bonus.

"Life is a journey,
not a destination"
- Ralph Waldo Emerson (1803-1882)

I am a seeker; curious; I always have been. I don't intend to ever stop questioning and seeking, both the world around me and the world within me. Over the years, I've read many stories of others who have had life-altering experiences. I believe those events always happen for a reason, which usually seems to be for the person to get to know their *Self* better and to learn something important in their development as a person. My grappling with the effects of PTSD and stress generally, certainly altered the course of my life, changing me forever.

"Progress is impossible without change,
and those who cannot change their minds cannot change anything."
- George Bernard Shaw (1856-1950)

It seems I had to be virtually debilitated enough to basically reach my personal 'ground zero' in some respects - to take stock, rebuild, and move on along an alternate path. I was given the time and space to analyse the cause and the effect; to face my problems and my *Self* - to take action I considered best for my own well-being.

There has been some pushing past and jumping over, but mostly it was *letting go* of the past and negativity, and *allowing* the new, creative and positive *energy* to flow. I had to learn how to get out of victim mode and out of my own way. I learned to new skills to fully participate in life with desire and intention, taking me to a state of *joyfulness* by surprise!

Through the process, I got reacquainted with that part of me that had forgotten how to have fun. Much of that growth came from allowing my curiosity to explore life in a variety of ways beyond what I had in the past. I could handle the adventure, no problem, but I had to come to terms with the notion that it really is okay to have *fun*; at any age!

I had often struggled with that throughout my life. I needed to go a bit easier on myself and simply lighten up. I was just too serious about life from an early age. I had to let go of the expectation and fear that a joyful experience would be followed by something that would wipe it out. I had to stop shooting myself in one foot or the other when that option was available. It can really slow a person down, as well I know.

Some aspects of my journey that I will share have been painful; however I am not going to pull you down into the trench I was in and drag you along with me. I really don't wish to go back in there to scrutinize and analyse. I see no need of it for either of us.

I want to move forward. The intention is ultimately to be uplifting in spirit and expansive in awareness and wellness. Whatever emotional or physical pain I may have encountered in my life, it is far out-weighed by wonderful experiences during my D-tour years alone when I **'got my life back'!** Despite the difficult and challenging times, part of it has been quite mystical, and much of it simply beautiful beyond words.

Breathe in/🐾/Breathe out/🐾/Breathe in/🐾/Breathe out/🐾

My Early Years

Soon after my parents were married in 1938, they built a house together in a rather idyllic setting. It faced north to a mountain on the other side of the Clark Fork of the Columbia River which ran past their front garden in Superior in western Montana. I was born in the local hospital in 1948, but my father's work had taken my family to the tiny town in Idaho with the U.S. Forest Service. Riggins sat on the Salmon River, and like my birthplace, was surrounded by mountains.

My sister Carol was older than me by about 4 years, and my brother George by about 7 years. My mother looked after all of us. Another sister Marguerite joined us when I was two and a half. Being closest in age, we became pretty much inseparable as we grew up.

My mother had been born and raised on a dry-land farm at Tarkio, fifteen miles to the east. Her parents, Grover and Anne Miles later started Grover's Café beside Highway 10 in Superior which proved to be a very successful business. When they decided to retire, my mother and her cousin Birdie Charette formed a partnership to purchase the cafe.

Changes in the Wind

January 1953 heralded a new year of great change for my country of birth and for my family.

- My parents celebrated their wedding anniversary on the 1st, as usual. It was their 14th.
- The newly elected president of the United States, former Army general, Dwight D. Eisenhower was inaugurated on the 20th. He had been the Supreme Commander of the Allied Forces in Europe at the end of World War II in December 1945.
- Three days after he became the Commander in Chief of my country, I blew out the flames of five candles on my chocolate birthday cake.

- Before I would blow out six candles on my cake, my family was to experience a tragedy which would be a lasting impact on our lives.

Marguerite

The progression of fateful events of the year started soon after my birthday. By spring, our family started the process of moving back to Superior so my mother could take over the café from her parents. My siblings and I accompanied her while my father initially remained in Riggins for a while with his work. Somehow we shared space in our grand-parents' small home until the house my parents had built became available to us from a family who had been renting it.

My cousin Toni, a year younger than me who had been living with us, Marguerite, and I had become the inseparable three musketeers. One cool cloudy day in early May, we ventured out of the house to make mud pies when rain had stopped.

Later it was decided that we play a bit of baseball, so my sister Carol took Toni and me in search of my bat, borrowed by a neighbour boy K.C. the day before. We were led by K.C.'s mother, Ruby. Marguerite stayed behind to continue making pies.

The water used to make the mud came from a hole in the ground partially filled with water. A water tap was at the top of a pipe coming out of the hole which connected to an underground pipe, deep enough at about four feet to prevent the pipes freezing up in winter. It had a stop/waste valve at that junction which was faulty, so it leaked water which filled the hole. It was easier to dip into that water supply than to turn a tap on and off.

I could reach in with a tin can to collect water, with no danger to me. Marguerite however couldn't reach down as far, but she tried. The hole was just big enough for her to fit into but too deep and narrow to get back out.

On our return a few minutes later, we were faced with the horrible sight of Marguerite head first into the hole. Ruby immediately retrieved her and attempted to revive her until an ambulance team arrived a short time later.

I can still see clearly, the events of that day over sixty years ago. My mother arrived from her work within minutes in her white uniform dress, with her long dark brown hair coiled on top of her head, covered with a net. She sat on the box that was trying to resuscitate life back into the body of Marguerite laying limp on the ground before us.

I really didn't comprehend the significance of what I saw that day. I had no concept of death. I kept asking my mom what was wrong with Marguerite, laying there on the ground before us, as the resuscitation attempts continued. She tried to explain through her remarkably composed grief, that she had gone to be with Jesus.

Because of attending Sunday school since I could breathe, I had a concept of Heaven and a perception of God. I just didn't understand why or how she could just stop breathing, moving and talking. I could see and touch her body lying in her pretty ruffled dress, but she didn't move or answer my questions. How could she be there *and* in Heaven?

There was a part of me that died with Marguerite that day. It was four months before her third birthday.

"Ever has it been that love knows not its own depth - until the hour of separation."
Kahlil Gibran (1883-1931)

Marguerite's absence left a huge void in both my life, and of course the rest of my family. My loss was felt even more so soon afterwards because Toni went to live with our grand-parents. Fortunately they were just across town, so we could still see a lot of each other for a while. We had grown very close in her time with my family, and was like a sister to me.

Soon after Marguerite's death, we moved into our own home. It was much larger than what I had been used to. On the ground floor, my parents shared one bedroom, and my sister Carol had the other. My brother George and I shared the attic 'bedroom' which was unfinished. Entry to it was a set a stairs off a hallway with a door which was kept closed. It was a separation that provided both privacy and an undesirable sense of aloneness, to which I had to learn to adapt.

There were gaps along the side walls of the room that was the length of the house, which made it feel very spooky to me. I was accustomed to the intimacy of a very small house, but my new home seemed big, and I didn't feel safe and snug in my own bedroom. I hated going to bed, often alone, after having shared a bedroom with others all of my five years. I avoided and delayed bedtime as long as possible. No wonder I was having nightmares and started wetting my bed.

It wasn't the cosy little house I had been used to. The feeling of joy I had known in Riggins was gone. So much had changed. Confronted by the loss of a loved one, there was a void within me that could not be refilled.

Eventually, there came a degree of understanding of one of life's inevitable truths at a very young age – the finality of our physical life. I also came to believe that our spirit lives on beyond our physical death, therefore Marguerite was still alive in spirit.

Through their certain pain over the incident, my parents had the courage to bring another child into our family just over a year later. She was a wonderful distraction that we could love and all embrace. Rita was such a blessing to us all.

*"**Trauma is** a fact of life. It does **not**, however, have to be **a life sentence**."*
- Dr Peter Levine

Life went on, but our family was never the same after that. The atmosphere in our home had changed. It was sometimes a big lonely house with my parents' away working for long hours, often into the night. My father's work with the Forest Service sometimes took him away for days at a time, particularly on fires anywhere in western U.S.

We would mention Marguerite but we really never talked about the incident. I didn't receive any counselling and I didn't know what it was or how to grieve. It wasn't a social tool available to our culture in those days. Consequently I carried that trauma and grief with me throughout most of my lifetime. A lid went onto my expression of joy that I didn't even realise. It became my seriousness, imposing an unconscious limit on me when that wonderful emotion tried to naturally surface.

I finally started tapping into my grief and dealing with it during the counselling and energy healing I started 47 years later with the Vietnam Veterans Counselling Service. Even though I have learned to accept what happened, it has only been in more recent times that I have re-discovered real joy and embraced it as my birthright.

I've also realised that there were actually some positive aspects for me from that experience. Inadvertently, even from that early age, I learned understanding and compassion for others who are dealing with the loss of a loved one.

I have also learned to recognize the feeling of joy that my short but sweet relationship with Marguerite gave me, and to truly appreciate that. Even though I am still affected by that tragedy, I now have the power, through what I have learned, to stop prolonged grief and sadness that had robbed me of my overall joyfulness for so long.

I've had glimpses of joy from time to time through my life of course, but I didn't feel that I deserved to *always* feel happy or good about myself or life in general. When I started feeling *too* good about things or myself I would nip it in the bud. I didn't feel comfortable with it; I felt guilty for feeling good! I actually thought that people who always seemed to be predominately happy and joyful were either uncaring about all the troubles we have in the world or that there was something a bit wrong with them!

What a tragedy to carry such a belief! Thank Goodness I've seen through that illusion, and as a result have come to really enjoy and appreciate much more of my life than ever before.

"The wound is the place where the Light enters you."
— Rumi (1207-1273)

Things can happen that adversely affect us emotionally with long-lasting consequences, particularly in our early years before we have an understanding of the significance. That incident was certainly traumatic and carried on as PTSD, but I didn't know the meaning or the consequences of it. It was simply a part of my life to me.

I had carried the guilt with me that, as the self-appointed guardian of my little sister, I had let her and my family down. That was obviously unrealistic since I was five at the time, but that thinking set a pattern that I carried with me for most of my life. Even later, after I could see it in a more rational way, I was still *feeling* it. A big chunk of my happiness had been lost, which I would seldom allow to surface, even when I would occasionally feel the urge to do so.

"We are not meant to stay wounded. We are supposed to move through our tragedies and challenges and to help each other move through the many painful episodes of our lives. By remaining stuck in the power of our wounds, we block our own transformation. We overlook the greater gifts inherent in our wounds – the strength to overcome them and the lessons we are meant to receive from them. Wounds are the means through which we enter the hearts of other people. They are meant to teach us to become compassionate and wise".

Caroline Myss (1952-)
Medical Intuitive and Educator

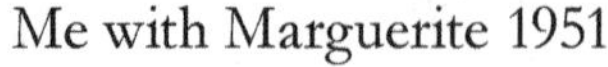

Me with Marguerite 1951

Marguerite 1952, aged 2

Breathe in/🐾/Breathe out/🐾/Breathe in/🐾/Breathe out/🐾

The Warrior in Me

Whack! Blood pouring from his nose, Ronnie ran back into the school house. It was all over with just one punch, even though he was taller and stronger. I was as surprised as he was. It wasn't my intention to actually hurt anyone - it was to settle a dispute over an issue at recess.

That seemed to become my way of settling a disagreement my first year at school. It was usually on the playground with other students which would turn from verbal to physical. Feeling frustration with my lack of communication skills and disadvantaged by my size, I would resort to more aggressive means of negotiating.

Being nearly smallest in my class, I quickly tired also of being bullied in that new, foreign environment. My father showed me how to defend myself - be fair, protect yourself with fists up. Don't back away. Get in the first punch if you can, and make it a good one. Most encounters didn't last any longer than that, often resulting in a black eye or a bloody nose, though not mine.

My father's experience and skills as an amateur boxer in the U.S. Navy served him well, which he passed on to me. I didn't look for a fight, but I found myself in many - simply standing up for myself or settling differences in that perhaps primitive way. It may have won the battle, but not the war.

Consequently I spent a good deal of time in detention or the principal's office in those early years of school, but I felt justified in my actions. Disciplinary action didn't seem to be a strong deterrent to me. Facing the additional music at home was more so, but that didn't come into my thinking in the heat of a disagreement. I wouldn't stand for being bullied and sometimes defended others being bullied.

I was learning more than the ABC's at school. Establishing a pecking order and bullying seems to be one of the laws of nature from chicken pen to horse corral to school yard. That instinctive trait hasn't seemed to go away with the so-called 'civilisation' of man.

Unfortunately, I too fell into the energetic suction of bullying others during those times. Nature – the 'kick-the-cat' response to being kicked – but that's no excuse. I feel sorry and embarrassed for those reactive actions.

Even worse, my memory can't erase one time in the third grade when I got frustrated with a girl at recess who grabbed my Cub Scout cap from my head and ran off with it. My answer for her playful taunting was a punch on the nose from me. My wonderful teacher Mrs. Lewis helped me to understand that was not appropriate action towards anyone, particularly a girl having some fun. I was a serious lad - and gender made no difference to me for invading my boundary.

On another occasion, in fifth grade, I 'washed' the face of another playful female classmate with snow on the way home from school in response to her pelting me with snow balls. Her tears and story to her parents meant I had to get past the meanest dog in town to knock on her door and apologize once my mother got a phone call from her mother. They only lived a few houses away from us, so it didn't take long, but it was a much slower walk to get there than it did to get back home.

Though I never received a black eye or bloody nose, I didn't always win and sometimes took a good belting from someone bigger and more skilful in battle. Perhaps not too clever, but I seemed to think it was worth the potential pain and consequences to prove a point or take a stand. Surprisingly, I gained the respect and often the friendship from many of those I fought, as with Ronnie. I didn't demand respect, but I inadvertently earned it the hard way.

Sometimes I would get caught by someone bigger and stronger than me that I couldn't outfight or outrun, if that course of action was an option. It rarely meant that I would be physically hurt, even though I might be flat on my back with that someone sitting on me. They would usually give me the opportunity to surrender with a bit of leniency, if not grace, in their victory.

If there was a glimmer of hope of getting them off me and not being 'killed' in the process, I would not utter those words, "I give up". It was bad enough to have to give in by simply answering "yes" to their question. Of course, once I was back on my feet, it was usually a case of taunting them at a safe distance. That bit of mongrel in me would never say die.

Fighting continued at school, but mostly outside it. That was life in a small town in western Montana in the 1950's. Just getting from point A to point B across town could be met with a challenge from bullies. The fighting skills I was fortunate to have gave me confidence in my defence requirements, but I was always on alert to the possibility of being confronted by a bully. Having a strategy for escape was becoming a greater consideration, if I felt that was a better option.

When I was nine, a kindly Native American man, Burt Burland, moved into town with his large, friendly family and started a boxing club. My mother was against the idea of me being involved, but my father and I won out. The tiger within me was gradually tamed somewhat with the discipline of training and time in the ring.

Burt had three sons about my age amongst his 'tribe'. There was a mutual respect and liking between us. They all helped me through their knowledge and skills. Thankfully my fights became more confined to a boxing ring as a result. We participated between other clubs in the region and I did well – until they moved a year or so later.

The club disbanded from lack of leadership, but by then I was becoming more civilized in settling differences with others. Challengers lessened, possibly in their perception of my improved boxing capabilities. Disciplinary measures from school office and home gradually made some impact on me, so they were no doubt factors in my change of behaviour. The value of verbal communication was beginning to dawn on me.

By the time I reached puberty, my fighting energy started to morph into an interest in girls. My parents tried, rather successfully to restrain that urge as long as possible. I left the fighting behind by high school, except for one memorable toe-to-toe dust-up at 17 that ended without too much injury to either of us. That was my last physical fight in those school years.

🐾🐾

By 1963, the looming conflict in Vietnam was almost a daily point of discussion in our classrooms that lasted through my high school years. Where was that warrior within me? I didn't want to kill anyone that wasn't a threat to me or my loved ones, and I had mixed feelings and concerns about the validity of the war there. The issue wasn't going away; it was escalating. I didn't like the idea of having to participate in a war I didn't understand, but I didn't want to shirk my responsibility to my country and other young people called upon for service. I didn't fear the possibility of going to Vietnam, but I certainly didn't want to be a combat soldier.

My cousin Rodger Miles had been corresponding with me from there as a Marine during my final year of high school, which convinced me that I wanted none of what he was facing. I considered the pros and cons of each of the services: Army, Navy, Air Force, Coast Guard, Seabees, and Marines. The preferable options had waiting lists with no guarantees, but the draft didn't allow me time to wait. Every U.S. male had to register for the draft at 18. My draft board had informed me I would be called into service for two years soon after turning 19 unless I was a full-time student or married with a child. I was neither.

Two days after my 19th birthday, eight months after completing high school, I entered the U.S. Army for a three year term. By enlisting I was given some choice of training which could potentially provide worthwhile skills, whereas not necessarily so with the draft. I decided not to gamble with the Army's choice for me.

Within a few months the Army had attempted to transform me from a peace-loving citizen in a society where killing another person is a crime, into a warrior with the training and authority to kill another human being. I hoped that I would never be faced with a situation to make that choice to employ those skills. The warrior within me during my early years had changed.

A couple of months after joining, I fitted boxing gloves on for the last time. My drill sergeant in basic training had me and another soldier settle our differences in a circle of the platoon members. They were heavy 16 ounce gloves designed for training and defence more than effective punching, so not much damage was done to either of us despite our best efforts. No blood or love lost there; another case of attempting to settle a dispute over a matter of my beliefs. Not the last, but never with gloves again. I had strongly objected to him following me in his rifle sights as I walked through the barracks after cleaning our weapons one evening.

Such was some of my recollection of being a 'warrior' before my Vietnam years. What I didn't realize was that I had a very good reason for not being able to verbalise and settle difference in a more congenial manner. The impact of a traumatic experience was locked up within me, so I may have been unwittingly reacting to in that aggressive way.

I still am a warrior at heart for the greater good of humanity and our planet, but I now take peaceful action now instead of using my fists.

My lifelong dilemma –

When does the 'peaceful warrior' within me have the wisdom, the moral right, and indeed an obligation, to become the 'outspoken warrior' - and to what extent?

Breathe in/ /Breathe out/ /Breathe in/ /Breathe out/

Another Devastating Loss

The tone of my mother's voice created an immediate sense of alarm within me. I could tell that she was upset about something, but she wouldn't say what. "I want you to come home right away," was her clear instruction, edged with a sense of concern.

'Something terrible has happened,' was her answer to my question 'why?' "I don't want to tell you over the phone,' was her answer to my question 'what?' My mind immediately flashed back to my last day with Marguerite. It was infused with thoughts of possible scenarios, in spite of no specific reason given.

🐾🐾

It was just one week before the summer solstice, but rather than hot, it had been a cool, overcast, and showery Montana morning on Wednesday, the 15th day of June 1960. My sixth year of school had finished in late May, with three months of summer vacation to enjoy. My day started in Missoula, sixty miles away from my home, where I was staying with cousins for a couple of days. In the afternoon I went directly to baseball practice after I returned to Superior.

Some of the players were missing, including my friend Larry, which we figured was due to the earlier showers. Afterwards, I went to my friend Tim's house to play some catch, so I rang home to get permission from my mother.

From the tone of her voice and reluctance to tell why I had to go home, I knew it wasn't good. I had immediate flashbacks of Marguerite's death, which had happened almost seven years to the day. Was there another tragedy with another member of our family? I could feel the adrenaline pump through my body and cloud my mind as I flew from Tim's front door without an explanation. "It's an emergency" were the only words I could put together as I grabbed my baseball glove and dashed past my baffled friend.

What could be the cause for concern to make Mom sound like

that and refuse to tell me over the phone? My head was flooded with possible disasters.

My legs were trying to keep pace with my racing mind, but they felt like rubber long before I could reach my house. It was about four blocks away but it seemed like four miles.

My body and breath wanted to quit as I ran past the Forest Service complex where my father worked, but I pushed on.

My imagination gave me no peace.

My mother was on the phone when I ran into our house through the back door. She seemed rather distressed about something. She briefly explained why when she got off the phone.

There had been a horrible accident at the front of our home with my best friend Larry, and she was trying to call his parents. No luck – both were on their way home, just a five-minute drive away. Their family car soon appeared at the front of their home next door.

We were all in a state of shock and disbelief as she broke the news to them of the tragic events that had occurred only minutes before. Through a bizarre chain of events, Larry was unable to escape from inside a car that had accidently gone into the river running past the front of our house. He was swept away in the high, muddy waters caused by melting snow in the mountains.

There was an immediate search for him by many volunteers in boats and along the river bank, joined by my father and me. It went on into the night and for days, but his body wasn't found until three months later, many miles downstream, after the waters receded and cleared.

Although his absence from my life had a very noticeable impact during that time, it wasn't until that sad day of his funeral that I faced the brutal reality of his finality, when I was honoured to be one of the young pall-bearers.

Larry had been my next door neighbour for the previous seven years and I spent a great deal of time at his house. He had soon became a replacement for Marguerite when we moved there just after she 'evaporated' from my life. We played catch and football in my yard and basketball at the back of his garage; we went fishing together; we watched his family TV, one of the first in town, well before our family had one; we occupied ourselves with woodwork and other activities in his home and garden or mine, often while our parents were away at their work; we built tree houses over the river bank down the street. We were in the same year at school though not always in the same class. Larry had been a big part of my life. Suddenly he was gone - like Marguerite, without warning.

Of course I felt an incredible sense of loss and grief, the events seared deep in my memory and being. June 15 was permanently stamped onto my internal calendar. My best friend and virtual brother just disappeared that day. Larry's home was no longer an extension of my own. The empty gap that followed was immense.

Apart from the trauma, the event also had a profound influence on the way I viewed life and death from that point on. It naturally reinforced the loss of Marguerite, but it went further because of the synchronistic chain of events that unfolded that day which challenged my perception of life and death.

The coincidences and outcome seemed to be virtually pre-destined. It was as if nothing could have changed it. It was obviously his fate, just as with Marguerite, but with much more complexity. It left me with a deep impression at the age of twelve, that when your time is "up, it's up" – it seemed there was no uncertainty about it. All the tumblers in the combination lock clicked into alignment. It couldn't have been a mistake – it seemed that it was *meant* to happen.

As was the case with Marguerite, there were no facilities in place for grieving, so those emotions got locked within me for much of my lifetime. As I travelled through life beyond that point, I didn't realise how the fuller extent of the trauma impacted me from that day on. 'Trauma' as a condition or even a word wasn't in my awareness.

It was through counselling over forty years later that the events of Larry's death quickly surfaced as a major component of my PTSD condition. The cumulative effects of that trauma, along with Marguerite's death and what I experienced in and following Vietnam, were all contributing factors.

Overall, those recurring thoughts and feelings of sadness, incurred by trauma, were more than just that. They influenced my behaviour, my restricted level of joy, and my attitudes towards life. Since they were not effectively treated near the time of the occurrence, they went onto to become part of my *D-Tour.*

The counselling I've received in recent years has helped me ease the sense of separation. I have learned to appreciate the wonderful times I had with Larry and the connection with his family, rather than focus on the pain of his early passing.

We may not erase the memories of a traumatic experience, but we can learn to accept the occurrence, heal the wound as much as possible, and move on with our lives.

"Live as if you were to die tomorrow.
Learn as if you were to live forever."
- Mahatma Gandhi (1869-1948)

I believe that someday I will let go of my last breath and my spirit will leave my physical body to go *'Home'* and will meet up with Larry and others again. When and where that happens doesn't really concern me. I would be living a very different, more restrictive and less exciting, adventurous life if it did. There is a great sense of freedom and well-being for me with that belief. Can we really fully embrace life until we lose the fear of our perception of death of our physical body?

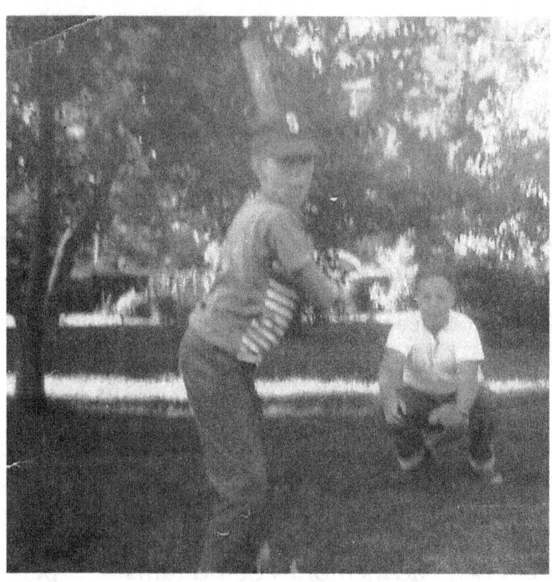

Best friends Tim batting and Larry – 1959

Breathe in/🐾/Breathe out/🐾/Breathe in/🐾/Breathe out/🐾

To Vietnam Veterans

This chapter is *especially for you* - men *and* women.
The millions who served, in or out of a uniform.
You are the reason I decided to write this book.

The Vietnam War Era

You and I were born at a time that put us right in the middle of an event that changed our individual lives and the course of history – call it fate if you will. The impact had huge consequences not only for all participants, the ripples were felt right across our planet in various ways. That continues today, as we veterans know, even if others have forgotten or have never known.

Like all wars throughout history, it created pain, tragedy, death and so much more, as they do. But the war in Vietnam was different to any other known. It was –

- Recorded and broadcast to the world by the media (largely government controlled)
- In your face war reality, both horrifying and yet captivating in a sense of curiosity
- Misunderstood – by politicians and public alike
- Mysterious – why were we involved?
- Mismanaged through disagreements between all concerned about how to fight it/win it
- Tearing apart the social fabric of the countries involved, creating great turmoil
- A time when the military people returning home from the battlefields were treated differently to any other war
- A powerful platform to question the human predisposition to warfare between people

- An opportunity for self-analysis resulting in the possibly of shifting values
- A time participants had to leave behind their innocence and face a new awareness with separation, loss, grief, anger, pain, mortality, and compassion
- A time for all concerned to find out their strengths and build on them
- A time for them to discover their weaknesses and correct them
- A time of transformation of values – for individuals and our world

Unawareness of the events occurring in Vietnam was impossible in the allied countries. Stories and reports daily penetrated every possible crack of society for years before, during, and after the war. Everyone knew something of it, whether it was accurate or not, if accuracy was even possible.

It changed us as individuals and nations. We all had to look at that war through different eyes. We had no choice. It was in our face whether we were there or not. I had to ask myself some very important and direct questions –

- Should our country and should I be involved in something I don't understand?
- Where does that leave me?
- What should I do?
- As a young man eligible for the draft – do I go on to college, into the military, or into Canada?
- If not the latter, then which college or which branch of the military forces?

The sum total of those thoughts and actions of individuals and nations over the past sixty years has truly re-shaped our consciousness about war and ourselves. My experiences there and afterwards, changed me dramatically, without realizing the extent at that time. And *you* no doubt as well. We have been, and continue to be, a part of that transformation into who we are as a result.

Upon my arrival in Vietnam in August 1967, I was dropped into a world I had not previously known or that I could possibly totally prepare for. My personal mission was to play my part to which I was assigned, and to *survive.*

In preparation for my assignment to Vietnam, the Army, in short gave me -

- suitable clothing for the tropical climate,
- a survival knife,
- a Vietnamese phrase booklet,
- orientations on the dangers of drugs, numerous venereal diseases, malaria and other diseases, and
- miscellaneous other information and suggestions.
- There was no mention of the potential of acquiring a condition called Post Traumatic Stress Disorder.
- There was no suggestion that a subtle black shadow would follow me home as depression.
- There was no suggestion that a tunnel rat undermining my inner mental and physiological world would surface onto my outer landscape with a new awareness and conditions years later – some of those symptoms coming sooner rather than later.
- There was no suggestion that possibly the biggest challenges I would face in my life was after I was discharged from active service.

Two days after I turned 19 -

- I entered the Army as a *raw* egg, shell intact.
- Eight months later I arrived in Vietnam as a *soft-boiled* egg.
- Another two years passed and I came back home as a *hard-boiled* egg.

My inner self had solidified and my outer shell had become more brittle. It wasn't possible to 'un-create' back into the raw egg I had been. **Giving up my protective shell around my emotions was the toughest but most crucial step in the whole process in my journey to healing of PTSD**. In order to heal, I needed to soften inside, which required peeling away the shell that was cracking. It was a process over some years, resulting in a breakthrough to where I could consciously transform that mess within me into what I wanted in preference. That is – my life in a form that worked *for* me instead of against me.

I couldn't move on until I let go of that protective exterior I held on to for my very survival in the military world. (That naturally also applies to anyone in a 'survival' situation in civilian life).

- That shell conceals an inner conflict that results in outer conflict.
- That shell is a hindrance to relationships of every description and to life itself, outside of war.
- All efforts to communicate in a transparent, bi-directional way are compromised until that barrier is broken down.
- That shell is no longer necessary to live in survival mode in a normal civilian world, but we cling to it through habit for a sense of protection and safety.
- That shell distances us from others and can make for a lonely existence, foreign to the potential fullness of our humanness.
- That shell and a cynical attitude towards many aspects of life were my shields to penetration

- I could not heal and truly come back to life until I got through our tough outer surface to the heart of the matter - a process of desire, effort and time
- I could then work on getting the necessary **coherence** between my heart and my mind to feel truly ***alive!***
- That **coherence** is an orchestration of those heart and mental energies to create balance - resulting in our ***wellness.***
- Trauma causes dis-connection and dysfunction in relationships of all kinds – between individuals and groups outwardly, between organs and cells in people – resulting in incoherence and disease
- Healing requires some understanding of how to make that happen beyond simply the desire.
- Healing requires allowing others with understanding and compassion to get inside the protective shell so they can help us in a way that feels safe.

The first step towards healing is simple in one sense – letting go and allowing, more so than working on ways of 'fixing'. But I had to get past my stubbornness I held onto until I reached a point of surrender. I was afraid to come to terms with the raw emotions laying behind my façade of being in control of them. They could unexpectedly unleash as frustration, anger, rage, confusion and tears connected to some indescribable feelings in unpredictable, uncontrollable ways.

The pattern became more frequent, less manageable, with more un-concealable tears. A few random tears became more . . . more often. Surrender wasn't in my backpack at birth, but I eventually sought help to get over the mounting challenge I faced.

Why my resistance to open up?

- The innate warrior within me, evident from an early age, didn't want to admit to such a sign of weakness to others or even to myself.
- I was taught from earliest memory to be determined and strong in the face of adversity.

- I trained to be a soldier. A *warrior first of all*; then skilled professional. Proud. Resilient. Ingrained training not left behind upon discharge from active duty.
- And I am human – not given to admitting to faults easily. My damaged self-esteem was in confusion. Who was I? What happened to my Self? That was not easy to answer rationally while in the *incoherent* state of survival mode.

In 2000 I was diagnosed with PTSD. That was my first awareness of such a condition. I had been, largely unconsciously, entertaining a nebulous of stress-related issues. Over the ensuing weeks, months and years of investigating and digesting the implications for me, I have come to see them as having some common traits that sometimes makes them hard to distinguish. A 'can of worms' or 'the Stress family' are probably appropriate broad descriptions which I use to reference them in general terms.

By about mid-2011, after several years of counselling and pursuing solutions and answers, I felt like I was finally getting my life back. The result by then was virtually a transformation of my health and happiness. I had learned much that helped me and I really wanted to share that knowledge in the hope that it might help others.

But I knew that I was still emotionally vulnerable in some situations when certain buttons were pressed. Since then, I have discovered and employed additional powerful tools more recently available to us all which have helped me further. The benefits I'm feeling have empowered me so I can help other people as well. Overall, I've spent over fifteen years on a journey of discovery and healing, along with the work to make it happen.

It is not the intention of my message here to dig up and rehash old memories or discuss the pros and cons of the Vietnam War. We all had a unique experience there - some better than others. My role there was in support rather than direct combat, so I faced less traumatic situations than for many of you.

I left there thinking the war and its effects were well and truly over for me. They weren't. Mentally and emotionally, I was affected without even recognizing the fact. Those effects created a lid on my happiness. Unknowingly, I came away from there with bombs ticking away inside my head and body ready to go off when the right button was pushed.

I believe that if we all knew then,
what I have learned since,
there would be no need for this book.

That knowledge would have perhaps saved me, and others like me, from going down many of the pathways I have. The ensuing experiences were sometimes difficult or even disastrous; it was my *D-Tour.* But of course it would have deprived me of invaluable learning and often wonderful experiences not otherwise possible. I have few regrets among any seeming setbacks. They would prove to be to my advantage through a change of time and perspective. I can now appreciate the overall journey for all its aspects.

"Life is very interesting…
in the end, some of your greatest pains,
become your greatest strengths."
- Drew Barrymore

❧❧

They say you can pick your friends, but you can't pick your family. While that is biologically true, you and I are related in another way we didn't choose. The moment each of us arrived in Vietnam, we formed an unconscious relationship; we became members of an exclusive club; a community as such.

Most clubs are made up of voluntary, like-minded members with rules and boundaries, sometimes by invitation only. That wasn't the intention in our case; it just was. The only requirement was simply to *be there*; to show up. Once there, you were in the club without a choice or even a conscious awareness of it at the time. Our club happens to have millions of members, each with a unique story within the confinement that defined us.

We were initiated and tarred with the same brush, which bonded us together in a way no one else can fully understand. Each of us had a unique experience there, but we instinctively have a *knowing* and *understanding* of a commonality only we can fully relate to.

When VN vets meet, there is an invisible key that unlocks the door into the club no one else can enter. There is a powerful connection that is felt without even speaking; a coherence of mind and body. Others have tried to get in to understand more fully, but it's impossible. No matter how hard they try, it is sealed to everyone but club members. No one else can get in, and no one can get out. Even so, the club is *only part of our life experiences – it is not who we are.*

Other people experiencing a common situation could also be regarded as members of a particular club with unique understanding.

Those invisible walls of the clubroom can sometimes both negatively and positively act as -

- A connection: the supportive and protective comfort of a brotherhood or community
- A powerful, valuable sense of increased mental toughness through surviving the experience
- A disconnection: a barrier to intimacy in other relationships that could bring us enjoyment
- A sense of separation of self from many potentially wonderful aspects of life
- A dampening effect on our life force, health and happiness
- A mixed bag of potential outcomes . . . negative or positive
- Love and compassion by others outside the club can break through those barriers for healing . . . but *only if allowed*

How can we allow and enjoy the connection we can feel in a community, and expand that connection to nurture our other relationships? I know that it is possible. I had to make choices. The essence of this book is sharing how I've been able to overcome that challenge and reconnect in order to move on to a happier, healthier life.

Whatever you are thinking about your life at the moment, you and I are some of the lucky ones to still be alive and perhaps to have learned to manage the symptoms and problems. But too many vets have already died post-war for many reasons, from slow self-destruct to more immediate forms of suicide. There are still those vets that are physically and/or emotionally wounded. Do we ever get totally over 'it'. I doubt it.

There are those that just *exist* in survival mode in parks, forests and under bridges. Others may have a roof over their head and appear to be okay to others, may be in a relationship and have a family, but they still live in their own world of **surviving** rather than **thriving**. Simply existing . . . but that *can change with desire!*

Our time in Vietnam put us all in survival mode with varying and lasting effects. Certain triggers re-create the adrenaline/cortisol impulses that still affect our behaviour to various degrees in civilian life. It is not possible to thrive in wellness while living predominately in survival mode because of the physiological and biochemical processes taking place which can override our conscious efforts to control our behaviour. I'll show the scientific evidence and reasons of that in another chapter.

We might -

- Feel emotionally disconnected from people or anything to varying degrees, often or always
- Think others don't understand us even if they have tried to do so
- Think only VN vets understand each other, but still don't want to engage in a connection
- Try to be mentally and emotionally bullet-proof for survival and self-esteem
- Have the feeling of being confined or trapped in circumstances or life in general

- Think that 'out of sight, out of mind' is the best solution and the stuff we are dealing with will just go away eventually
- Be fearful of feeling emotionally vulnerable

i.e. Will I: get angry; explode with rage; feel overwhelmed; get teary over 'nothing'?

- Be fearful of what others may think of us if we become emotional and 'let go'?
- Think we will appear to be weak by admitting the need for help
- Be fearful of how far it is to the bottom of the canyon of emotions if we take steps to investigate and take action about our feelings

We might have thoughts like -

- Is it 'safe' to open up?
- Can I get back out if I do?
- Will I break down?
- Will I lose my identity?
- I've made it this far, why should I bother to change?
- I'll play it safe and remain a 'clam'
- I don't want to think or talk about any of my Vietnam experience

Those are a few of the reasons I can remember that held me back from taking action for so long. I could probably add more and elaborate at length on each. I could also give you my version of a very long story laced with my political take, along with any drama I experienced that could possibly suck you right down with me into an angry, black hole. They are all my perception of course. But what is the good in doing that?

- It keeps me enmeshed and embroiled in it
- It doesn't free me of all that and help me feel better about myself and my life

- I can't move forward if I am locked in my past
- It certainly wouldn't help you, which is the focus of this book

❧❧

I arrived in Australia in January 1972, not knowing a single soul. One of the first people to be-friend me was Stan Haas, a workmate in my first job and a vet of the Australian army in Vietnam. There was that instant connection as a 'club member' that lasted through thick and thin. He was a great friend and really instrumental in my integration into my new life.

Stan was a friendly, cheerful, and intelligent fellow who had injuries incurred in Vietnam. He didn't talk about them. He never complained or blamed anyone for his circumstances or whatever condition he was dealing with. He preferred to just wear it inside for whatever reason. Sadly for me and all that knew him, Stan passed on my birthday in 2012. There is no chance of me ever forgetting our wonderful memories and friendship which I celebrate along with my birthday.

What's the point of Stan's story? His loving partner Helga encouraged him to address his health more attentively, but he seemed to resist for some reason, as seems to be the case with so many vets. Helga, his family, friends and Stan himself, really wished that he would have gotten the help sooner that he eventually sought.

I think a lot of vets don't really care too much about their own well-being and mortality. We don't always value our self-worth – influenced perhaps by the treatment we sometimes received on our return from the war. It seems to be common amongst us. Others often care about us more than we do about ourselves

❧❧

I'm sure *your* Vietnam story affected you a great deal in many ways. We all *changed* - prior, during, and after. We had to. We were trained in order to do a task put before us and to hopefully survive whatever we experienced. We were then left to adapt back to civilian life with our own devices. There wasn't an awareness of the problems I carried out with me and no way to treat them had I *been* aware. I continued to self-medicate my demons with alcohol and occasional marijuana use, neither of which cured anything beyond a temporary relief. I would think my efforts were the common path for most vets.

Later, many of you got some form of help outside your own survival methods as awareness of PTSD and other health issues such as those around Agent Orange became known. That help may have been very effective for you, but chances are, it probably simply helped you to cope enough to get by. Counselling was very beneficial for me for some time. What is known and available today in treating the 'Stress family' of anxiety, depression, and PTSD, has expanded greatly and is more advanced to what was available to me in 2000. They allow for greater self-responsibility, self-awareness, and self-treatment in our overall health.

There are a wide variety of methods now that approach those problems very differently and effectively, usually without medication. They often have an immediate improvement in how we feel and on our mental clarity, without the side effects that I struggled with using anti-depressants. Many are simple do-it-yourself techniques, which we can easily program into our life. There really is a smorgasbord of effective help available to us now.

Regardless of our past experiences, whether military or otherwise, the important questions to me are:

- Am I happy with my thoughts and feelings i.e. do I enjoy peace of mind and feel good in myself?
- If not, am I prepared to consider possibilities that can possibly help me reach that?
- Am I willing to *change* to improve my wellness?

"Knowing is not enough; we must apply.
Willing is not enough; we must do."
—Goethe (1749-1832)

Whether we arrived in Vietnam by our choice or someone else's really doesn't matter any longer. That is past. The only moment in life that *really* matters, is the one that we are in at this instant. That is the *only* one we can *change* and *manage* in order to feel differently about our self or anything else – through intention and the breath in the present moment. That is *conscious change*. ***That is where our power lies.***

That requires -

- Desire
- Intention
- Action

I would love to tell you that my 'stuff' is totally erased from my memory and feelings, but that is not the case. Writing this book certainly brings up memories and emotions I wanted to forget and some I thought I had forgotten. As with so many things in life, it seems to be a case of learning good management, rather than 'good-bye' in some cases.

My Vietnam experience is no longer my mental prison – it is my teacher.

Fortunately I've learned to be able to accept and re-process them to transform some of them into a more positive light. That is freeing and empowering. The more I do that, the more my fears shrink and release their hold on me. I had unconsciously been putting all those memories, deemed 'bad' in my mind, into a box together to avoid. Once I eventually opened the dreaded imaginary containment to face those issues individually, they became more manageable, enabling me to let them go so I could move on.

In the process, I have also recalled some excellent memories of that time and can see how some of my experiences, perhaps previously perceived as 'bad', were ultimately beneficial to me – even strengthening. Either way, I've had to accept them and take ownership, and consequently feel enhanced in ways by the experience.

Moreover, the battle of dealing with the thoughts and emotions has empowered me in ways that would never have happened without that conflict within me. It was my human nature to sometimes avoid confronting issues if I could duck and weave my way around them, rather than face and take up the challenge. Affirmative action helped me to expand my awareness and grow in strength as I let go of 'stuff' and moved on. It also helped me *feel* better in my self, the magic ingredient of better overall health.

- All of us had a *drastic change* when we arrived in Vietnam - in environment, behaviour, thinking, feeling, experiences, and consequences.
- There was a more *subtle change* that actually started well before we put on a uniform - it started in high school for me. Discussions in classes and elsewhere on the topic of U.S. involvement in Vietnam - based primarily on what we learned through various forms of media. It was unavoidable.

A conversation with my mother took place perhaps a year or so after my return from Vietnam when she showed concern that I had 'changed'. I figured it probably didn't really take the perception of my very astute and remarkable mother to work that out, but I queried her remark further. Not by choice really - she had me cornered.

In essence, she was saying that she felt that something in me had diminished or died during that time since I had left home (after high school). I had lost some of whom I had been and that my behaviour had changed. Of course her perception rang true. My attitude and feelings couldn't be concealed.

How could I have *not* changed? I couldn't un-see, un-hear, un-learn, un-do those thoughts and feelings easily that had moulded me into someone different. I just hadn't realised how apparent it was to others; someone who I really cared about in particular. And how much it concerned and hurt her to witness that, unable to help.

Why do I emphasize *change*? Because we all *changed* through our military and Vietnam experience - outside of our control. It requires further *change* in order to alter the effects on our well-being by our own conscious positive action. Do I want to remain in a rut - or *change* so I can move ahead?

I was changed from a '*civil*'ian -

- Into a military programmed body and mind in 3 months
- By two years, seven months and five days of active duty
- Two of those years in a war environment
- By decisions I made during those times

During my final days of military service I was 'debriefed' on how to adjust back to civilian life; probably the same for you. I wasn't even aware of most of the *changes* that had taken place in me during my time in service. I had laughed at the suggestion that 'de-briefing' was even necessary before my discharge. I probably appeared to be alright on the surface; at least through my eyes that see what they want to see.

The disciplined routine so necessary in a military environment with regular prepared meals, work, sleep, and behaviour learned quickly and forcefully, was suddenly swapped back into a reality left behind nearly three years before.

The military machines and attentive Vietnamese domestic help looked after me in many ways. Then suddenly I was put out into the world to look after myself. No problem I figured, but I needed to learn or re-learn how in some respects. The world had changed and so had I. My outward persona was an altered image, reflecting my new state of being. What were the chances of changing back to an 'unaffected civilian' to any degree?

It wasn't simply a matter of slipping back into my old mould. I had to adapt in ways I didn't see coming. In addition, the craziness of the ongoing war, government actions and the attitudes of society towards the mix, had a dramatic impact on me that I wasn't expecting to face upon my discharge. The sometimes cynical young man I was becoming, could not always mask those feelings of suppressed anger at some aspects of the world I found myself in.

"The only permanent thing in this world is change."

That oh so true quote in 1898 is credited to an Italian actor with an expansive name who shortened his tag to Toto. I would suggest that similar words have been expressed long before. Human beings know that life is a process of *constant change*; of the world around us and in our being - *everything!* So why did I struggle with it?

It's usually easier to *change* when it is for something that we want than what we don't want. I think we can deal with the constant, subtle *changes* going on in our world; stable; balanced. It is the drastic *changes* that most of us don't feel comfortable with. It can wobble and topple everything from relationships to stock markets and governments. It can be traumatic if our body and mind can't adjust. We can get stuck in a sense and can't move on in step with the world around us. Such is the effect of trauma and PTSD.

Ironically, I have lived a life of virtual *constant change* since leaving high school in 1966. Apart from nearly two years in Vietnam (in one location), I have since lived in dozens of locations in two countries, had dozens of jobs, owned dozens of vehicles, and been in numerous relationships, including two marriages, both ending in divorce.

Change has been a pre-dominate characteristic for me, with its positives and negatives. Apparently that is not uncommon for Vietnam vets. I can see how it was actually a way of coping with an underlying dis-satisfaction with things by being a frequent distraction in the adjustment process of *change*.

I am okay with it now, but I wasn't always when I didn't initiate it. Mostly though, it seemed to satisfy an urge within me when I chose the *change*. Once I accepted and balanced that trait in me, life got much better for me. Fortunately, *change* has served me well in moving my life forward in ways when it pleased a desire within me, overriding the unfavourable uninvited events that have created *change*.

Life throughout nature is cause and effect. Whenever possible, I try to use my intention and tools to *cause* the effects I desire, and ride the waves of that which I have no control.

❧❧

Change is Energy in Motion (*E-motion*)

According to scientists, the *energy* imprint and impact that any traumatic experience has on us is influenced by -

- The strength of the *energy* of an event
- How much of that *energy* we absorb
- How effectively we can release that *energy* from our physical body
- How we deal with that *energy* psychologically

That can be wonderful or problematic. In a war situation, the *energy* is massive, on and off the field. We absorb some of that *energy* which we take away with us regardless of the role we played in the overall drama. It's unavoidable. It seems to carry some level of trauma for nearly everyone who connects to it. We were all part of the machinery and *energy* of war. I believe that some understanding of *energy* and its effects on our body, (also *energy)*, is very beneficial in our healing and maintaining our wellness. (More on that in another part of the book)

The trauma can be quite obvious or absorbed subtly into our being with little degree of awareness at the time. Simply discussing the topic creates an *energy*. Just those two words, Vietnam War, in fact, set off an emotional reaction (releases an *energy*) within me, often beyond my immediate control.

The real problem lays in not realising the presence of the effects on us and not doing something about them. That energy having those effects is best to be released as soon as possible to avoid long term effects. Our VN experience occurred a long time ago, but I believe that *it is not too late to get help if we want it.* We *can* shift that trapped *energy* within us that dictates unwanted behaviour beyond our conscious control.

The whole question is:

- Do you want to be different from your current state of being and/or behaviour?
- Are you prepared to *change*?

It is a process. It doesn't have to be dramatic or traumatic. You need to -

- Want to
- Believe that you can
- Be prepared to learn
- Take steps that will take you forward towards a new vitality for life

A change in your *energy* will cause a shift in your relationships; a ripple effect -

- It may take some time to adjust for all concerned
- The relationship with yourself is ultimately the linchpin – address it first
- A happy relationship with anyone else starts with your own happiness and desire

As I come to complete this book, I am seventy years of age. Most of you would also be in that age bracket. We are getting to the pointy end of the stick of life, though I feel I have much more living to do. I am not afraid of dying, but I am in no hurry. I don't wish to have a miserable death or have my loved ones around me putting up with a grumpy old fart in my final years, sometimes a trait of the 'elderly'.

These should be some of the best years of my life in many respects – enjoying what is left of it with my family and friends while striving to ensure I have the best health and wellness I can maintain. I am the only one who is responsible for making that happen. It has meant I had to let go of blaming my circumstances on anyone or anything and accept full responsibility for my decisions and actions. I had to let go of someone else nagging or pushing me into a course of action, whether that was through a partner/family member, or my doctor. That in itself was empowering.

I had to take off the emotional armour that was a protection against a situation which no longer serves me. The 'Who', 'Why', and 'What Was' of those events are no longer important. *They were a part of my experience, but they are not who I am.* Sure, that can still make me vulnerable at times to emotional triggers that can suddenly appear when I least expect them, but that is a small price to pay for the benefits I now enjoy.

It is important to accept what has happened and let it go in order to put our *energy* into healing. That means letting go of the hurt, the anger, the pain, the guilt, and any other toxic *energy* sappers holding me back from moving on with a new sense of self in a positive direction. I can't move ahead if dwell on the issues of the past. I must work towards solutions through my desire and intention for what I want now.

My Vietnam experience was a holiday in comparison to many of you. Yet the effects of PTSD still caused me to feel *dysfunctional* enough to *D-tour* me and to look for ways to correct that. I hope what I have shared in this book doesn't appear to be too simplistic to overcome a complex condition you may have. The measures I've suggested in this book are often simple, but don't be fooled into thinking they aren't effective.

We all have had individual journeys, but I believe that our passage out of the darkness is still along a similar path (like life itself, it starts and ends with the simplest tool - the breath!)

You and I are not to blame for our PTSD -

- but it is up to us to work our way out of it –
- in our individual way with some help.
- No one else can do it for us.
- We don't need or want sympathy –
- We just need help to find our way out of the tunnel we each find ourselves in –
- but we have to admit to ourselves that we have a problem -
- and to *be willing to receive that help.*

Vietnam is past. We can let go. We can give up our persona of the wounded warrior living in *survival energy*. We can move forward in an empowered way of *invigorated energy*. We are in the *NOW* – the *only* time with the ***power*** to act and the potential for finding *peace of mind*, *wellness* and *happiness*. **It is the *only* time in which we can take your life back!**

The Realty of my Search for Solutions

I still haven't found a magical fix for PTSD. Everything that helped me required some effort from me. There has been wonderful assistance from many sources, but no one has been able to do anything for me that hasn't involved my own desire, allowance and effort. I had to search, listen, learn and try with an open mind and an open heart. In the process I have found many very effective methods of improving my condition.

- It's been realising it is a complex physiological condition that requires a multi-faceted approach to healing
- It's been about re-establishing communication throughout my body, humanity, and nature
- It's been about changing the energy through my *body* physically – whether from stagnant to movement, or erratic to coherent.
- It's been about calming my *spirit to find peace* within me.
- It's been about bringing the energies of my *mind into clarity*.
- It's been about learning to constantly *balance* those energies of my *body, spirit and mind*
- Life in the army was disciplined action to be an effective soldier; dealing with PTSD is the same – get up, move, do what you gotta do, going forward and upward – every day. Simple strategy for a complex condition. That's ***LIFE!***

Suggestions:

- Focus on how **you** *want* to be – *complete and whole* – rather than past or current state

- See yourself *being* that way ***now***
- ***You*** are ultimately *the only one* who can make that decision and take that action.
- We have to *let go* of those thoughts and emotions that keep us from moving forward
- We can use those *strengths* we gained in the military time of our life
- We can't just *think* our way through the fog past the intention and desire
- We have to get off the mental merry-go-round that is characteristic of stress, through the *breath*.
- We have to *open our heart* and get back in touch with who we were before the shit hit the fan.
- That may be a point in time before we ever put on a uniform
- It requires some *guidance*. Have a mindset that is *open to all possibilities*
- There is an amazing *abundance of support available* to us
- But most of all it requires our *desire* and *allowing* some assistance.
- It is ***your*** decision.
- I hope that the contents of this book will help you in some way
- **May you be blessed with the peace and joy and overall good health** I have found in my search for **wellness**

Breathe in/ /Breathe out/ /Breathe in/ /Breathe out/

My Vietnam Experience

What Was It Like?

If only I had a dollar for every time I've been asked that question regarding my experience in Vietnam. Such a simple question, yet so difficult to answer in short form – or any other form for that matter. You virtually had to be there to relate. It's a bit like a man asking a woman what it's like to give birth. As a man, I can *try* to understand, but I can never *really* know without experiencing it. Probably not going to happen.

If there was any hope of being able to paint an accurate picture, or to put it into a few words, and then to be understood, it might be worth the effort. Generally it was a feeling of "why bother?" Consequently, like most vets I knew, I would tend to close the door on the subject through much of my life.

In all fairness and respect, I would usually try to come up with something to satisfy the seeker without getting in too deep before perhaps my emotions got too uncomfortable for me. I can understand the curiosity, but I preferred not to have to deal with it emotionally, and it was basically 'mission impossible' anyway. It seemed that only people who had actually been there had any real idea - and they didn't need to ask.

❧❧

My Arrival in Vietnam

I shuffled along in the queue towards the rear door of the Boeing 707 with a slight nervous excitement in anticipation of what awaited me. Little did I realise, as I stepped outside into another world, that my life was about to change forever.

The flight from the U. S. Air Force base near San Francisco had been long but comfortable enough aboard the chartered commercial airliner. There was only a short refuelling stop at the tiny island of

Guam. I was thankful it wasn't a no-frills air force plane like the C-141, which is a bit like being strapped into a jet-propelled 55-gallon barrel. I was also thankful to be arriving in such a civilized manner rather than in an amphibious boat with a rifle in my hands, onto a beach with a hail of bullets and mortars as a welcome.

I stood for a moment at the top of the stairway leading to the steaming tarmac, stopped in my tracks by the humidity and heat of the day after the air-conditioned comfort of the aircraft. No one seemed in a hurry to disembark to an uncertain fate, so I had a moment to look around at the surrounding environment and take in what I could.

The immediate thing that had the most impact was the pungent odour that was an unforgettable assault on my sense of smell. It was to become a familiar companion which varied in strength at different locations, but seldom left me. I was told later that it was a blend of rotting vegetation and smoke from the crematoriums and fires used for cooking in the huts and houses hugging the airfield.

I was oblivious to another invisible companion with me that day as well. I'm sure I had a guardian angel on my shoulder as I walked off that plane. That would become apparent to me at times in the ensuing weeks and months.

We had landed at Tan Son Nhut on the outskirts of Saigon (now Ho Chi Minh City) which was reported to be the busiest airport in the world at the time. There seemed to be every type of aircraft imaginable using the facility, shared by military and commercial aircraft alike. It was built by the French in the 1920's during their occupation, later expanded and jointly controlled by Vietnam and the U.S.

It was early September 1967, 8 months after I had entered the U.S. Army at Butte, Montana. In contrast, that had been a bitterly cold morning in January, two days after my 19th birthday. So, there I was in a very different environment to what I had been in hours before, on an assignment of twelve months that turned into nearly two years.

What awaited me that day wasn't really a shock. We had been preparing for the possibility of going there for months and had been briefed as much as one could be. Yet my new world had a sense of unreality about it, as if I was an actor stepping out from behind a curtain onto a stage in a production of make believe. Was this all just a dream? Would I wake up at some point back in the 'real world'? That sensation or perception was to remain with me during my tour of duty.

There was a range of personnel on the flight, mostly additional or replacement troops (as opposed to a complete incoming unit). Some were new like me and some returning to duty from leave or a previous tour of duty. I was surprised to see that there were also a few civilian workers such as technicians on contracts amongst the military. I hadn't previously been aware that they also played a vital role in the war effort.

The other army personnel and I were taken to a facility to receive a briefing and to be issued with a range of suitable tropical combat clothes and equipment. It took a few days to get an assignment to a unit in the field.

While there, I could hear the sounds of war going on around me, but no one seemed to be too concerned about it, as we were not being directly attacked. Some of the time waiting was hanging out at the club talking with others that were incoming, or those more knowledgeable of the situation. It was a time of curious anticipation.

It was general scuttlebutt that the further north and closer to North Vietnam, the hotter the action and therefore more dangerous. I got my orders to go north along with another 'greenie' to the same unit as we were both avionics technicians, trained to maintain the electronic communications and navigation systems on aircraft. He had trained to do repairs in a workshop, while I learned to maintain the systems on the aircraft, primarily helicopters and small fixed wing types.

We flew up on an Air Force Hercules C-130 to a place called Nha Trang, which was about halfway up the country and reported to be a fairly peaceful location. We arrived at the company headquarters, which was on an airfield just near a beach. It was also used as a bit of an in-country R & R (rest and recuperation) centre for battle-weary troops, so a choice assignment as they go.

However the company had another facility further north where it was decided one of us would be sent. The choice of which one of us was to go on was left to the two of us. The other fellow was married and figured he'd be safer at Nha Trang, so he helped me decide (so to speak) that I should be the one to go north. So after a day or two in the sun, I was off again.

My New 'Home'

Qui Nhon, though smaller than Nha Trang, was a fairly large coastal city numbering maybe two hundred thousand. I arrived there late in the afternoon on a post WWII C-47, picked up by office clerk PFC Shoemaker, who was a willing fountain of information. We reached our facilities on the northern side of the fenced airport enclosure by jeep in about five minutes.

The office had closed for the day, so Shoemaker took me to the enlisted men's quarters and told me to pick any available bunk on the bottom floor of the barracks. We dropped my gear there at a bottom bunk near the back door leading to the adjacent shower/toilet block and went off to the mess hall for the evening meal. He gave me a bit of a briefing on facilities, procedures and rules and answered my questions.

Upon returning to the barracks after eating, I started to make the bed and unload my belongings in my new 'home'. While in the process, a group of guys came walking in from the other end of the 'hooch' on their way back from chow at a different mess hall. One of the voices I could hear sounded just like Ed Schultz, a friend I had known most of my life from our little home town of Superior. I couldn't believe it – it was Ed! And of all the spare bunks, I had picked the one under his! He had been in Vietnam some months, but he had only arrived at that platoon a short time before me.

So what were the chances of two people that grew up together in a small town in Montana to be put in that situation out of hundreds of units and some 500,000 troops there at that time? The odds were incredible! We couldn't have planned it or organised it within the Army that I knew.

There must have been an angel on my shoulder that answered the prayers of my mother and others that I would be safe and looked after. It certainly made my arrival in that new environment a much happier experience. Ed was invaluable in teaching me the ropes, having his companionship, and sharing news from home. Thank you God or 'Events Orchestrator' of the Universe!

My Unexpected Job

On my arrival there, Shoemaker asked, 'Can you type'? My answer of course was, 'Why'? He had been seconded into the clerical role he held until he could find a suitable replacement at which time he would be allowed to go to work doing radio repairs as he was trained to do. He was very keen to get out of the office and ply his trade before his tour of duty was over. He pointed out that the monsoon season was still in force and that work out with the flight line crew was in the unrelenting wet. The office however was air conditioned, and there were other perks, such as no guard duty.

It was a rather convincing argument he put up, apart from the fact they didn't need another body on the flight line crew at the moment until one of them completed his tour of duty. My records showed that I could type about sixty words a minute. That and a quick interview was enough to convince the commanding officer that I was potentially a suitable replacement.

It wasn't my choice. He made the decision for me, probably due to unrelenting nagging from Shoemaker. It came with the understanding that it was a temporary situation and that I would be allowed to do my trained job when a position became available.

My job as the office clerk came after a short training stint with my predecessor. I was typist, mail boy, and go-for. It had its advantages and privileges of sorts, apart from working conditions mentioned. More importantly to me, there was a degree of freedom to explore while on my trips in the jeep to the postal distribution centre to exchange our bag or bags of mail. That was unauthorized but tolerated if kept within reason.

The position was naturally one of trust since I was often privy to inside and delicate bits of information that few in my platoon were, apart from the commanding officer (a major), a lieutenant, warrant officer and top sergeant That could be both a blessing and a burden, as I was of sworn to secrecy of all knowledge I held. That set me apart from my peers and therefore something that could sometimes be uncomfortable for me, but not a real problem. The accompanying privileges made it a worthwhile experience, but as a bonus, I learned a great deal that both empowered me in a sense, and dismayed me in other ways, about things I could never have known of otherwise.

🐾🐾

The Qui Nhon airfield was used by both military and Vietnamese civilian aircraft. Air Force transport planes larger than C-130's were rare and there were no fighters. There were various Army helicopters there but no gun-ships stationed there. The airfield was about one mile, or 1.6 kilometres long, running roughly SE to NW and perhaps half as wide at widest point, and was surrounded by a barbed wire fence. There were limited access points with permanent guards and patrols of the perimeter at night.

Our barracks or 'hooch' ran alongside the barbed-wire fence less than ten metres away from huts of locals against the other side with only a low wall of sandbags around our building. It was a very easy target for a hand-grenade with no chance of finding the thrower. It appeared that we were in a location of low risk, but we did our best to remain friendly with the families on the other side of the barrier for what it was. Rolls of barbed wire weren't too effective in stopping bullets. We also had above-ground steel bunkers covered in sandbags near each end of the hooch we retreated into during occasional alerts.

The concerns regarding being further up-country meant increased dangers were soon put to rest. Apart from the U.S. Army present and the air force base with fighter jets at nearby Phu Cat, there was the presence of the U.S. Navy in our port. There was also a contingency of very proficient South Korean soldiers in the valley on the outskirts of the city. They all provided a comfortable sense of security.

Vietnam was a situation where there were few enemy lines as such.

The 'enemy' could be a soldier or an innocent looking child or elderly person - anyone, anywhere, and often not in a uniform, regardless of where I would have been sent.

Secret underground tunnels existed throughout much of the country that ranged from simply a safe passage or sanctuary to virtual cities with accommodation and hospitals for the Viet Cong and North Vietnamese Army. That made for very difficult warfare, despite the massive weaponry and firepower at our command. It was enough for me to think I would be building a raft and chance the high seas in the event that our enemy had similar warfare assets being fired back at us.

There was occasional sniper 'pot shots' directed at the airfield from the safety of the dense vegetation covering the nearby mountain and some terrorist activity around the area, but overall Qui Nhon was considered to be fairly secure area.

Occasionally gunships would be called in for air support on nearby activities when required, which would sometimes put on an awesome display of firepower visible from our hooch, with flares and tracers in the night sky.

Peace was usually restored in the coming light of day, although there were sometimes airstrikes nearby from jet fighters, which again, were impressive to watch in action. However, not long after my first birthday late in the following January, all hell was to break loose in our peaceful bit of war zone.

The TET Offensive of 1968

TET is a holiday that celebrates the Vietnamese New Year, with times varying according the lunar calendar. It is observed every year for several days.

At the start of it on January 30, 1968, the occasion was cleverly used by the Viet Cong and North Vietnamese to strike US allies while things were at a relative commercial standstill. They were also able to capitalize on the explosions of the usual accompanying holiday fireworks. No doubt many of those that were taking a 'holiday' from their 'day job', had greater energy for their 'night job' – as Viet Cong.

Attacks on our facilities were expected to some extent, but that year it was extremely well planned and executed with major impact on our forces. Our usually peaceful location was under attack for several days. We were on high alert before and after for some time. Overall, our forces took a hammering around Qui Nhon and throughout the country, which changed the direction of the war. It woke up the U.S. to the reality that it was dealing with more than poorly armed and poorly organized armies who would soon be overcome by mighty firepower. Our forces were under attack around us and throughout the country. A lot of people on all sides were killed and injured.

Since we were a support company, as opposed to a combat group, we provided security guards to airfield security, but we didn't take part in combat missions. It was the only time I can remember being directly part of the action as we laid low behind a low wall of sandbags along our barracks.

We could hear bullets flying, some of which hit our buildings and wall beside us. I laid low . . . very low! That was in broad daylight after a long night. The seriousness of war became more of a reality during that time.

We had one man from our unit on permanent guard duty assignment with airport security, who tragically, was killed point blank when an enemy soldier got through the airport barriers. Tommy paid the ultimate price in protecting us that first night, for which I feel eternally grateful. His sacrifice shocked us. !t was a vivid reminder that despite being a unit of technicians, we were still warriors above all else, participating in a real war of life and death.

There was damage done to some aircraft and facilities and sadly, some injuries and some lives were lost in the region during the attacks, but security was restored on the airfield fairly quickly.

Some of the Vietnamese civilians working by day on our base didn't return to work after they were eventually allowed back to work in days following. One of our onsite barbers had always given me an uncomfortable feeling, so I avoided him at the shop if I could. He was killed on the streets during the fighting - a Vietcong as it turned out.

My Early Months

My new learning experience seemed exciting and rewarding to some degree to begin with. I felt a sense of pride in being of service to my country. However I soon had questions regarding the purpose of us being there and the way we were going about fighting the war.

Naturally, each of us that went there had a different experience viewed through a different set of filters. Everybody's story was his own. It's probably safe to say that the one thing we all had in common was the pain of separation from our loved ones and the countdown of days until we could return home.

My memory was that I was reasonably okay for a few months, apart from some homesickness. For me, missing home started when I got news that my grandfather Grover Miles had passed a few weeks after I had arrived. It was a shock, so soon after seeing him while I was on leave.

Ed Schultz and I
Christmas 1967

My treasured 'spoilers' – cleaning my living area, clothes, even my boots

One Sick Puppy

A couple of months after arriving in Vietnam, I was playing basketball on an outdoor court set up near the clinic one evening following dinner. Soon after starting I started getting a pain in the left side of my abdomen. I thought it was from playing on a full stomach, but it quickly developed into much more when I began feeling feverish. The pain became very intense within minutes. One of the other players, a medic, and my friend Eddie got me off to the military hospital on the other side of the airbase.

At the hospital they wasted no time giving me their attention. They were soon poking and probing, both physically and verbally, with questions about what and where I had been eating. They kept asking if I had been eating the local food. The answer was "No", but they kept asking. I guess they couldn't believe anyone could have the reaction to our mess hall servings that my body was having.

It didn't surprise me too much, considering some of the disgusting foreign objects that occasionally appeared amongst the overall good stuff. I had soon learned to check it out before indulging. Fortunately my healthy appetite could surmount virtually any challenge and I became capable of stomaching just about anything; mind over matter for survival.

My temperature became very high and I was feeling rather delirious. I was soon lying on an operating table, lower abdomen shaved and ready to undergo an appendicitis operation. Apart from my own bewilderment at what was going on, there were concerns from the medical staff. The sharp pain I was feeling most was coming from my left side, opposite side of my appendix.

I have no idea how long I was laying on that table; I could hear chatter and laughter. I was rather incoherent. What was going on? Was I going to die? I was praying to be free of the pain and to be okay. I made promises to Heaven above that I would be a 'better' person if I lived.

Anaesthetised in prep, I was awoken some time later to be told that they had decided not to perform the operation. My fever had subsided somewhat for some reason. They thought the problem was probably some food poisoning causing the pain as well as the rectal bleeding I wasn't aware of. They weren't sure.

Bowel blockage or constipation? The one affliction no one ever had after arrival in the country. We could sh— through the eye of a needle at 20 paces. A rare solid stool was something worthy of mentioning to others, which could bring up jealousy, or applause - certainly amazement anyway.

That night I was put into a ward as the temperature and pain subsided. I was exhausted but my senses slowly returned somewhat. I spent the following week there, hoping to get back to normal; I didn't. I just wanted to lie in bed and get better, but a military hospital is not a rest and recuperation centre or holiday camp.

I lost about 30 pounds (14 kg) in that time and consequently I was very weak. Still, I thought I'd be better out of that place than in. I had to be up at the crack of dawn to make my bed for inspection by an officer later inspecting the wards, and then wait for permission afterwards to lay on it.

After a few days I was given something to do to amuse me. I got to help clean the area occupied by the hepatitis patients further down the room with a special disinfectant. No lazing about if you could breathe. I couldn't wait to get out of there, ready or not.

I was eventually given permission to go - against the advice of the hospital and my unit leaders who came to see me. I thought I was much stronger than I actually was, which I soon found out on returning to my unit. I could hardly walk, and would be tired just getting to the office across the road from our barracks. I just wanted to lie in my own bed and recuperate, but that is not the military way.

If you're sick, go to sick bay at the clinic. If you're deemed bad enough, you'll end up in hospital with its own version of nurturing as I already described. Either way, you were under scrutiny to make sure you weren't feigning it. In the ensuing days I was kindly allowed a few times by my superiors to retreat to my bed for a while when I was pretty useless at work.

Over the following weeks, I gradually improved, but I never gained back all the weight I carried into the country. I was still over twenty pounds (10 kg) lighter on discharge nearly two years later than I was prior to my illness.

Was that episode in my life traumatic? I don't know if it falls within the definition. I didn't really consider it to be until I thought about it more recently. I'd pretty much forgotten about it.

Perhaps it was. Whether realistic or not, I did have great concern for my welfare. And I really did wonder if I would survive at the height of it, albeit in a somewhat altered state. I did negotiate with God in my heart and mind, whatever state I was in. And I did lose 20 percent of my body weight in less than a week. No doubt a shock to my system, but was that 'traumatic'?

So that leads me to the question, "What is trauma and when is it actually a problem?" Here is a simplistic online dictionary definition for a complex range of possible answers:

Psychic trauma *a psychologically upsetting experience that produces an emotional or mental disorder or otherwise has lasting negative effects on a person's thoughts, feelings, or behaviour.*

I really don't know if that would be clinically classified as traumatic, but it may have added to the overall accumulation of trauma in my life that lead to more of a deadening of spirit by the time I re-entered the civilian world. In any case, it was part of my experience there I thought I had forgotten, but didn't.

Out on 'the Line'

Eventually I was able to get to work on the flight line crew in the area for which I was trained, and stayed there for the duration of my tour of duty. We had a small team, usually about four, based in a little hut near the runway, with a light truck for quick response to calls for help from aircraft. I enjoyed the freedom from the office environment and my new work for the most part despite challenges from weather elements and the demands of workloads at times.

My unit was there to provide avionics support for two air transport companies we were attached to, as well as any aircraft that came in from outlying areas for immediate attention. Our flight line crew had an obligation to repair problems with communication or navigation systems on army (and some air force) aircraft that presented themselves to us, as quickly as possible and keep at it until problem solved or able to get them airworthy. It was often just a matter of changing a 'black box'.

There was also a list of repair and maintenance activities to get through as our general activity. We always welcomed the occasional Korean plane that would come in for attention. They would usually pay us with a carton of Korean beer in token payment. We had a New Zealand plane or two at times as well.

The office Quonset hut
and our workshop

My flight line crew
in my latter days

Cheap Thrills

As a flight-line avionics technician, I maintained aircraft radios and navigation equipment on some fixed-wing aircraft, but mostly on a variety of helicopters. During part of my time in Vietnam, I gained flight status in order to check out the aircraft radios and instruments while in flight. That was a privilege for a few with extra pay, which I appreciated in all respects. Flying was my favourite form of escape from my mundane captivity – anywhere, anytime I could.

One of the helicopter test pilots was George. His flights were always a thrill. Part of the post-maintenance checks on the craft was to go up to 10,000 feet and switch off the engine, allowing the blades to auto-rotate as we floated back down. The engine was switched back on at a particular point and hope all went well. George loved to push the margins and level out as late and low as possible. He was a legendary terrorist. Farmers in the rice paddies would hit the deck and the water buffalo would run for their lives. The only one amused was George, but I can't say it wasn't something of an adrenaline rush for me in the other front seat. Unfortunately, he wasn't the only pilot I experienced that harassed innocent civilians and animals during my time there.

At times I was also able to act as an observer in the little single-engine Cessna 'Birddog' planes used by both the Army and Air Force. The pilot sat in the front with the observer in the rear seat, both packed tightly in. We would be assigned to fly above a convoy of trucks to look out for enemy activity or perhaps provide coordinates for artillery or strike aircraft. Sometimes the pilot would allow me to take the controls when we headed back to base, so I got a bit of flying experience in as well which I enjoyed. Unfortunately, after a few experiences, that form of freedom came to an abrupt halt.

I was called into the office one day and shown a UHF radio unit that had come in for repairs (salvage.) Turning it over, the impact of a bullet in the bottom of the very solid unit greeted me. That 'black box' had resided under the observer's seat of an Air Force Birddog that we supported. We had a very short discussion about how that bullet might have made a mess of the backside of the observer had it been a bit different trajectory. I suggested the observer was very fortunate, it had been a great form of protection, and chances were good it would never happen again.

My commanding officer saw the very same thing - yet very differently. He immediately banned me from further observer activities since it wasn't my assigned role. I had stripes on my sleeve, but he had bars on his collar – he squashed my appeal and terminated that extra-curricular form of my enjoyment. Fortunately, I still had an escape route when time allowed. There was an occasional call to ride gunner on a courier chopper flights going to headquarters in Nha Trang, Pleiku, DaNang or elsewhere – anywhere was fine with me.

A Bit of Adventure

During my second year in Vietnam I was sent to an in-country avionics school in Vung Tau for a few days. There was some new equipment I was required to learn about we would be maintaining on the navigation systems. Our team leader, who was about to complete his tour of duty, was also sent. Perhaps I needed an escort and chaperone? The Army does as Army does; don't waste time asking why. His mind was already on board an aircraft heading home, ahead of his body. In my eyes, it was a rare and privileged junket which got no resistance from me.

Vung Tau was convenient to Saigon and considered a 'safe' area if there was such a thing in that country, hence a good location for in-country training. It was also a primary short R&R location for battle-weary troops, and the incoming/departure point for Australian soldiers.

While there, I was approached on a road through our camp by a soldier in a different uniform to mine, which included a slouch hat. He asked me if I knew where a man could have a slash. I didn't quite understand the accent or the term, so he repeated it and explained when he saw my puzzled look. I directed him to a convenient typical open outdoor 'privates hidden' style urinal along the road. That was my first and only encounter with anyone from the U.S. ally country that would unexpectedly become my new home about four years later.

Our base at Qui Nhon was far to the north which required flights connecting through Tan Son Nhut airbase near Saigon. We arranged to conclude our escape from normal duties with a night in Saigon on the way back. We indulged ourselves with dinner at the exquisite restaurant in the beautiful Hotel Continental, built by the French during their fateful occupation of the country. The setting, with white linen covered table, and elegant candles served by impeccably mannered waiters was impressive and fun in our bazaar reality.

During our meal, we thought about engaging in some female companionship for the night to cap off our adventure. That led us to Cholon for some 'shopping' - to 'look' and to convince us one way or the other on the idea. It was a busy area of Saigon that was a commercial centre by day and off-limits at night due to the fact it was infested with Viet Cong and their sympathisers. Military Police patrolled the streets, particularly during hours of darkness and warned soldiers away. Despite the obvious risks, we managed to slip through and find some 'ladies of the night' to our liking who 'convinced' us they would keep us safe during the night. We were all locked in as darkness enveloped the city.

During the night there were the sounds of war, as usual. Occasional single shots and automatic weapons sounded nearby, with mortars and rockets off in the distance. It really didn't matter to me. I left the safety of our cocoon in the daylight the following morning, promises fulfilled. I was feeling sleep-deprived but nurtured by the sensual intimacy of a woman who looked after my emotional needs. In return I looked after hers, with respect and appreciation. There was a beneficial mutual exchange of assets which brought rewards to us both. Such was a human side of surviving the demands that war places on its participants and its victims.

Love and War

Aren't they similar in many ways – fear, passion, and battles etc.? War can be hell, but there is a more human side of war, which is very much a part of it, but seldom gets revealed - the emotional aspect. That of course covers a vast area from fear and hate to love and . . . simply sex.

Historically there have been sexual interactions during war from brutal rape to passionate love affairs and marriages, with everything in between. A warrior, male or female, could be away for very long periods of time, thus making the absence from loved ones a challenge for all concerned.

So how does war impact on the lives of service men and women during their time away from their nest? I can't speak for all wars, but I am going to share some of my observations and experiences during my time as a soldier in the theatre of war in South Vietnam.

I was one of millions of military and civilian men and women that served in that war lasting several years, half way around the world from our homes. It employed half a million personnel at that time in a game of tag where thousands landed every week as replacements and others departed, usually after a 12-month tour of duty.

What emotions and desires we were each dealing with through such a long period of separation from loved ones - the loneliness, the thoughts of partners and families and what they were doing? Were they safe? Were they managing alright? Did they still love us? Were they being faithful? Were the eagerly awaited letters bringing reassurance or bad news? How did we cope with that ever present powerful drive within us all, when for most, was at its lifetime peak? The majority of troops had yet to see Christmas 21 times.

Many of us were married or had a partner back home in some form of relationship, even at that young age, or at least had a steady girlfriend. Some were newly-weds in a last minute act before departure to secure their loved one. Others such as me, were alone in that sense, which had its obvious downside, but I saw it as a preferable position to be in. I didn't want the stress that a close relationship might cause me, in spite of the emotional support it could give from afar.

The first few months of my assignment were spent as the office clerk and mail man for our unit of about fifty men. A range of emotions with anxiety, joy, relief, disappointment, and even anger were evident when I distributed the letters each day. Emotions could be very real. One fellow we called Pooh Bear, threatened to kill me on more than one occasion, if I didn't deliver the news he hoped for. He was big enough to do it with his bare hands and sounded like he meant it, but of course never did.

On the bright side I got the pick of the letters from people in the homeland wanting a pen pal, so I established lines of communication with some lovely people offering friendship and support who sometimes were also in search of love.

On rare occasions someone would get a dreaded 'Dear John'

letter, telling them that their relationship was finished. That could be particularly devastating since there was no opportunity to discuss it face to face with the writer. One of the young fellows in my unit, who had gotten such a letter, shot himself in the foot while on guard duty in expectation of being sent stateside to recover and win back the heart of his lady.

However, the military machine takes a dim view on doing damage to government owned property, intentional or not, so he was charged, fined, and busted to lowest rank. He was sent to a military hospital in Japan to recuperate sufficiently to return to duty somewhere and fulfil his obligations with the time lost not counting towards his discharge date. It was very painful no doubt, but thankfully he didn't have a handgun or he may have gone for the heart or head.

I received a 'Dear John' letter during my months away from home while in training before leaving the U.S. That was difficult enough to deal with, since we'd planned to eventually marry, but thankfully it didn't occur while I was overseas and married.

But enough of all that for now – what about the sex aspect right? Well . . . like any situation of separation or isolation in the human experience, you just deal with it as best you can, taking into account accessibility, personal, moral, and religious beliefs and so on. Obviously that can play out in a variety of options and appeared to do so in the case in Vietnam.

That was taking place alongside the social revolution occurring in much of the western world during the '60's and '70's - drug use and so-called 'free love' - probably making it different to any war in history.

The military establishment tried to discourage troops engaging in sexual activities and getting emotionally involved with the local people for obvious reasons, but it was like trying to stop the rain during the monsoon. Sexual attraction, with or without love attached, happens anywhere and anytime, at any rank, war or no war. It's a bit hard to reign in what's natural for millions of young virile men and liberated women also engaged in atmosphere of the social changes and sexual freedom. Personally, I was in 'recovery' status from my broken relationship, therefore a free agent on a discovery tour, so to speak. I managed to find some lovely 'friendships' to ease the pain.

Naturally enough some guys fell in love with local Vietnamese women, occasionally resulting eventually in marriage. That created a number of problems for all concerned in the short term at least, with various outcomes, but hopefully happy ones in the long run. Who is to know how many of those relationships were based on true love, or just the desire of a woman to escape a war with a willing or perhaps unwitting accomplice?

Some guys established relationships, both casual and reasonably permanent, with native 'girlfriends' off base. It appeared that officers were unofficially 'allowed' the privilege of inviting 'guests' to their quarters when safe to do so. Some people would have a random quick fix with a local 'lady' at an establishment designed to accommodate such needs, perhaps after a few drinks at a local bar. Some would visit a spa/massage parlour that provided a range of services.

Some guys probably felt like it was a compromise in attending to the condition, but perhaps even with a degree of acceptance by an understanding partner back home. There was probably a lot of "ask me no questions, I'll tell you no lies," during those long absences from home.

Some people had affairs with other military or support personnel like nurses, which didn't seem to be much of a problem in the eyes of the military machine since it accommodated officers' natural desires primarily. That meant less chance of them getting intimately involved with the potential enemy (Viet Cong) I suppose.

Married personnel were allowed to meet their wives in Hawaii for a week of R&R midway through their tour of duty, which was a huge help in morale and holding marriages together. There probably wasn't much focus on rest and recuperation; or at least the rest aspect. Most returned with a smile on their face and determination to see them through to the end. It was beneficial in keeping their sanity and sometimes resulted in seeding the ground for expanding their family.

What were the effects of relationship interactions at any level with the local population? Firstly, there was always the risk of catching one of the many forms of venereal diseases available. Some were quite horrific - not common back in the homeland and not a desirable gift to take back to loved ones, present or future. Some were said to be incurable. That may or may not have been true. It may have been a story used as a deterrent to sexual activity with limited success by the powers that be. They stressed the dangers of venereal diseases before and after our arrival.

Cases of gonorrhoea were not uncommon with people who refused to use protection. One fellow in my unit would usually use the communal shower when no one else was around because of a large lump on the side of his penis. That was an effective visual reminder that worse things could and did happen.

Probably for some troops, sex was a meaningless act or a fling to help them get through a difficult time in their lives. Those in relationships always faced the risk of being exposed either during the course of their tour of duty or when they returned home. That of course could potentially ruin a marriage through their 'extra-curricular' activities – particularly if the trooper had contracted a lingering venereal disease.

There could be a nurturing exchange of emotional energy with someone that helped pull them through that difficult time regardless of the depth and permanency of the situation. Emotionally, it was not too unlike a relationship anywhere else where two people meet, so there could be wounded and broken hearts upon departure at the end of a tour of duty. Who knows how many of us made love with one or more of the 'enemy'? No doubt many of us did.

Overall

We looked forward to the mail call each day in the hope of getting news from that loved one or anyone. We would talk about our plans and dreams upon returning to home shores, particularly if we were getting close to reassignment or discharge. We discussed families, what university we wanted to attend, what career we wanted to pursue, or what super-car we wanted to buy. We built up hopes and fantasies that were probably often unrealistic, but it helped us to deal with the situation at hand.

The time spent during working hours was generally good and often rewarding. Morale was generally pretty good since we were all in the same situation and formed some excellent friendships. It was off duty time that could be a problem if not spent constructively like reading books, doing an extension course, or writing letters. Playing poker was a popular past time for some. We had a radio and TV station broadcast by the military and live performances frequently at the 'clubs'. There was plenty of cheap alcohol and dope available to help take your mind off things. Off base there was some female companionship – but not always accessible, depending on circumstances.

Drugs

My level of awareness of anything outside of alcohol was and is pretty limited. Totally so with any hard drugs. Marijuana was illegal in military eyes. There would be an occasional shakedown inspection for contraband, particularly if someone caused an 'incident', but it was basically tolerated to some extent if not obviously abused.

I used alcohol on a regular basis and sometimes to excess in retrospect. I hadn't considered it a problem until I returned to the U.S. and civilian life when I realised the degree of my dependence on it. I encountered marijuana for the first time in my life soon after arriving at Qui Nhon. I was only an occasional and light user which limited the degree of impact on me. It was good for a laugh or to chill out.

The percentage of people smoking dope, at least occasionally, was probably fairly high as a guess. I knew a few regular users that seemed to sort of 'cruise' – others took it too far and got 'messy'. Most users were probably quite discreet about it so hard to tell outside their circle.

Those that used alcohol were more obvious because it was acceptable to the establishment. It was likely to be more that did – probably more often. Most of us that drank did more so there than we would have back 'home', I think most of us handled both forms of escape fairly responsibly. There were a few exceptions in both those methods of 'escape' who had to face the music. Ultimately, we all just used whatever devices we had at our disposal to get through our time there in the best way that we could.

Morale Boosters

Our avionics unit was attached to two air transport companies in Qui Nhon – the 79th and the 540th. Each had facilities like a mess hall and a club we could choose between for meals and socializing. That gave us access to more entertainment appearing at the clubs, which was provided on a fairly frequent basis. From memory, the majority of evening shows were of Asian origin – Vietnamese, Thai, Philippine – but some were from the U.S. and Australia. Regardless, they lifted our spirits with laughs, music and dance. Virtually all touring entertainers got everyone on board with the hit by The Animals, '*We Gotta Get out of This Place*', which became the anthem of the time.

The highlight for some, any year, was the annual Christmas visit by Bob Hope, flying into various sites around the country on the big day with his USO entertainers. I was fortunate enough to amongst those present at the Phu Cat location in 1968 when Rachael Welch, footballer Rosie Greer, Miss World, and numerous others toured with him. Ann-Margaret capped it off with a very moving and unforgettable, '*Silent Night*'.

Christmas Day 1968

Aussie entertainers at our local club in Qui Nhon

There have been countless numbers of people who have served, supported and entertained the troops and continue to do so with love and selfless dedication far beyond a sense of duty. Some famous, but mostly unknown, yet all showing their appreciation for our service. Thank all of you for lifting our spirits and letting us know you care, even now, long after the event! I certainly appreciate it and know that we all did!

Turning One Year into Two (or Two Years into One - in my Mind)

When the end my 12-month tour of duty was approaching, I received orders for my next Army assignment which would take place following a 4-week leave. In the months prior to that, we were asked to put in for destinations we might prefer if we weren't being discharged. My request for Germany obviously didn't match the needs of the Army as much as my desire. The avionics school at Fort Gordon, Georgia where I had trained wasn't on my list of choices – but guess what. I don't need to tell you - the Army does as the Army does.

- The exact role I would play there wasn't clear.
- It would be very unlikely that I would be actively engaging in a flight-line requirement.
- There was the likelihood of becoming an instructor, but then again that wasn't a guarantee since the number of returning technicians would certainly outnumber the teaching positions required at any given time.
- Did I want to be an instructor even if I was assigned to that role?

- I had seen other returnees from Vietnam there that were fundamentally killing time until discharge in a variety of jobs unrelated to avionics, often feeling unvalued and bored.
- I didn't want to be back there in any case. No!

That left me with two choices – stay on in Vietnam – or go AWOL went I got back to the U.S. on leave (with nowhere to hide - a joke).

As you probably know - marijuana, apart from relaxing the body, affects the human perception of time and space. Those attributes are no doubt much of the attraction to it. Could one make the year in Vietnam detention seem like a tropical holiday of shorter duration? Ha! Ha??? My efforts failed, but I can assure you, some of us captives tried to do just that.

With that in mind, I was faced then with the 'crazy' challenge of making an even longer time of seclusion from my 'real world' seem shorter than it actually was, and not go 'completely crazy' in the process - a 'catch 22'. Time is an illusion anyway according to the genius Einstein. It is a dance, is it not?

There were several good reasons to keeping on keeping on where I was -

- I knew and enjoyed my job and preferred doing what I was trained for
- There was a sense of purpose and fulfilment in what I was doing
- The environment was tough but so was hot, humid Georgia
- Despite being in a 'cage', there was greater freedom in military sense – no spit and polish
- Better pay with hazardous duty and flight status
- I was in line to take over the lead of the flight-line crew with a promotion, including
- Upgrade to sergeant ranking; same pay as specialist but with more privileges and respect
- A month at home at the end of the current year tour

- Another week R&R to a great place after 3 months of a first six months of an extension
- Best incentive of all – get discharged five months earlier than my 3-year commitment

In truth, it was a fairly easy decision to make. It was a stacked deck. By breaking up the 11-months extension into acceptable time frames and activities, I managed the illusion of time/space to get me to my desired goal. In the process I had –

- A month of magical summer in Montana
- Another wonderful week of R&R in Singapore (had one there during my 12 months)
- A 'gift' R&R to awesome Australia after that
- A greater overall military/life experience than I believe I would have had elsewhere
- A completion of my military and Vietnam time together to start fresh as a civilian
- An opportunity upon discharge to have a Fall term start at the course I wanted in Seattle

So, "What Was It Like"? In short, it was literally millions of experiences, peering through the perceptions of millions of minds – how can anyone accurately convey that to anyone else? That was a peep at some of mine through my senses.

Breathe in/🐾/Breathe out/🐾/Breathe in/🐾/Breathe out/🐾

An Angry Young Man

Adjusting to Civilian Life

"How much is a postage stamp?" I asked. Such a simple need, but it hadn't been part of my reality for two years. I had forgotten.

The world I left behind at 19 when I departed for Vietnam in September 1967 seemed a very different world to the one I walked back into 24 months later. I had worked at Boeing Aircraft in the three months before my enlistment, living near Seattle with my brother George and his wife Pat. I had wanted to get a job there in the computer department but they would only employ me as a riveter on the bodies of 727 aircraft because of the draft hanging over my head. The horrible job I started in October of 1966, was deafening and boring, but I stuck it out until I went home for Christmas in Montana and my active enlistment a month later. I was soon marching around Ft Lewis in basic training, back to within a few minutes' drive from where I had just lived for the previous few months.

Two and a half years later, I was given a physical check-up, fitted with a new Army uniform and given my marching papers out the door. I carried my duffle bag out the gate about 9:30 the night of August 30th 1969, picked up by my brother George and taken to my family at his home. We were very happy to see each other after a very long day of waiting to be released. No wife, no girlfriend, no brass band waiting. I didn't expect any of them, but I did have an expectation that I would resume life much as it had been before I entered that same fort.

Back in the 'Real' World

Early in the morning of the first day as a civilian again, I was fishing from my brother's boat on Puget Sound. The fog cleared into a beautiful sunny day and the one and only salmon anyone caught stayed on the end of my line and into the waiting net. What a great start for my return to freedom!

In the following days, I was on my way to Canada on another fishing expedition, again with my family. The entourage consisted of my parents, my brother and his wife and their newborn baby Marla, just eight weeks old. We were all travelling in a car and a pickup with a camper on it . . . towing George's 17-foot boat. The incentive to travel so far, be it into British Columbia with a newborn baby, was the 'promise' of monster fish in Shuswap Lake my brother was told about; maybe once, maybe over and over, I don't know. That's all it took. George fell for it hook, line, and sinker. Any excuse for a fishing adventure, or adventure of any kind really, and I was a good enough reason.

There was one instance as we trolled around the lake that I actually saw a very big fish leap out of the water in the distance behind us, my lure trolling in the murky depths far below it. It was to be the only visible evidence of anything that resembled his stories. But . . . we had a great time!

It was wonderful to be free and out in the wonderful world of Nature with my family. The beautiful scenery and fresh mountain air were a welcome change to the war zone and humidity I had recently left behind just days before. But there was a degree of restlessness and sense of suppressed joy I couldn't quite understand. There seemed to be a part of me mysteriously missing.

What I very soon discovered was something that I hadn't left behind in Vietnam; my dependence on alcohol. It started to become apparent to me when we reached Canada and our short supply brought from home which soon ran out. It wasn't as easy to obtain alcohol as it was in the U.S. It was only available there through liquor stores as opposed to any supermarket, so we had to find a source.

My Dad and brother enjoyed a beer as well, but it was much more of a demand by my body for me. I started to feel agitated by the noticeable absence of it. I didn't want to show that to my family once I began to realise that need. There was a desire within me that needed to be satisfied.

We eventually were able to locate a source to supply us, but in the meantime, it was a real awakening for me. I had an addiction that I hadn't seen in that light until then. It was to become a crutch to help me adapt to the lifestyle I thought I would simply slip back into.

Perhaps it also served to hide my emotional ripples through the time of readjustment to civilian life.

❖❖

Things happened very quickly from there. Before I knew it, I was attending classes at Highline College, midway between Seattle and Tacoma. I was very fortunate to get in on a late entry to the Computer Science course I wanted, studying programming and system analysis, towards an associate degree in two years. I bought a beautiful used car, I really couldn't afford, to make good my dream, and to stroke my unrealised damaged ego – the ego associated with another world.

I was in for a shock I hadn't expected. The country I just re-entered had changed, my perception of it had changed, and I had changed. Nothing ever stays the same in our revolving world, so why did I think that it would?

Having grown accustomed to the lifestyle in Vietnam, I soon felt uncomfortable trying to fit into the one I thought that I knew. Military life in Vietnam was far different from civilian life in the U.S. of course, but it wasn't as regimented or strict as the army structure outside of the war zone. There was a reasonable degree of freedom and flexibility not enjoyed in other military duty locations around the world that helped us keep our sanity in that situation. It was as casual as possible, yet disciplined enough to get our jobs done with professionalism; a question of balance to keep up morale amongst the troops. There was the comradery and a sense of purpose I surprisingly began to miss - our common situation that had provided the sense of a large family.

That was replaced by living alone in a 55ftx10ft trailer house, just across the street of a trailer park from my sister Carol and her family, whose company I enjoyed. I was happy to be free of the 'green machine' and Vietnam, and yet there were adjustments I needed to make in some ways I didn't expect.

Gone also was the almost daily connection I enjoyed with the Vietnamese people. There was always a degree of fascination I had with their simple lifestyle that reflected something desirable in their smiles and cheerfulness that camouflaged the pain of their circumstances.

While I enjoyed that interaction, I couldn't wait to get away from that world, and certainly didn't expect to miss it. But I did. It was the *energy* I had grown accustomed to, as we humans do in order to function in our surroundings, whatever form that may be. It wasn't until later in life that I came to better understand that.

Very soon, I felt like an alien in my own land. I didn't know the cost of a postage stamp because mail was free from Vietnam. I didn't know the price of a beer, or how to do some simple things anyone would know. Western women no longer appealed to me in some respects in the way they had before. I had enjoyed the soft gentle nature of Asian women and felt the loss of that tenderness. What hadn't been communicated with them in words was felt in the power of intimacy. Where the hell did I fit in to all of this? I began to feel that I didn't - much to my surprise and sense of tarnished self-esteem through the discomfort of feeling out of step with my '*real*' world.

Being a community college, most of the other students attending classes were straight from high school; none of which I had attended, being from Montana. They hadn't served in the military and must have found it hard to understand the complexity of the raging war. Attitudes towards it and veterans varied from curiosity to disapproval, though it was not usually openly expressed to me. Didn't I just leave all that conflict between disagreeing people and inaccurate deceiving bullshit splashed out in all the various media behind me? It became an irritant I didn't expect to face which stuck like a case of measles that wouldn't go away.

I soon gravitated towards other vets I discovered on campus, obvious by their age, manner, and dress, some wearing their fatigue jacket less the badges. Though we were not working together as in active service, there was still a sense of connection through familiarity that brought a degree of solace to what I was feeling. There was a veterans group which I joined.

There was still very much a part of me that was used to functioning in military mode. I didn't get programmed into that discipline in one day or week or month, and it wasn't as easy as flicking a switch to change back into a civilian way of life as was my expectation months before.

Suddenly I was dropped back into a world that I had been familiar with all my life prior to service and looking forward to re-engaging, which now seemed foreign, undisciplined, soft and vulnerable to enemy attack; an easy target for any attacking force to my military-trained mind, as unlikely as that may have been. Was I safe in this world without a barbed wire perimeter and guard tower to watch over me? It was more of a feeling than it was a conscious serious thought, but none-the-less it was there.

Thoughts of survival take precedence over all others that penetrate the human mind through the bio-chemistry of fight/flight reaction to danger, though I didn't understand that at the time. Rational thinking cannot function alongside thoughts of survival and are relegated to the passenger seat in the mind. That feeling lasted for many years, particularly when I was in heavily populated locations. The later events I witnessed on TV of 9/11/2001 validated those concerns in my mind. I was not totally surprised as I watched the horrors of that day unfold. Like being in Vietnam, it didn't seem real as events unfolded through the medium of a television.

Having been used to simply appearing at the mess hall at meal time to be fed, having my clothes laundered, and my living area cleaned and tidied up for me, I was re-entering the realm of self-responsibility cold turkey. No problem; the fridge was always full of cold stubbies to help deal with whatever as I gradually came to grips.

Ideas of having a relationship with a young woman was problematic; a lack of finances beyond my basic needs which included beer, my car, and my new-found romance with skiing for a start. I couldn't divest the time and energy given to the studies I was focused on and loving, to other types of loving pursuits. There was drinking and dancing venues aplenty to pick from on Friday and Saturday nights with friends. That helped to partially fill the emotional need for female companionship to some extent . . . and to drain my resources that I had little idea how to manage in my 'new old' life. There were occasional dates and even romances as such, but I found it difficult to relate or commit myself in a genuine committed way. Still, there was a deep longing to be a nurturing, emotionally satisfying relationship, but I knew it was unrealistic to add that dimension to my life at that time.

Shortly after I got back, I went to see a lovely young lady from the Seattle area that I had been corresponding with for months from Vietnam. She was younger and very sweet. After all the thoughtful letters she invested her time and energy into, I just felt uncomfortable in person, unable to relate to her world. I still feel ashamed to admit to never contacting her again, even to explain how I felt. I just didn't know how to. I did find out much later through her sister that she was very puzzled and hurt. I am so sorry Pam.

Unfortunately, that was an act which I repeated on a number of occasions in the years that followed. I just didn't seem to have the guts or the skills to say "good-bye" in a civilized manner. So likewise, I apologize in spirit to any other women I have left wondering. Blessings to you all.

What I didn't realize while I was in Vietnam was the adrenaline kick I was getting from a number of activities, including the sense of always being on alert for my own safety and survival, even though I was hardly conscious of it. The occasional 'alert' warning of attack or possible attack, nearby gunfire, flying observer in a 'bird dog' light plane, or being hidden from patrolling Vietnamese 'white mice' police by my 'girlfriend' in a secret closet in her home - off-limits to me. I wasn't getting that in Seattle.

Unconsciously, I sought ways to get a buzz; to replace those hormone stimulates on a daily basis for two years in another world. Driving at ridiculous speeds in my powerful set of wheels, sometimes intoxicated beyond sensible levels, was the easy way.

A more responsible, acceptable way was flying down a ski slope. I would get up before dawn and drive to Crystal Mountain near Mount Rainier to have a few hours of joy via terror, alone in the crisp invigorating winter air whenever I had the opportunity. Skiing lessons were an ignored option. It was great therapy to something I didn't consciously realize yet that I was dealing with. It was just a fun relief in my attempt to adjust to life back in the U. S. of A. as they say.

Had a psychologist put a camera over my head and a monitor in my mind with another in my heart for a period of time, he would have easily detected the depression I was dancing with. I didn't know that at that time. I just didn't feel at peace within myself or what I could call happy. *Something* was missing.

Things seemed to be going so well and smoothly for me with studies and my outward life as it might have appeared to others, yet I had times when I simply wanted to fly off the road in my car into a another world. Or to go to sleep and not wake up. Alcohol and occasionally marijuana were my remedies to help with an acceptable way to deal with those irrational feelings.

Looking back now, I can see the symptoms of PTSD wrapped up in the blanket of more obvious depression. Had I been diagnosed then by an expert with today's knowing in PTSD awareness and knowledge, it may have been nipped in the bud. Such was not the case, or even possible then, so my journey unfolded as it has, no doubt for my own development as a soul with many lessons to learn.

In the two years of post-war life, my thoughts and emotions towards the government I had always held in the highest regard and respect, continued to eat away at me internally. They were powerful and eventually couldn't be contained as they bubbled to the surface and increasingly exploded. What I had seen in Vietnam had shocked me initially, not believing what I was seeing and hearing. It shattered the image and beliefs I had all my life for what I thought was the bastion of democracy and an example to the world.

The dots of truth supposed to connect between what was happening and what was reported from my government through the various media, were scattered like chaff in the wind. The acts of war were blatantly manipulated to confuse the enemy, and the public at home, alike.

Propaganda has always been a part of warfare, but the whole spectacle saddened and angered me in my disbelief. I may have been only 19 and naive, but I wasn't deaf, dumb, or blind – the military machine only accepts those that are healthy.

Two years there provided me with enough vision to see through some of the illusion with greater clarity, but I don't know if any one person then or still alive now could provide those answers in truth. There was an incredible complexity to the situation that was in full swing during my time there.

In the years since, many of the observers and primary participants have tried to provide answers and expose the truth, filtered through their perceptions and degree of knowledge, in interviews, documentaries and books. There is so much conflicting views and debate, the truth may have been buried with the players.

It did happen. I was a part of the cumulative *energy* of that war, simply in a support role as I was, repairing communications equipment on aircraft on a relatively safe airfield haven, just as was a grunt under great danger and stress carrying on warfare in the rice paddies. I was part of that machine. Unaware, I carried that *energy* back to my homeland as life went on for me, unaware of the extent that it was enmeshed that energy as well at a distance from the battleground of Vietnam.

At college, I knew I'd picked the right career path to prepare for. I loved it and had thrown myself into my studies, making the honour roll and securing some scholarships in the process. I also was given a part-time job at the computer centre as an operator, a rare opportunity which proved very beneficial later. Everything seemed to fall into place for me somehow.

As time went on, I was concentrating on my education, but the emotional war within me was competing for my attention. Ranting and throwing my shoes at the TV when I became upset with the news I couldn't resist watching was not a remedy for anything. If only television was interactive eh? Still, I suppose those outbursts did help me release some of my inner agitation. The constant feed to my emotional upheaval was around me too much to avoid, regardless of the attention I gave to watching the news, or observed on campus. It certainly didn't help me to contain it.

Nearing the end of my time in college, it was decision time for me to go on with studies in business at a four-year college/university, or pursue employment out there in the field of life with the skills and associate degree I earned at college. I had grown tired of study and really didn't want to continue without a break, but friends had enrolled at Ellensburg, so I did as well as a backup plan.

By then, I had made enquiries in response to newspaper ads about jobs in Australia that grabbed my attention. I just wanted to get as far away as possible from the tension and turmoil I felt building in America - and in me. For some reason I couldn't just let go and put it all behind me.

A Ray of Sunshine

A few weeks before I finished college, a response eventually came back about the supposed jobs in Australia. I hadn't realised the tiny 3-line ads were actually from the Australian government. It sent vague details for a work/permanent residence or an immigration visa. I filled out and sent back what seemed an application that didn't provide a lot of information on what would happen next.

I waited with some excitement at the prospect of finding employment in the country I had been fascinated with since my early teens. I'd just gotten a whiff when I visited Sydney on a lucky R&R granted to me in April of '69, just four months before my discharge from service. I had vowed to myself to return. Those thoughts never left me.

Meanwhile, public awareness of the truths about Vietnam had been growing as the veil hiding the lies became thinner, making them harder to conceal. Government officials couldn't agree on what strategies to take in either trying to win the winless war or simply get out with a glimmer of dignity if possible. Both prospects seemed very unlikely.

People from all walks of life were starting to demand more truth about the war from the government and cries to get out were getting louder as the peace advocates had done for years. The generally peaceful activists were having huge public rallies and demonstrations around the country, challenging authorities that wanted to project a strong stand which often resulted in violence, bloodshed and even deaths.

What I was witnessing in my own country horrified me. I was an angry young man who wanted to live a life of peace, but I was living within the war zone of my homeland that tore at my heart. I was in a war within myself that wasn't there while I was in Vietnam.

The successive governments over the war years refused to give in to pressure, trying to put up a strong front and plans for an acceptable outcome that seemed more impossible by the day.

❧❧

It was time for me to go. Moving back to my parents' home in Montana at the end of college in June 1971, I started looking for work while waiting impatiently for the visa to come through. More forms to fill out came without what to expect after that. Having found a job on construction work for a few months of summer, I sent the forms back to the Australian consulate in San Francisco and waited. My job finished but I found work at the local sawmill to keep the money building in my savings account towards getting away.

A security/crime check form arrived. Why didn't they send that first I wondered? It could save a lot of time and process efforts in some cases, couldn't it? I got a good reference from my local sheriff and sent it off.

I continued to pull boards off the never-ending supply coming down the chain belts at the saw mill as autumn turned into winter. Each board I stacked carried a picture in my mind of Bondi Beach. I was wishing the money I needed to go, if my application was successful, would stack up as quickly. Too late to join my friends for the fall quarter at university should the visa never eventuate, I waited; in hope . . . impatiently. If only that visa would come!

An envelope with the long-awaited prize finally arrived just weeks before Christmas without fanfare or warning. My U.S. passport contained a permanent resident status visa rather than just a working permit as such from the Australian consulate. Plans and preparation kicked into gear as I worked right up to Christmas to try to have as much money together as possible. I had been counting on the proceeds from the sale of my car which didn't happen, but I forged ahead regardless. I booked flights to leave from Missoula just after the new year with short stays in Seattle and Hawaii in-route to Sydney

Winter in Montana is not a good time to sell virtually any vehicle other than possibly a 4-wheel-drive or a snow plow. Unemployment is high during winter with inevitable shutdowns in the timber industry, the backbone of the local economy then. The money I was asking for my GTO wasn't being met, so I left it in the care of my parents to sell in the spring when the market would be better. My parents loved driving the car so ended up keeping for themselves, perhaps with some hope of me returning.

As it was, family and friends had to join me in coming to face the fact that the talk for much of the year was becoming reality. There was a mixture of reactions, from sadness to declarations of jealousy. I loved them and Montana, but the pull by my vision of summertime beaches in Sydney versus the snow and near zero degrees temperature I was experiencing was not much of a contest. The focus of getting away from the turmoil was of course my paramount driving force to go. The effort I had made in pursuing an intangible dream, had been rewarded with the valuable permission to bring that to fruition.

Suggestions by my mother to wait until I could sell my car for a better price still didn't win me over, nor did the desire and plan-in-progress by my good friend Del Kamhoot to come with me.

I knew Del was serious about going as well, and was working to save money to join me, but I also knew how quickly things can change in a person's life that can distract and derail the best laid plans. I wasn't going to let that happen to me. I left my car, and part of my heart behind on that cold winter's day of eight degrees F for sunnier climates that were calling my name too loudly to ignore. A new chapter in my life was beckoning and about to unfold.

Breathe in/ /Breathe out/ /Breathe in/ /Breathe out/

My New 'Home' Land

The Pan Am flight from Honolulu departed on a balmy evening, and touched down in sunny Sydney a few hours later on the clock - and two days later on the calendar, Saturday the 8th of January 1972.

After a polite interview with Australian Immigration at the airport, I was taken to a migrant hostel at East Hills, nearly an hour to the southeast of downtown Sydney. The chauffeured Commonwealth Mercedes seemed a pretty special treat I didn't expect! In fact, I didn't know quite what awaited me. (In reality just a government taxi). I checked in at an office, was given a bed and a small personal space in an open area Quonset hut, an evening meal, and a kiss good night - the latter by a beautiful sunset.

The next morning I heard the laughter of kookaburras just before the dawn in the most ancient land on our planet. The iconic call made me think I was in a South American jungle. Upon awakening from my dream, I realised the truth. What a wonderful, classic start to my new life on a new day of the week, the first month of a new year in an amazing country! Two weeks later I was sharing a flat overlooking Bondi Beach with another American, also looking for work in the infant computer industry.

🐾🐾

Fast Forward

Jump ahead from 1972 to 2000. In the years since my arrival in Australia, much had happened. Events, jobs, relationships, marriages, children – 'life'. A very full life. Often challenging, but very good and largely satisfying in most respects, especially after having a family.

The laughter of kookaburras was often a wonderful wake-up call throughout those times, which helped me to drown out the inaudible internal echoing cries of the pain of separation from my birth 'home' land.

I loved my new life, but I also missed my birth land and its people – my family and friends. It felt like I was trying to live in two worlds simultaneously for many years, with a leg straddling each side of the Pacific Ocean, both feet trying to keep in touch with solid ground. It wasn't really possible. I had made my bed on the far southern side of the big pond.

As my years advanced into my fifties, the suppressed cries and reasons for them were starting to surface and drown out the kookaburras. Suddenly I awoke from another dream to discover I had a condition called Post Traumatic Stress Disorder (PTSD) which I knew nothing about.

Breathe in/ /Breathe out/ /Breathe in/ /Breathe out/

My Pathway to Healing

Most Vietnam vets I've known have a tendency to not want to discuss their experiences with others, particularly with those who have no connection to the situation. It was a different world and it was too difficult to try to explain to someone who hadn't been involved.

Therefore vets typically closed up and held it within, whether by a conscious intention or as a result of communication channels choked by emotion, as I did. I assume that to be the case with most veterans of any war. Perhaps due to the complexity of it, there was a feeling that you just had to be there in order to even commence a dialogue preface.

It can be an uncomfortable topic of conversation at the best of times, but of course unknowing people were curious or even fascinated by war. Talking about their experiences can probably benefit those vets able to talk about it. That is good, but that can possibly wear a bit thin with the listener if it is too much too frequent.

For most of the previous thirty years, my experiences in Vietnam and the army were not often spoken of, particularly after my arrival in Australia. It was too hard and it would often bring up an emotion for me that I sometimes found difficult to control, be it anger or blatant dis-comfort. I would feel the blood rise to the surface, my face flush and perspiration appear.

I simply avoided the topic and not many people even knew I had a connection with it. That subject was an obvious emotional trigger for me, so it should have been no surprise to discover that I had a stress-related problem connected to it. The stressful events of the previous few years, and the prior few months in particular, were the catalyst that finally brought the condition to a head in mid-2000.

It manifested in a level of increasing anxiety - confusion, cloudy head, increasing cranky disposition, occasional angry outbursts, mild depression and my memory playing frustrating games on me.

There is a rule in carpentry, 'measure twice; cut once'. I would measure and re-measure - and re-measure and re-measure - get ready to cut and measure a few more times! And I would *still* sometimes get it wrong!

I would forget instructions almost instantly, whether it was something I was told or had read.

I would walk from the house to the shed and forget why I was there when I arrived.

Or I would get distracted on the way when I would remember something I wanted to do to the car as I went past it, so I would stop to do that instead.

I was suffocating in confusion. What was happening to me? Why couldn't my conscious, positive mind restore order to my thoughts and behaviour? I was dysfunctional and that realisation depressed me. It frightened me.

Fortunately I was still coherent enough to realise I needed to get some help before it crushed me mentally. **I** knew it was stress. I knew I had to act before those symptoms took me to total dysfunction.

I was trying to avert the images of myself sitting in the foetal position in the corner of a room on the floor. I had to surrender my resistance to getting medical assistance before that became my reality. I had seen glimpses of that when visiting people in mental facilities, so I was determined to avoid that with its potentially horrendous consequences.

Medication

Help came promptly when I finally gave in and visited my doctor. He only had to ask if I had served in Vietnam, which he guessed as a possibility due to my age and his experience. I immediately felt agitated with the emotions coming to the surface. Tears unexpectedly appeared, my cheeks flushed, and I choked on the words in response to his questions.

His diagnosis suggested that I had PTSD, so he got treatment underway with an anti-depressant as first aid to my anxiety. He also arranged an appointment with a psychiatrist to confirm his suspicions. I ignored my life-long resistance to the use of that medication and accepted it. They proved to be a blessed relief within hours. The squirrel in my head soon got off the wheel and laid down – we both got a rest.

The solution was great in the short term, with a break in the anxiety energy whirl. However, within a few days I wanted to reduce the dosage to restore my energy and awareness, which had been significantly dampened. My doctor put me onto a milder script that seemed largely okay for a while. We tried a few over the ensuing months in an effort to get the right balance of anxiety suppression while maintaining the ability to think coherently.

My doctor had suggested that I approach the Vietnam Veterans Counselling Service about the possibility of receiving counselling from them. I soon found out that there was a reciprocal agreement between Australia and the U.S. which made certain services available for veterans. They gave me approval to have an interview and I commenced counselling soon after. That became the cornerstone for my recovery treatment from issues around PTSD.

The counsellors there had not been through the experience of Vietnam by intention, but could relate to our situation. My initial counsellor, Phil was excellent in establishing a good connection and getting on with some positive results.

I was soon slotted into a regular, frequent session. It was really crucial for me in letting go of what was bottled up inside of me and learning about the condition I knew nothing about. I wanted to understand it and why I had it.

The time of the next appointment couldn't come around quickly enough to begin with as I tried to come to terms with it all. I wanted to be fixed and move on. Little did I know that it was going to be a longer process than I had expected.

Soon after I started the counselling sessions, it became apparent that there were other traumatic events in my life, besides my war experiences, that had contributed to my condition. They were events that I was certainly aware of and could never forget, but I didn't fully realize the degree of impact of the cumulative effect that they had on my life. It was a revelation I didn't expect to appear.

🐾🐾

Some six months passed. Medication and counselling had been helping me, but I sensed that progress towards the recovery I expected was slowing after the initial relief that had seemed promising. I was still somewhat emotionally 'fragile' and still lacked mental clarity. I began to wonder if that was going to be my new sense of self for the rest of my life. The thought troubled me. I felt sure that people I knew who had faced difficult circumstances and trauma, were more mentally 'together' than what I seemed to be. I wondered if the remedy for my trauma was worse than the condition itself, but for the time being I felt like I had to go along with the generally accepted way of dealing it.

A Rude Shock

In February 2001, my then wife Kris attended a retreat with a group of service veterans dealing with PTSD, and their partners. We were told by an established psychologist that if we were expecting a miracle cure, *don't* - because there wasn't one!

As a typical bullet-proof male in regards to my health, which I thought was otherwise pretty good, that statement stunned me. I had expected to reach a full recovery in a relatively short time and get on with my life. I felt like I had just been handed a life sentence without hope of parole.

I don't think I heard much of anything being said after that. He did say that there are ways we can learn to manage it through medication and other means such as meditation. I've always tried to be pretty responsible for my well-being. Suddenly, I saw myself as damaged. That added further to my sense of not understanding what I was facing, my diminishing confidence and my loss of self-esteem.

The anti-depressant tablets I took reinforced that outlook. In taking them, I became less anxious, but mentally foggy and indifferent about a lot of things. I was still concerned about the loss of work and income, and felt a huge lack of confidence for some reason I couldn't understand. I felt less competent with my carpentry skills and incapable of conducting a business as such or being a potential employee carpenter. Was that because of the condition or the medication? It was a downward spiral.

❧❧

I used to say I was flat-lining – basically emotionally flat even if I may have appeared to be relatively 'okay' to others. I have always been sensitive to drugs which would sometimes set off a reaction - from pain-killers to allergy medication. I tried different anti-depressants in search of one with fewer side-effects. They tended to deaden the anxiety and lift my mood initially, but I would eventually feel somewhat depressed after each new remedy anyway. It really impacted my whole sense of being, which shattered my initial hope of a speedy recovery which further depressed me.

I coped, but I knew I couldn't stay on that path, so I decided to wean myself off the medication. I eventually reached the point where I wouldn't take any more anti-depressants and began to work my way through it by other means I found.

I began to feel more energetic and clear minded straight away. It was a bit of an emotional and energetic roller-coaster at times but I resisted going back onto them again. However, on a couple of occasions I took the anti-depressants for a short burst when it seemed to be too stressful for too long. That was something I was warned against by my GP, but it worked for me. Meanwhile I kept looking for alternatives. A beer or two at appropriate times could temporarily lift my mood, so that was the easy remedy when I felt the need.

The counselling continued for several years on a regular basis, then more spaced and sporadic. I gradually wound it down to a halt. It was certainly crucial, especially initially, and very beneficial overall, but it eventually was no longer an effective healing tool for me. Sometimes I would reach a point where it seemed to be re-hashing old issues. That made it difficult to let go of thoughts and the attached emotions, and allow me to move on.

🐾

Through much of those early years of treatment, I was sometimes emotionally fragile, particularly for a while after I stopped using the anti-depressants which had de-sensitised me. The emotions would uncontrollably well up and tears would appear and sometimes flow. There would usually be a reason I could see, but sometimes that could happen for no apparent reason. It could be from seeing or hearing something that touched my heart more likely than an angry response to something. In any case, it was often embarrassing to me because it seemed to be out of my control - the triggers and the responses to them. I learned to avoid known triggers.

When it was during a session of counselling/healing, I could often understand and accept because it was in a private setting. But when it was in public, it was frustrating and concerning at a deeper level. I felt emotionally sensitive to comments, sad or even beautiful stories or movies, or simply thoughts which could trigger a reaction, often with a tear or a few.

There seemed to be some wound I couldn't see or touch in order to heal. Physical wounds are tangible, so there is hope of addressing them, but when they are often linked to an intangible emotional wound, the reason may not be so evident. I couldn't begin to realise then just how deep and extensive that wound was. I was struggling to work it out and find balance.

🐾

That First Step

"You really need to get out – to go for a walk and get *moving*"! Those were wise words from my wife I didn't want to hear, though I knew it was true. Seemingly, not that long before as a carpenter, I had been active and full of *energy*. I had become a couch potato and found it difficult to move beyond a chair in the morning. And for the rest of the day - and evening. The recliner didn't need to seductively beckon me - it had its tentacles attached to me. The only other chairs that attracted me were in front of my computer and the dining table.

Why? Was it an aspect of PTSD or was it a side-effect of the anti-depressants I was on, as suggested by another veteran. He said it was common knowledge that they cause you to gain weight and take away your ambition and *energy*. Others agreed, yet talking with other people on such medication afterwards who seemed to have similar problems, most hadn't realized the connection either so I guessed the knowledge wasn't that 'common'.

One day I finally gave in to Kris' suggestion of taking our beautiful cattle dog Cookie for a walk. She would rather do that than launch into a bowl of her favourite dog food. The word 'walk' brought her out of her meditation on the tiled lounge room floor, looking at me with enthusiasm and amazement. She was up and at the door before I could get up from my comfort; there was no turning back now without having to deal with my very disappointed friend wagging her tail in anticipation.

So out we went onto the quiet street in the little rural community where we lived. The cows in the paddock across the road mooed in amazement at the sight of us. Cookie's joyful excitement was virtually pulling me down the street as she raced ahead to checkout each property along the way – sniffing and squatting and occasionally looking back at me to see if I was really doing this, and still coming.

Feeling puffed after only a block, I couldn't believe I could feel so unfit. I pushed on for a while longer to try see if my burning lungs and tired legs would improve, but it was a short walk because I was soon exhausted. Cookie and I arrived back home, both of us in disbelief.

It wasn't that long before, I could work for hours without feeling like that. What happened to me? Where had my *energy* gone? I decided then and there that I really needed to improve my condition.

With Cookie's engaging pull of joyful exuberance, we went further and further on our outings. I had no choice; she was demanding more of the same each day, and gradually my body was as well. I began to look forward to it perhaps as much as my faithful friend who wouldn't take 'no' for an answer to her begging at the door each day. I had to give in to those beautiful beckoning eyes touching my heart. 'Yes Cookie, I'll just get my shoes on'.

It took a push from Kris and a pull from Cookie, for which I am grateful, to wake me up to my pathetic state. I had reached a point of laziness unbecoming to me and somehow I had felt uncaring and stagnant in my lack of *energy* and motivation. That first step out the door with my dog was what led me to eventually feeling much better in myself. Within months I was amazed to find with *energy* to spare. It started with one step out my door – and a transformation of my state of being I didn't see coming.

A More Spiritual Direction

With me not working much during those early years from 2000, I had more time to attend to tasks that needed my attention, along with communication and reading. My wife Kris would go to the library and come home with a stack of books, mostly on her passion – gardening - so she decided to grab a couple she thought could interest me.

She started bringing home books on spirituality, death, after-life and near-death experiences by people. The books in that vein continued beyond her initial exploration. Had the library run out of gardening books? I began to wonder if she thought she was dying.

The Celestine Prophecy was the first book she brought to me. For some reason it intrigued me in spite of thinking to myself that it was a bit of fantasy. That book planted a seed of curiosity, which led me to follow up with a sequel and then other books of that nature. Apparently I wasn't the only one drawn to it. By 2005, 20 million copies had been sold worldwide.

By the time I was about five years into my D-Tour, I had gradually improved somewhat in what I saw as getting myself back 'together'. The degree of recovery hadn't reached what I had hoped for or expected at the initial discovery of PTSD, but I was managing better. Life was moving along and dragging me with it. Although I was functioning better, I still lacked my confidence and self-worth of old.

I didn't feel good enough or fast enough with my carpentry skills, which made it difficult to find lasting employment. Somehow we managed to get by better financially after selling our home, and buying a cheaper one, but there seemed to be something missing within me beyond the material aspects. The books I had started reading of a spiritual natured seemed to spark a renewed longing for a connection in that area of my life.

Kris and I had been going for a couple of years to a placed called Rainbow Lodge which held a gathering on a rural property every three months. It was a social fun day, usually with 20-30 other people from far and wide to listen to talks on various interesting topics - generally on wellness, environment, or spiritually oriented subjects and enjoyed the amazing food we brought.

On one such occasion, a woman named Rosie gave a talk about a spiritual centre she belonged to, which attracted my interest. It offered courses on a variety of subjects relating to spiritual and physical wellness. Kris and my daughter Amy and I enrolled in a course at The Harmony Centre in Cooranbong called 'Ignite Your Spirit' in June 2006. It was to become the start of a major shift in my self-awareness and healing.

From Medication to Meditation and Transformation

That was my introduction into a very supportive spiritual community, which soon played a very significant part in my life. That brought a great deal of soul searching and getting very involved in expanding every aspect of my Self. I became more Self-ish in my search for healing and spiritual direction.

I learned various meditation and breathing techniques and became much more conscious of my diet and health in greater detail. Learning about our bodies of energy and how to heal them and to receive healing was both fascinating and empowering.

I gained a much better understanding and 'energy' of Spirit – mine and in the greater aspect, various religions and their connectedness, the one-ness of humanity and all beings on our planet, relationships to everything - and so much more. It helped me to heal much of my emotional pain and find my joy, which had been somewhat dimmed for much of my life.

My spiritual 're-birth' was like the passing of virginity – once gone there is no going back to before. That long-stifled energy of my spirit was launched in a new direction with passion.

There was -

- a strong pendulum swing to the spiritual aspect of my Self
- an eventual re-balance of body, mind and spirit
- an insatiable thirst for knowledge and awareness of Self and Oneness, or All That Is
- a look at my inner world of Self and the outer world around me through new eyes
- a new-found perspective of everything like looking through a turning kaleidoscope
- a large amount of time and energy committed towards my new direction
- a reassessment of all my values
- an attraction of love and learning
- a passionate burst of expansive energy seeking greater awareness
- a realisation of beauty and lessons in all aspects of our lives; it's a matter of perspective

- a very fulfilling time of learning, fellowship, and healing, but after three and half years
- a sense that my time at that school was over - I needed to go apply what I had learned
- a decision that I wanted to create my own path
- a sense of separation from the centre and many friends that left a void I had to deal with
- a realisation that the sense of loss was an illusion. Love is ever-present if I allow it to be
- a greater acceptance of what was, or is, or will be
- a letting go of memories, emotions and possessions that were obstacles to healing
- a greater allowing of myself to love and to be loved in order to heal
- a greater awareness of the energetic make-up of our physical and non-physical world
- a greater desire for being of service to humanity

Though I haven't participated there since 2010, I still practice what I learned. I am forever grateful for the teachings, lessons learned and love exchanged with so many then and since. Thank you Shakti Durga, Hugh, Sioux, Rosie, Greg and so many others for your love and wisdom shared.

Breathe in/🐾/Breathe out/🐾/Breathe in/🐾/Breathe out/🐾

Changes on the *D-Tour*

"We are not meant to stay wounded. We are supposed to move through our tragedies and challenges and to help each other move through the many painful episodes of our lives. By remaining stuck in the power of our wounds, we block our own transformation. We overlook the greater gifts inherent in our wounds – the strength to overcome them and the lessons we are meant to receive from them. Wounds are the means through which we enter the hearts of other people. They are meant to teach us to become compassionate and wise."

– Carolyn Myss

Transform

1. to change in form, appearance, or structure; metamorphose.
2. to change in condition, nature, or character; convert.

I believe both of the dictionary definitions would suit the transformation I have experienced over the years on my *D-Tour*. PTSD creates a dramatic change in our Being that *has* to be addressed in order to heal and move on. Once aware, I wanted more than that. I wanted my life back!

There was a gradual process that took place over a number of years, where my whole being, body, mind and spirit shifted and reorganised. There were also several experiences that were more profound and evident during that time which were more of a spiritual focus. That of course impacted my whole Being.

At the time my life went off on a *D-tour*, so to speak, I was 52 years of age. It was a point where I felt that my life should be less struggle with more family enjoyment and activities while our three teenage children were still with us. Despite the difficult challenges I faced with providing an income to finance our lifestyle, in most respects we were doing reasonably well on the surface – fairly typical I would think of other families in a similar stage of life.

For some time, I felt trapped and facing a wall on every side. I didn't know which way to turn to start climbing out of the trench I found myself in. But before I could start climbing, I had to find the bottom of the pit. I had to acknowledge and accept that I had a problem that was bigger than my capacity to overcome on my own. I had to surrender to it and seek help outside of myself.

That brought feelings of failure and inadequacy resulting in loss of self-worth – feelings that I was not familiar with at that level during my life except on a couple of occasions of sustained unemployment. It didn't worry me much as an individual, but the pressure was different when others were depending on me.

I always worked my way through difficult situations before, but this time was different for some reason. It seemed overwhelming to me in spite of being able to mask it to others much of the time. Many of the people I knew or met would probably not have known that I felt quite dysfunctional in some ways and varying degrees for several years overall.

The process through it all was ultimately a blessing. It became a transformation of my body, mind, and spirit that certainly wasn't a glimmer of a blessing in the early stages, and a very long time after, from my perspective.

The overall transformation was really an unconscious intention that resulted from a conscious effort to get my life back on track. I was discovering the dance with my mind and emotions required to address my *spiritual energy* in order to rebalance my life overall.

If I wanted to get out of my depression and my anxious state I needed to change and to be open to it. It was the only way out. No body or no thing could magically fix me without my desire and intention and effort to change my condition. It required me to want to change to wellness more than accepting my debilitating condition.

- I knew I didn't want to stay in that situation that was sucking the vitality out of me.
- I realised it was diminishing my sense of self and my quality of life.

- I knew I was better than that.
- I knew it was ultimately up to me to change the situation within myself regardless of what help I could get medically. I had to change!
- I knew I had to change from what *was* happening to what I *wanted to be* happening.

I just didn't know how that could happen. A cloudy head and lethargic physical body from the anti-depressants didn't help me to focus and think clearly, in spite of their ability to lower my anxiety.

Angel or Demon?

As I mentioned earlier, getting the help from anti-depressants was initially a God-send. They helped me break through the anxiety I had been experiencing to a manageable level. The anti-depressants I took were powerful and effective, but they also sort of tranquillised me into a degree of uselessness anyway.

The cure became almost worse than the condition itself, so I tried a number of different prescriptions over the following months. I wanted lessened side effects while attempting to rid myself of the anxiety and its impact on my life. Eventually I weaned myself from "momma's little helpers" and was able to handle the stresses in more effective ways with fewer side effects as the anxiety was lessened. Moderate use of alcohol seemed to be the best antidote until I later discovered meditation.

A Major Setback

The biggest challenge and casualty during this period was my relationship and marriage to Kris. We both had changed over the course of 25 years together, as people do, but I really didn't see that coming. The 'transformation' of my 'self' was very difficult for her. My outlook on life changed dramatically during my *D-Tour*. Through the shift, caused largely by my dealing with the effects of PTSD, which took me on a more 'spiritual' direction, our relationship needed to adapt as well.

It was a real test of personal values and priorities in life for us both. We both compromised as far as we felt we could and still be true to ourselves. It wasn't a situation of either of us being right or wrong – we just couldn't walk side-by-side any longer. We chose two different paths to follow.

We separated and reunited several times in the final five years of our marriage, the first time innocently while I was working away. There was never anyone else involved. It was a recognition of the difference in the way that I felt about myself and thus our relationship during the times together and apart. It was a surprise to me. It was staring me in the face each time I went away working.

We had to talk about it which was painful. We separated. We tried again. And again. We thought we could get through it, but we couldn't seem to be truly happy under the same roof for a variety of reasons. For me, it was as if I had a new 4-wheel-drive and wanted to test it out, top down, hair in the breeze. Kris didn't want to go for the ride.

Eventually we had to accept the fact that even though we loved and cared about each other, the differences were too much to allow a harmonious relationship. Mutual co-existence wasn't acceptable without the sense of peace and happiness. There is a price for everything.

It seemed ultimately the right decision for me to finally divorce – the 12-month process legally finalised in 2011. A BIG 'D' on my *D-Tour*. In spite the painful consequences of it, we went through that period with as much ease and grace as humanly possible, allowing us to move on with our lives. It created upheaval, but we had had many good years together we could still value. We were friends before we married and are still good friends. We were a good team together but we couldn't agree on how that could continue to be.

Our children and grandchildren are of ultimate importance to both of us. I acknowledge and appreciate her huge contribution to my life. She always was, and still is, a lovely person and great mother who provided us with four beautiful children.

She had supported me throughout our largely productive and

mostly happy marriage. Unfortunately, she certainly wore a good deal of my stress-related behaviour with undeterminable consequences - for which I am sorry. There was counselling available for her and all my family which she did try. Like all the partners and families of PTSD people, she was, and is still, a silent victim.

Breathe in/🐾/Breathe out/🐾/Breathe in/🐾/Breathe out/🐾

Landmark Education - Boot Camp Revisited

In the months following my decision to leave THC, I kept very busy. I paid a visit back to the land of my birth, which pulls me back to the womb from time to time with those innate cords of attachment. I did some work, I connected with other like-minded people, and I did some writing.

One day I received a phone call from a close friend, Janneia, who invited me to a meeting that she thought would interest me. She used words like integrity, self-empowerment, commitment, inspiration, and transformation to describe an event that she had attended. I couldn't resist the pull to investigate.

Not really sure of what I had agreed to over the phone with a person she had referred me to, I showed up to a gathering in Sydney. It was at a large conference room at Landmark Education near Darling Harbour. There were about ninety people there from memory. Within a short period of time, the MC who was a very dynamic Indian woman, had people in tears, including me. And mostly not from laughter.

People were called up on stage and asked to share relationship issues in their lives. They were then pushed to deal with those matters that had been causing them emotional pain, or disconnection, sometimes for years.

Some had suppressed feelings from past situations which were stewing in the pits of their stomach, and others had current situations and confrontations causing them anxiety, sadness or anger. People were handed a phone and told to ring that parent or sibling or child they hadn't communicated with for years. Often one or both of them said something in anger that they wouldn't forget or forgive, or whatever reason.

"Ring your partner - tell him or her you are sorry for that hurtful argument that created a rift in your relationship. If you love them, tell them so. Forgive your father for not being in contact for the past ten years, regardless of who is to blame".

Barriers were penetrated or broken down within minutes. Emotions and tears erupted, for both those on stage and those in the audience. Fears were overcome and replaced by joyful reunions! People were transforming their lives for the better before my very eyes. It was *powerful* stuff!

Whenever people from the audience were picked, I sat there in silence, avoiding the searching eyes for the next player to be up on stage. I was too gripped by my fear to stand in front of that many people in my most vulnerable state. I'll just wait I thought until I am more composed.

One of the agreements, if you attended, was to participate – to interact. I didn't. I couldn't let the emotion bottled up within me out into the public arena like those I was witnessing. Every time I built up the courage to get up there, I'd cave in to fear. I had gone through army boot camp, but this was tougher.

It was emotional hardball with no glove. The leader wouldn't take no for an answer to her demands to make contact with the other person in that relationship. A few people bolted at the first break. Others never returned from lunch. At the end of the long first day, I was emotionally worn out just listening to the stories of drama others told about, the action they took, and the results they got. Many had successful outcomes, but not always. Yet it was inspiring, and the potential for positive change in my own life made it enticing.

The next day a few more people were missing. I vowed to myself to participate on stage, but somehow I managed to avoid selection again. Still, I rang a few people with apologies for some of my actions with them. They all responded with, “What? No problem”. It was very empowering and encouraging just being there.

After the third day, we had a few days break until the following weekend when we met for our ‘graduation’ ceremony, open to the public with family and friends encouraged to attend. We had been given instructions to continue trying to heal broken connections in the meantime.

When I finally put my hand up that night to be called upon, I was passed over. Oh well, I had the courage to put my hand up. It was still a great time in celebration for those that faced their demons and resolved issues. They could move forward with their lives and relationships. Their victories and transformations were very inspiring.

❖

For myself, the protective shell around my heart I had *thought* had been open, was softening up. I realised that I needed a blow torch to get me fired up to confront my fears and heal my emotional wounds. I signed up for more events. I did several more courses over the two-thirds of 2011. It was baptism by fire, but it’s just what I needed. I had struggled for years with emotional breakdowns at times. I had never been really comfortable with public speaking, even as a class and student body president in high school.

The two courses in communication were especially excellent and very beneficial for me. I gradually got more comfortable with speaking from my heart in front of others, and I was able to maintain my composure better. It was a time of further healing for me, and I came away from the experience more empowered and balanced in my self.

It gave me the framework to further define me, my purpose, to gain inner strength and direction for my self. When I decided I had gone as far as I wanted to go with it, I no longer continued. The learning, healing and transformation that I experienced at Landmark were certainly a different style to my much gentler Harmony Centre approach. They always tried to ‘encourage’ going further with courses – ‘pushed’ would probably be more accurate, but that was what I needed at the time.

Landmark never claimed or even suggested that they had a *'spiritual'* basis. Any reference to that, God, or religion, seemed to be absent, but I was *'inspired'* by the teachings and the experience there. Eventually I had enough 'pushing' through barriers and left their programs.

Thank you Landmark Education and the people involved, for your inspiring, effective and transformational programs for my personal development, giving me another link on my road to recovery. Thank you Janneia for the invitation and support you gave me through that time.

Breathe in/❀❀/Breathe out/❀❀/Breathe in/❀❀/Breathe out/❀❀

Cutting Edge Help

By the time I completed my time with Landmark Education seminars in 2011, I had been learning, healing, and transforming for several years. I had changed a great deal through that. If I wasn't attending a course or seminar or meditation, I was reading a book related to wellness in various forms. I invested a substantial amount of time and assets towards that endeavour. My addiction to television was a thing of the past; there wasn't the time or interest in the majority of programs. My *D-Tour* had long since become my new and permanent pathway; there was no going back; it wasn't a detour, but a new way of living, onward and upward.

After doing so much to overcome the effects of trauma and strengthen myself in all respects, I still felt emotionally vulnerable at times, but I couldn't quite understand why. I pondered the questions, "Has my body, i.e. nerve cells, been physically damaged by the energy of trauma beyond repair? If so, does that leave me susceptible to disease, as it is known that stress to be? How can I scientifically prove my condition one way or another? What can I do to overcome any effects if there to be fully healed?" I felt that getting answers to those questions was my next important step towards reaching optimum wellness.

My belief system is that the human body is able to recover from virtually any condition where the body is still intact, to a state of wholeness. I'd had enough personal experience and witnessed that in others to fully believe that. I didn't know it, but my long, seemingly slow, yet interesting path was about to enter into a new phase of greater understanding and healing methods.

It seemed that I was dealing with life and my PTSD quite effectively. In spite of my divorce from Kris that year, I was otherwise generally happy in myself. The legal process took twelve months after application, but the break-up was on and off over some four years with recurring efforts to make it work. The love we still felt for each other couldn't overcome our differences, so we had to accept that a permanent parting would probably be the best option for our greater good.

The wonders of Nepal and Tibet pulled at me and I succumbed to their magic for several weeks of unforgettable experiences. The time with those wonderful people in the Himalaya was a welcome break, during which time my divorce was completed. A good time to contemplate my life. And to start writing a book on how I had "gotten my life back."

Dr Peter Levine

My sister Rita came to visit me in Australia from the U.S. a few months later in April 2012. She brought a book for me on healing PTSD called '*Waking the Tiger: Healing Trauma*' by Dr Peter A. Levine. It supplied me with a wonderful 'aha' moment when it so undeniably provided the clue to the feeling I had been sensing that I needed to go further with my healing. Moreover, he claimed that he was actually able to rehabilitate a client from long-term PTSD to wellness.

I think it is fair to say that Dr Levine was acknowledged as being one of those at the forefront of understanding and treating the effects of trauma. His highly acclaimed books and works, including his follow up book, '*In An Unspoken Voice: How the Body Releases Trauma and Restores Goodness*', published in 2010, gave me a much better understanding of trauma. His findings and conclusion with his following statement which concurred with my inner belief was terrific news from such high authority:

*"**Trauma is** a fact of life. It does **not**,*
*however, have to be **a life sentence**."*
- Dr Peter Levine

The accepted view of the medical world at that time, seemed to be that PTSD was basically 'incurable' – you could only try to effectively 'manage' it through medication, counselling and good health practices. Whether true or not, it was a viewpoint that I found unpalatable and preferred not to believe. It shattered my hopes of getting past what I was feeling when I was given that 'incurable' message in 2001. The inability to think clearly and the lethargy of my body motivated me to seek other options in hope of ridding myself of those inhibitors, potentially for rest of my life.

The medical method of treatment may have worked well for many other PTSD sufferers across the world, but unfortunately, some gave up the quest for improvement after hearing that prognosis. I know of one veteran who terminated his life when he was given that message by his doctor. He left behind a grieving wife and two children. He felt he had no hope of overcoming the symptoms that held him in its grip. Thank you Dr Levine for providing solid evidence that, at least in some cases, the condition could not only be managed, but actually be cured! ***Gold!***

As Dr Levine points out, we all encounter trauma in our life. It can start with our birth process. Trauma is virtually a daily occurrence for some people, experienced either directly or indirectly. The important part of his message is *one of hope* and a way to overcome the condition so that it doesn't detrimentally impact us forever; it is not the trauma itself that is our real problem; it is *how we deal* with it.

Dr Levine's message gave me a far better understanding of trauma and how to overcome its impact. He took me on a quantum leap upwards with his insight and advanced techniques of treatment into the 21st century. Great! So how could I get access to that treatment in Australia? Time marched on as I wondered about a way to make that happen.

🐾🐾

Dr Levine had used a bit of trickery in a sense to enable success in his treatment with his client told about in his book.

- He engaged her into a state of re-living her traumatic experience in a very real sense from her memory, and then
- He basically convinced or 'tricked' her sub-conscious mind to overcome the energy of that trauma that was locked into her body's cellular memory.
- He helped the client produce a more powerful emotion of courage to take flight instead of freezing in the moment of confrontation with danger.
- The action of *flight* released the stored-up energy created by fear and allowed the sub-conscious mind to believe the body had escaped, thus complete the traumatic event in a positive way.
- The client could then let go of the attached emotion and stop going through the thought-loop that held her in that state when it was triggered by a certain circumstance –thus curing her of the symptoms and effects of her traumatic event!

One day the thought occurred to me that if the mind could be tricked in such a way to clear the effects of trauma on the body, it was effectively a placebo, so why not create that for myself somehow. Later on, I read Dr Lissa Rankin's great book, *Mind over Medicine: Scientific Proof*

You Can Heal Yourself, and Dr Bruce Lipton's also excellent book, *The Biology of Belief* which confirmed that it had been proven truly possible to do just that – create a placebo healing with mind over matter. I just wasn't sure how I could do that. Then another feather dropped at my feet and a door opened in early 2014, figuratively speaking, when I picked it up.

Hello 'Dr Joe'

A newsletter from Chris Hooper, who organises wonderful events around Australia with some of the most interesting people from Australia and world-wide brought some good news. Dr Joe Dispenza was returning to Australia to do a workshop in Sydney, based on his work and new book *You Are the Placebo: Making Your Mind Matter*. If you don't already know, Dr Joe, as he is affectionately known, is a neuroscientist, lecturer, author of several best-selling books, and featured in the thought-provoking films *The Secret* and *What the BLEEP Do We Know!?*

I had attended one of his lectures in Sydney in 2011, and have been fascinated by his research findings on our brain/mind function and our human behaviour. My thoughts of why not use our mind to create a placebo effect for ourselves was being used by Dr Joe! I booked in immediately to the workshop in June 2014.

Since then, I have attended several of his workshops and retreats, read his books, listened and watched his material in various forms, and practiced his methods. He seems to be at the forefront of discovering and sharing successful leading edge approaches to healing the mind, body, and spirit. He is constantly taking awareness of our body and healing to new levels. He works with other like-minded scientists who are in a class of their own, breaking down barriers of secrecy that science has often hidden behind over the centuries. His laboratory has been his own experiences and ever-evolving workshops where he measures, analyses and shares.

His approach to communicating his vast understanding and knowledge is the best and most thorough of anything or anyone I have found. He explains our neurological system structure and function so well, putting the scientific view into a much more digestible language. 'Dr. Joe' teaches *how to heal the self* rather than doing it for us.

I continue to use and expand myself with the ground-breaking, empowering techniques he has developed. He has measured the incredible results through his scientific measurement of participants in his gatherings, which he has used to understand and develop further. Again, the breath is a key part of the meditative process.

Using his techniques has definitely has been transformational and effective in my healing and expansion of awareness. I love and appreciate Dr Joe for his openness and putting his heart and soul into his work. He has dramatically changed so many lives right around the world in many profound, empowering ways, including spontaneous healings. Another important step in my journey.

Breathe in/ /Breathe out/ /Breathe in/ /Breathe out/

Alcohol and Marijuana

My Mood Mellowers

"Hey Greg – the 'arranger' has some unbelievable new wacky weed you've gotta try! How about we come over with a few of the gang to your place to try it out?" My friend was enthusiastic, as he always was, especially when it came to dope, drinking and women. He always seemed to have an ample supply of each and often mixed the three.

He wasn't easy to say no to whether I was keen to engage or not. Participants for the gathering 'magically' appeared within an hour. There were only about eight of us, ready and eager to try this "blow your socks off" batch as the latest on offer. It was more like 'blow you head off'. We were all soon laughing hilariously at nothing, which was fairly normal when smoking, but this stuff took me beyond where I wanted to go. Most of the others were worse, in no condition to hardly function, much less drive away.

Wiping myself out on pot was never an intention for me from the first time I had it back in Vietnam about five years earlier. To some extent, I had given in to peer pressure then, but as an infrequent user with light indulgence, I had no fears about what long-term affect it might have on me then, or with any of the experiences afterwards. There was enough reassurance from the group I was with initially and enough evidence over the years from many sources to convince me.

It was just to have fun, chill and relax or perhaps forget about the situation I might happen to be in. It was fairly easy to manage its effects on me. I had no trouble saying no to LSD or other hallucinogenic drugs I feared could be detrimental to my health – my mind in particular. Or any with the possibility of creating an addiction to anything I couldn't control.

On this occasion, the pot had apparently been laced with hashish, as I was to find out. The effects on myself and on all of us that night made me reconsider my use of marijuana at all. I had enjoyed the times I'd used it in the past, but before I went to bed that night, I'd wished I hadn't smoked it this time.

The various members of the gathering disbanded fairly early, so I started running bath water for a relaxing soak. Although I hadn't over-indulged, the full effects of the drug were yet to hit me. Before I could get ready to enter the water, one of the group returned to the house to ring a taxi. He'd drive two feet forward instead of reversing, smashing the plate glass window of the shop he was parked in front of. I found out the next day that another thrill-seeker realised before he reached the end of the street that he would be much wiser to take a cab as well. He parked his car and did just that.

An Awakening

I continued with my intention to have a bath. Settling into my envelope of watery bliss, I began to imagine that I was in a canoe travelling through the blood vessels of my brain. That was interesting, but my head began to pulsate and I began to feel uncomfortable with that. I wanted it to end but I couldn't manage to control those thoughts and feelings for some time, which was a concern.

Looking back, perhaps it was a good thing, as it made me stop and think about what had taken place and the effects it had on me. That was the impetus I needed to decide that I would not touch that concoction again.

Following that unpleasant experience, I continued to have a smoke occasionally, but I was very cautious about what was contained in the joint. Pot for me, and other party goers I knew during that period of my life, was a convenient way to enjoy myself in a manner easier to manage than beer in that sense of controlling its effects. It was also much easier to take to a party environment where beer stashes would be discovered and pilfered or totally disappear. Putting one's beer into the fridge or the tub full of ice was often a gift to other drinkers who may have forgotten what belonged to whom.

Why did I begin and keep using marijuana? The same reasons I suppose that I started using alcohol at times from my late teens and more heavily in the Army, particularly Vietnam. Apart from being convenient, it had reasonably reliable and consistently predictable effects, and it was relatively cheap. I could alter what I was thinking into concentrated thinking or into non-thinking. I could alter how I felt into feeling better.

Whether to alter perceptions in the pursuit of a sense of freedom and escape from the present moment, or simply to relax, it was my opinion that it was fairly harmless at the level at which I used it. That was both from the point of any given time and my cumulative use.

My view was that it was less disabling mentally and physically than alcohol, with potentially fewer negative consequences when used sensibly. It didn't take me on the more deceptively elevating mood build up as alcohol would, and then dump me with a hangover.

Alcohol effects depended much more on what I was drinking, how much, over what time frame, whether with or before, how much food or without food, and how tired I was - more so than with pot.

Of course drinking was, and still is far more socially acceptable, with alcohol easier to acquire. I rarely drank hard liquor because of the taste, inconvenience, effects on my wallet and after-effects on my body. Beer was my preference generally for taste and convenience. Occasionally I would have wine, usually with a meal rather than for general consumption.

Both alcohol and marijuana, in reality, were basically used to feel in a brighter mood as in party mode, or to deal with thoughts and emotions I wanted to disengage from. That could include to forget about the war environment I was imprisoned in, the homesickness at times in Vietnam and later in Australia, or to soothe the emotions of anger and depression during those years in America between those faraway places from my homeland. Would have I have ever begun smoking marijuana had I not gone to Vietnam? I can't answer that knowingly of course, but I think it would have been unlikely.

Eventually I stopped smoking it altogether about the mid-70's, as it became known to be hydroponically grown giving it more powerful but unpredictable effects. That seemed to become more frequently the case with some unfortunate outcomes reported from about that time in Australia, resulting in behavioural or health issues – a risk I wasn't prepared to take.

My alcohol consumption was moderated considerably when I married – both times. These days it ranges from nothing to very little for different reasons, with periods where I couldn't be bothered. I enjoy a drink occasionally when I do have any, particularly at a BBQ, a meal, the end of a hot day or hard work. However I rarely have more than a couple of beers or a glass or two of wine at any given time. I'm happy enough already in the moment I am, and I don't need the after effects if I overdo it.

Breathe in/🐾🐾/Breathe out/🐾🐾/Breathe in/🐾🐾/Breathe out/🐾🐾

Rage

That is been an emotion that I have expressed a few times in my life that seemed to virtually consume me. It would literally take over my being, as if possessed, leaving any rational thinking or behaviour in the ashes of the fiery explosion. I could usually feel it approaching with rising frustration and anger over something that I was trying to do, but wasn't able to for some reason. Perhaps it was the absence of adequate patience.

My body would become agitated and the heat come up the back of my neck to enflame my head and face before I would explode. I could generally catch it and take control before it reached that point to walk away and cool off, avoiding any contact with anyone if possible.

However, once the lid flew off and the cyclone unleashed, it was difficult to rein back in. I had to expend that energy until it dissipated of its own accord and I could recover some composure. Any previous semblance I previously had of dignity would be in shreds.

As a child I had a pretty wicked temper at times, which could flare up and be gone rather quickly. But that was not the rage I mean. What I'm talking about here was a slow build-up like the contents of a pressure cooker on the stove, resulting in an explosion when the lid blew off.

The first time that I can distinctly remember it happening, was while working on an old car I'd bought when I was seventeen. Laying on my back under the car just about touching my face, I was trying to perform mission impossible. The position of the pistons needed to be in a certain position in order for the oil pan to be removed. That crucial bit of information wasn't known to me at that stage. The frustration was building and building and my patience was diminishing in equal degrees. Despite the cool of the autumn night, I lost mine. I *totally* lost it.

Little did I realise my girlfriend had come out to my garage to see how the project was going. She got to witness me at my worst.

There were words of venom coming out of my mouth that I didn't even know I knew - probably could make a bad-tempered sailor blush. My behaviour was a shock to her and even to me. How do you un-do a performance like that to restore the original image? You don't.

The next memorable time before an audience was many years later in Australia. A grown man with some living and Vietnam behind me, nearly thirty years of age. Rational and mature? Again it involved a car.

On a long drive of 600 miles or 950 kilometres from Sydney to Brisbane, our car started acting like it had a faulty fuel pump or dirty fuel. It eventually stopped and wouldn't start. It was in the middle of the night in the middle of nowhere. Very tired and battling the flu and fatigue, I totally lost it as we sat in the silence of the winter's night. Fortunately I managed to resist my temptation to smash the innocent windscreen. Still, there were consequences.

My first marriage was about a year old. Michelle had never seen such craziness coming from me. She was shocked, horrified and perhaps even frightened. That few minutes of madness quite probably contributed to the failure of our short marriage. Another scene in my life story I wanted to erase. I couldn't.

Another pathetic performance I can recall was one of several that took place in the early years of my *D-Tour*. Another vehicle and another fuel pump issue – trying to fit the replacement back to where I'd easily removed the faulty one. The same mental and bodily symptoms presented to the similar circumstances. My second wife, Kris, came out of the house to where I was working in the driveway. She simply asked 'How's it going?' It was like putting a match to the powder keg. Unfortunately she was standing next to the explosion rather than at the safe end of a fuse trail.

We had been married for nearly twenty years by then, so it wasn't a total surprise for her to see an angry eruption coming from me. Still, not pretty or impressive. She survived to go back into the house and shrug it off - or absorb it? Again. Sometime it's just best not to ask the question if there is steam coming out of the ears.

The ute survived my kick and I retreated to the house for a beer to settle me down and later find the tools I projected at the earth. The neighbours acted if they didn't hear me. They must have been deaf. It wasn't the first or the last time I 'lost it' during that period, but usually not with someone immediately around me that had to wear it. I'm pleased I didn't have to see myself, although had I done so, it may have stopped the repetition of such behaviour from me.

❧

My uncontrolled displays throughout those years were beyond a little temper tantrum. That in itself could startle someone not expecting that sort of behaviour from someone that normally seemed pretty casual and composed – those monumental explosions were out-*rage*-ous!

It seemed to happen mostly trying to repair something which would go wrong beyond my ability to accomplish a task, not at people. A vehicle I might be working on was usually the poor innocent recipient of my wrath if it went that far.

It was usually just throwing some tool or other handy object around, before storming off in a horrific verbal barrage. Thankfully I seem to be past those terrible tirades. Sadly though, I think the consequences were costly.

What 'possessed' me to behave like that? Did I inherit that trait from one or both of my parents? Did my childhood traumas cause or contribute to that as they did with my early inability to express my feelings, resulting in anger-fuelled fights? Did the pent up anger of post-Vietnam contribute? I can only guess. Thankfully, it seems to be resolved now regardless of the cause(s), which I think is largely a result of my 'inner' work on my 'Self', rather than simply growing out of it. Time will tell.

Rage can be scary because of its intensity and unpredictability, even my own. Fortunately I didn't inflict any physical harm to anyone or even want to. Regret doesn't fix the past, but I hope those people, dogs, cats, cows, birds and whatever else that may have had to witness my bad behaviour and rage, were able to recover and can forgive me.

Breathe in/🐾/Breathe out/🐾/Breathe in/🐾/Breathe out/🐾

An *Empowering* Side to Anger

In February of 2001 my wife at that time, Kris, and I arrived at a five-day live-in retreat/workshop facilitated by the Vietnam Veterans Counselling Service for Vietnam veterans diagnosed and being counselled for PTSD. It was intended that all participants and the group in those relationships would more fully understand, appreciate, and manage the condition. Nearly twenty of us were there for most of those days, which included eight partners. My wife had come along rather reluctantly, but finally agreed which was very important – and compulsory in order for me to attend.

I had been diagnosed with the condition about seven months earlier. I was prescribed anti-depressants and had commenced counselling soon after with the Vietnam Veterans Counselling Service (in Australia). The counselling I had received by that stage was already helping me to understand the condition and starting to restore more order for me.

At that point I was beginning to feel a bit better about the prospects of a recovery from the messy state I had been in prior. When first diagnosed, I had thought the situation would all be over in a matter of weeks or months and I could get on with my life. Unfortunately I was, very wrong, as I was to discover beyond my early realisation that it could take a bit longer than expected.

Up until then, Kris hadn't really accepted that the problems I had were significant. Like many partners, we were to learn, initially don't realise the turmoil going on within us. She was also fearful that if I sought medical help, I could end up in hospital with it, treated as mentally ill.

- She couldn't think and feel what I did
- She seemed to think that I simply had stress, which was nothing new to either of us
- She had symptoms of severe stress herself she didn't seem to realise
- I wanted to help her with that

- I wanted her to understand for both our sakes
- I wanted her support

🐾🐾

We arrived in the afternoon to settle into our rooms, meet the others over a few drinks and a meal. Afterwards we all gathered in the games room for some more drinks, fun and bonding, and taking turns playing team pool. By then, we were more relaxed and getting to know each other somewhat.

After a few games, it was the turn for the team with Kris and another vet's wife. By then Kris was losing her sense of shyness, as she sometimes did with the right mix of alcohol and the right company. She was unknowingly becoming the life and the focus of the now party. As she engaged in the game, she tended to spend more of her time sharing her sometimes comical sage advice to others, rather than focusing on the game itself. She had to be told when it was her turn and which balls were hers to shoot at. She became an easy target for a prank from her opponents, a couple of men who would stealthily put the balls she sank on rare occasions back onto the table from the pockets. When her partner twigged to the mischief from her husband, she went along with the great amusement for all watching the game.

She eventually began to think that she or her partner may have already pocketed some of the balls reappearing on the surface, to the denial of all players, including her partner now fully in on the fun. She eventually caught one of them in the act and had a few "I thought so's!", and "I knew it's!", and a good laugh about it all.

By then, she had won the comedian of the night award for her great unwitting performance, as well as the admiration of all for her being a good sport. It was a great way to break the ice of fear about meeting others and what the next few days might hold for us. It was also a good start for Kris in feeling a bonding with the group, particularly the women who helped her to better understand so much in the coming days about PTSD and their relationship to it with their partners. It was to be a challenging but beneficial time for us all.

One of the focuses of the week was discussion and education around self-medication through alcohol to deal with stress, trauma and PTSD. It is probably the easiest, most used and abused, socially accepted form by veterans. That already well-known fact was pointed out, along with the consequences and suggestions for moderation and responsible levels. Despite our disregard for that warning during that week, I must say that what I took away from that time was literally quite sobering for me.

The following morning gathering was more subdued than the departure from the games room the night before. Apart from a few sore heads, the apprehension of what was to come reappeared to some extent. As more formal introductions and a brief statement about what we hoped to get from the coming days passed in sequence around the room, Kris and I both struggled with our emotions. It was very obvious that we both were in need of support, which was offered by others. We were fortunate to be in the right place to get that. We left at the end of our time there with a much greater awareness of the condition of PTSD and ways in which to address the symptoms. We also formed valuable friendships that we held on to for some years.

Looking at a Life Sentence

Something else occurred there in the first days of the retreat which had a huge impact on me. A renowned psychologist and expert on PTSD spoke to us. It was a statement coming from him in his address to us which he said that he had some news for us that we probably didn't want to hear. He was right. It both shocked and angered me!

The context of his message was that -

- **There was no quick fix to PTSD**
- I had believed that I would be back to 'normal' within months – whatever 'normal' meant.
- (I felt better after seven months, but didn't realise the extent of the time and effort and what measures were necessary to overcome the problems or symptoms).

- **The symptoms could be managed and you can get on with life, but …**
- **There was no known 'cure' for PTSD; it was with you for life!**
- I didn't hear much of anything beyond that point; I was in shock at those words!
- I thought, ***"That's bullshit!"***
- I thought, ***"That does not fit into my belief system. I refuse to believe that!"***
- I thought, ***"Everything and anything is possible!"***
- I thought, ***"I will prove you wrong! I will heal from this condition!"***

🐾

Breathe in/🐾/Breathe out/🐾/Breathe in/🐾/Breathe out/🐾

A Potentially Powerful Energy

Refusing to believe that message was a defining moment for me in setting the intention of finding reasons and solutions to that condition we call PTSD! He was a recognised authority on the subject so why would I not believe him? Something in me wouldn't accept it. Years later I learned the science of that shift in me -

- The *energy* within the emotion of anger I felt then, empowered the thoughts I had in those moments to change - to take the action that I did in order to make the necessary changes in me.

  There was an amazing potentially *positive energy* in that emotion of anger that *empowered* me!

- I have never stopped believing those thoughts and
- I have never lost sight of that intention!
- That turned my D-Tour in a direction of looking for solutions beyond medical treatment

- His view was based on his experience and that of others in the field of psychology and medicine
- The thoughts of disbelief, defiance, and refusing to believe his opinion or perception allowed me to create my own reality - regaining my wellness through my positive beliefs and actions to find solutions and healing modalities has proven to be successful for me
- Whether or not I ever become totally free of the symptoms of PTSD, doesn't really matter to me any longer. I have successfully learned to manage them if and when they appear. I feel I have empowered beyond what I have ever been in my overall wellness. That has been made possible by that decision and action to find alternatives
- I am truly grateful to Dr X for motivating me to search of my own methods and truth
- I am also in so much appreciation to my loving parents who instilled in me empowering attitudes along with the courage of my convictions to act; to trust in myself and in a Higher Power

Early in my life I had witnessed healings, both in myself and others, that defied the expectations of medicine through the power of prayer and positive belief. I knew that connection to the Divine was powerful and effective in healing and bringing myself into my wholeness, when I *allowed* that to happen. (The Divine Power is always available, I just have to allow it to heal my body through my spirit).

I had been absent from that focus in my life for most of the previous twenty years. Could that link be re-established? There had been a resistance to do so during that time for a number of reasons I'll share in another part of this book. However the powerful emotion of what transpired that day dropped a seed of potential re-birth onto the hard ground of my heart that I didn't realise then. I was just angry, defiant, and determined to find a way to recover from what I felt in my weakened body and cloudy, confused mind over the previous months. There *had* to be a better way!

What was I angry about? I really didn't analyse why at the time, but

- I felt trapped by the state of body and mind I was in – like a cornered rat
- Caused by being told that essentially, there were ways to manage PTSD, but that there no known end to it
- My hopes of both a soon-ish and a long-term recovery were dashed by what an expert had said
- Who wants to live without hope of feeling good and having mental clarity?

So the anger? Probably the result of the sense of entrapment I felt in the situation and the frustration feeling that *I had lost control of my life.* But . . . it kindled the fire within me to seek ways to *re-gain that control!*

🐾🐾

Anger had been a powerful emotion throughout my life that sometimes had been difficult for me to control, creating some bad outcomes in my behaviour and health. Fortunately, during my *D-Tour* years I learned that, like the amazing energy of a horse, it can be brought under control to be mastered to actually be an effective tool. It can be used in a negative manner to manipulate or even harm others, but on the positive side of things, it can shift negative thoughts or stagnant energy within our body into movement in a positive direction.

I have also learned how angry emotions can create dis-ease in my body if not released in some way. As a youth, I had very bad acne that plagued me through my teens and beyond, in spite of going to great lengths to control it with skin care, diet, and medication. Even x-ray treatments were tried with some success but which years later created extensive skin cancer (basal cell carcinoma) on me, requiring the removal of dozens upon dozens over time, from my face, arms and back with various forms of treatment. It was pretty clear, even back then as a teenager, it was an emotionally based problem, but I had no idea it was probably due to the unresolved impact of trauma in those earlier years.

Perhaps the fighting and boxing I engaged in from the age of six until about the age of twelve was more beneficial than the suppression of anger. Those pent up emotions needed to be released in a more positive manner than fighting, but I wasn't able to do that consciously or effectively in my ignorance.

I am very pleased I have that understanding and tools now that have enabled me to take effective action to release that energy, and to use them to prevent further problems. I feel a great sense of appreciation to my many teachers with many methods over the past few years.

Breathe in/❀❀/Breathe out/❀❀/Breathe in/❀❀/Breathe out/❀❀

Post-Traumatic Stress Disorder (PTSD)

Statistics on anything can be tricky and misleading so those on PTSD are no different. However they do give something of an idea to the extent of the problem if you can read between the lines. Stats are generally documented clinical cases so many people possibly with the condition aren't counted. Since many people never get diagnosed, I would suggest that there are far more people dealing with that and related issues than we could ever know.

According to the National Institute of Health in the U.S., in 2009 there were 7.7 million adults affected by PTSD in a population of about 310 million at that time. In Australia it is suggested over 6 % of the adult population of 22 million, or roughly 1.4 million people. The numbers compared between the U.S. and Australia seems disproportionate with 1 in 40 affected in the U.S.; it's 1 in 20 in Australia. Is that a true indication?

The U.S. Department of Veteran Affairs states that 31% of Vietnam Vets are affected by PTSD. In Australia it is estimated at 56% for that group. Again virtually double for Australia to U.S. What are the figures as we enter 2019 with governments admitting they are increasing?

What is Post-Traumatic Stress Disorder or PTSD?

The simplest description can be found in the extensive works of Dr Peter A. Levine who is a world recognized leading authority on the subject. He has worked for over forty years in his passionate search for answers to the mystery of trauma. He describes trauma as **"a highly activated incomplete biological response to threat that is frozen in time (and) is physiological."**

Stopping our flight impulse in the face of threatening danger is the root cause of distress-anxiety. The anxiety emotion generating an urge to run that is stopped, becomes a fixed emotional state of anxiety, especially if one feels trapped or powerless. The threat creates fear in order to run away. If unable to run, anxiety results.

Dr Levine has written many papers and articles as well as two very helpful books on the subject, *Waking the Tiger Healing Trauma* and more recently *In an Unspoken Voice* where he explains what PTSD is and how we can overcome its grip on us. He has proven that this crippling condition is often actually ***curable***! It is not the life sentence I and so many others were led to believe by medical authorities that have held that belief for some time. There are people who have taken their own life after being told that it was incurable in the belief that they had to put up with the debilitating efforts and mental torment forever and felt powerless to change it.

The trauma and the condition known as PTSD can be created in a countless number of ways which affects everyone differently, so effective treatment on the individual can vary considerably. My treatment started with the use of prescribed anti-depressants to somewhat suppress my anxiety, and working with a counsellor experienced in that area. I believe both of those standard approaches proved effective in making my life more manageable for a period of time.

I cannot claim to have clinically conquered PTSD. Emotions can still sneak up on me from nowhere when I least expect it, but the worst of them like rage and anti-social behaviour have been conquered. I manage both the symptoms and effects very well now. Stress has an impact on our health beyond our conscious awareness, so I still consider myself to be a work in progress until I can reach a point where its impact at every level of my being is virtually undetectable.

"Trauma is a fact of life. It does not, however, have to be a life sentence."
— Dr Peter A. Levine

How PTSD Affects the Veteran

The following article is presented with permission of Susan Barr
PTSD Support Group located in Albuquerque, NM.
Susan is a trained counsellor and the wife
of a U.S. veteran with PTSD.
I believe she is very accurate in her assessment of what
PTSD veterans, their partners and loved ones face.

PTSD is a very complicated syndrome and can affect the veteran in many ways. As explained in last months' column, there are many symptoms and the combat veterans don't all have the same symptoms. The degree of trauma affects the degree of effect on the veteran.

The re-experiencing of a traumatic event, or flash-back, brings with it all of the effects that came with the original experience. If the veteran was in constant danger for his life, for instance, the fight-or-flight response of high adrenaline output would have been pretty much constant. Some veterans experienced that for long periods of time and some of them for more than one tour of duty.

When a flash-back occurs, so does that effect of high adrenaline. It can soar from a high which is normal to them to extremely high in the time it takes for that event to flash into the mind. This frequent soaring of adrenaline has a huge effect on the physical health of the vet, not to mention how it affects his emotions when the flash-back occurs. (irritability, health problems, exaggerated startle response).

Quite frequently, it seems, these flash-backs also bring feelings of anger, or even rage. After any engagement with the enemy, the resultant numbing and rage would increase. But what do you do with all that anger, with the reality of your experiences when you are thrown back into civilian life with no de-programming to prepare you? However, this numbing of feelings which served a purpose at the time, continues.

Unless and until there is a safe place where these feelings can surface and be felt and dealt with, little by little, they fester and explode with little provocation. The least little thing will cause them to erupt.

The vet feels out of control and isolates himself to try to keep these outbursts to a minimum (explosive aggressive behaviour, fear of losing control, panic attacks, social avoidance, job instability, difficulty in parenting and bonding, phobic-like avoidance behaviours)

They returned from literally life and death situations; from terror and horror, to everyday activities that seem mundane and pointless. They frequently feel that no one but other combat vets can understand what they experienced and continue to live with. They are right. Even their spouses often don't understand why they act the way they do. These feelings of alienation, of being "different" also make the veteran want to isolate.

They have learned what it feels like to kill and to have someone want to try to kill them. They lost, at an early age, most of them, all innocence and trust in their fellow man. They learned to survive by watching their backs at all times…and most of them still have a hard time sitting in the middle of a room, with other people behind them. They don't feel comfortable in crowds, their eyes darting about, always aware of anything or anyone that could be a threat. (loneliness, distrust of authority figures and the system, lowered trust of others, hyper-vigilance, persistent anxiety, paranoia)

There is a lot of self-blame and guilt associated with combat. Some of their buddies didn't survive; why did they? There was a lot that they saw and had to do that makes them feel guilt. They know that they did their jobs, what they were trained and sent to do, when you are fired upon, you shoot back. But how do eighteen year olds get a grip on having to kill?

Men tend to associate with their jobs. Does having to kill make them killers? Does that make police killers? These are extremely difficult issues to come to grips with. (intrusive thoughts, decreased intimacy, personality disorders, self-destructive behaviours, depression)

They also feel guilty about raging at their families. They don't want to feel constantly angry and irritable, they feel helpless: the symptoms are crazy-making for them, as well as for their spouses and children.

The constant re-enacting of traumatic events, the constant ebb and flow of adrenaline in their bodies makes it almost impossible to maintain an even mood. The constant, for some, nightmares, year after year, means that they don't get peaceful sleep. This also causes irritability. (memory and cognitive impairment, insomnia, sleep disturbances, impaired concentration, sexual dysfunction)

Some veterans try to cope with the symptoms of PTSD by self-medicating: they try to keep the flash-backs and nightmares at bay by taking drugs or alcohol. They cope by running: if you stay busy enough, long enough, you fall into bed so exhausted that you might be able to get a few nightmare-free hours of sleep.

The frequent coming and going of flashbacks, keeps them off-kilter, not quite knowing if they are there or here: is it then or is it now? They exercise immense effort of will trying fruitlessly to control this.

I understand that trauma can affect a person in other ways. The person can become stunted in their emotional growth at the age at which the trauma occurs. For instance, if the soldier was eighteen when they went into combat, (a very formative and vulnerable time in their lives), they could continue to behave and think as an eighteen-year-old would, ten, twenty or more years later. In other words, somehow their emotional growth can stop there, or continue at a much slower pace.

Sometimes the horror of their experiences will wash over them; especially at anniversaries of particularly horrible events, and it will feel unbearable. They can feel overwhelmed by them and feel as though they cannot endure one more second of it. They feel, right then, as though it will never end. (suicidal or homicidal thoughts, depression)

Holidays are particularly hard for them to deal with. Others around them are feeling joyful and happy. They, on the other hand are re-experiencing horrible events, death and destruction that happened during those holidays, events which super-impose themselves over today. (emotional numbness)

This is not just bizarre behaviour, it is the normal result of experiencing tremendous trauma. But some of these symptoms can be controlled to some extent and the veteran can learn to have some quality of life.

If you would like to ask questions of Sue and the members of their PTSD Support Group located in Albuquerque, NM who have been, or are in a relationship with PTSD husbands, please join their online forum at http://www.theveteransvoice.com/ptsd-and-wives

I would like to acknowledge Susan for sharing her first-hand experience in involvement with PTSD and to thank her for kindly allowing me to include her article here. Although I was not facing some of those horrors of war personally in direct combat, most of those symptoms have been remarkably similar for me. I would suggest in my case they are not as intense or overwhelming compared to many participants of war, but it was still debilitating enough to greatly impact my life. I believe many, if not most, Vietnam Veterans would identify with her assessment. I wish that all people dealing PTSD could receive the level of support her organisation offers.

Breathe in/🐾🐾/Breathe out/🐾🐾/Breathe in/🐾🐾/Breathe out/🐾🐾

Symptoms and Characteristics of Trauma or Post-Traumatic Stress Disorder

- Has many faces; can be obvious or subtle; not easily detected
- Heightened awareness - in 'fight or flight' state - seldom to virtually continuous
- Re-living a traumatic situation in the mind resulting in emotional and physical response
- Can be dis-empowering, debilitating, or disabling
- Nervousness or anxiety
- Racing thoughts
- Can't focus; can't think clearly or concentrate thoughts
- Can't get to sleep or stay asleep; poor sleep
- Unable to control behaviour; twitches, erratic eye movement, tapping feet, can't stay still
- Shallow or rapid breathing
- Increased pulse rate
- Perspire more than normal
- Use of distractions to ease nerves i.e. cigarettes, alcohol, drugs, chatter
- Feeling depressed or hopeless
- Worried; concerned about and focused on a negative situation or possibility in the future
- Unable to relax
- Letting future concerns overwhelm current reality that hasn't yet or may not ever happen
- Fear - whether substantiated or not
- Feeling unwell, particularly in stomach or mind; possible pain somewhere in your body
- Feeling dis-abled and dis-empowered; inability to cope with a situation/overwhelmed

- Panic attacks
- Inability to gain control of thoughts and emotions
- Loss of confidence and self-worth
- Sense of dis-connection from others and your world
- Loss of ability or desire to communicate with others
- Loss of affection and intimacy; de-sensitised
- Feeling suicidal – not wanting to face the world or exist
- Feeling stuck – unable to motivate body, mind or spirit
- Seeing the world as grey or black

Breathe in/🐾/Breathe out/🐾/Breathe in/🐾/Breathe out/🐾

Anxiety

Possible Characteristics and Symptoms

- Nervousness
- Racing thoughts; many thoughts competing for attention; can't stop thinking
- Repetitive thoughts in a loop or pattern can't break out of
- Can't focus; can't think clearly or concentrate thoughts; can't keep thoughts on track
- Can't get to sleep or stay asleep; poor sleep
- Unable to control behaviour; twitches, erratic eye movement, tapping feet, can't stay still
- Shallow or rapid breathing
- Increased pulse rate
- Perspire more than normal
- Use of distractions to ease nerves i.e. cigarettes, alcohol, drugs, chatter
- Loss of confidence
- Worried; concerned about a negative situation or possible situation in the future
- Uneasiness
- Apprehension
- Allowing future concerns to overwhelm current reality that hasn't yet or may not ever happen
- Fear, whether substantiated or not
- Feeling unwell, 'butterflies' in stomach; possible pain somewhere in your body
- Disabling and dis-empowering thoughts; inability to cope with a situation
- Feeling a sense of overwhelm
- Panic attacks

Possible Ways to Deal with Anxiety

- Take a few deep breaths
- Breath control exercises
- Meditation
- Focus thoughts on good feelings or memories
- Stay focused on the present
- Avoid thinking about stressful situations by focusing on the breath and loving thoughts
- Trust that everything will be okay regardless of how bad things look; have faith
- Herbal medication
- Prescribed non-addictive medication if required
- Listen to soothing music
- Sports activities
- Exercise
- Yoga
- Walking
- Dancing
- Talking with a professional practitioner, psychologist (counselling)
- Talking with an ordinary understanding, caring person or a trusted friend
- Time in Nature
- Try to get enough sleep but not too much; try to keep it in balance
- Do activities you enjoy
- Avoid stressful situations and activities
- Read uplifting, feel-good books
- Watch TV programs and movies that are uplifting rather than negative or stressful
- Eat healthy food in balanced amounts according to your need
- Avoid sugar and sweet foods; it is scientifically proven sugar adversely affects 'happy hormones'
- Avoid addictive food, habits and behaviour

- Keep alcohol consumption within reason
- Enjoy what you eat
- Spend time with a pet or other animals
- Believe in your own ability to deal with all situations

Breathe in/❖❖/Breathe out/❖❖/Breathe in/❖❖/Breathe out/❖❖

Depression

What is Depression?

You could get a vast variety of answers to that question, depending on whom you ask. A trained authority on the subject, may give a more clinical view than someone who has simply experienced the condition in one or more of its myriad of forms. Because it is such a complex subject, and because I fit into the latter category above, I will try to keep things simple. There is a great wealth of information available through a variety of sources, particularly books and the internet for further exploration of this fascinating topic. For our purposes here, I will give a brief definition from Australia's Macquarie Dictionary and supplement that with my own experience/viewpoint.

Depress:

- To lower in spirits, deject; dispirit.
- To lower in force, vigour; weaken; make dull.

Depression:

- The state of being depressed; dejection of spirits; state of despondency, characterised by a feelings of inadequacy, lowered activity, sadness and pessimism.
- In severe cases, unresponsiveness to stimuli, self-deprecation, or delusions of inadequacy and hopelessness.

Just by simple definition alone, you can see it is a very broad area. Who of us would claim to have never experienced any of that? I'm sure we all have, to varying degrees, at some point in our lives. I can say yes to virtually the lot.

However there were times I was knee deep in it and didn't recognise or appreciate the fact.

- I didn't realise I was supposed to be much happier all of the time than I was only occasionally.
- Or that my self-deprecating sense of humour was really a lack of appreciation of myself,
- Or that the emotions of sadness I had buried deep within me which would surface occasionally, could actually be released and transformed.

Depression covers a vast range of symptoms and degrees, so it is not always easy to determine, diagnose, and categorise for several reasons:

- The ability to assess a person cannot be measured in black and white terms generally, as in viewing a person's blood under a microscope. Assessment may be done, at least initially in many cases, by a time-deficient doctor who listens to a patient, makes a quick judgment, and may cover his/her bases with a script for an anti-depressant.
- Suppressing the symptom may clear the problem and they can move on; but I believe it may mask the real problem, delay the solution, and may not be in the patient's best long-term interest.
- More severe cases of course are more obvious, but it may be masked to some extent in some cases and therefore not obvious to anyone, even the sufferer. I was dealing with a form of subtle depression for many years, as a companion or component of PTSD, without really realising it, which impacted my life in a negative way. It becomes the accepted behaviour of the person, as I can testify. I believe that to be quite common. At what point on the invisible chart do we call it depression?
- Regardless of the extent of a person's depression, clinically diagnosed and labelled or not, in my view it really boils down in the end to feeling bad or feeling good. If I'm feeling bad, I naturally want to do something to make myself feel good.
- If I feel 'bla', I may not be clinically depressed, but if that feeling lasts more than a few minutes, it is impacting my ability to function in an effective and happy manner.

- Allowing my self to veg out or just relax occasionally for awhile is fine; but when my mind goes into a state where it cannot process a thought from go to whoa, and take action, I am 'depressed'.
- It's just as debilitating as an 'official' diagnosis of depression, depending on the depth of feeling and the length of time I spend there. It is probably more of a state of stagnation. If I stay there long enough, I can beat myself up about it and then have good reason to feel depressed; right?
- When I get into that non-productive, non-feeling, 'bla' state, I reach for the energiser: music; movement – stretches, exercise or a walk; water; conversation with someone uplifting; anything inspiring! That is usually enough to snap out of my 'state'. Generally, the resulting oxygen and bio-chemistry get things moving and feeling good again.

Possible Characteristics and Symptoms

- Feeling dispirited
- Unable to experience or express love or joy
- Feeling despondent
- Feeling sad
- Feeling pessimistic or negative
- Un-feeling
- Feeling hopeless
- Feeling inadequate
- Feeling unresponsive to life; flat, blue, down
- Possibly feeling like harming self
- Possibly feeling suicidal or not wanting to be alive

Ways of Dealing with Depression

- Move; get active; go for a walk; sports activities, exercise
- Take a few deep breaths/breath exercises

- Breathe; breathe in; hold 2 seconds; breathe out; hold 2 seconds; repeat 10 times
- Meditate
- Try to focus thoughts on good feelings or memories
- Try to stay focused on the present; use the breath exercise
- Get a relaxing massage, sauna, or spa treatment
- Avoid thinking about stressful situations by focusing on loving thoughts
- Trust that everything will be okay regardless of how bad things look
- Herbal medication
- Prescribed non-addictive medication if required
- Play an instrument; drum; sing
- Listen to relaxing, soothing music
- Yoga
- Talking with a professional practitioner, psychologist etc (counselling)
- Talking with any understanding, caring person
- Time in Nature
- Try to get enough sleep but not too much; keep it in balance
- Do activities you love to do
- Avoid stressful situations and activities
- Watch TV programs and movies that are uplifting rather than negative or stressful
- Eat healthy food in balanced amounts according to your need
- Keep alcohol consumption within reason
- Enjoy what you eat
- Spend time with a pet or other animals
- Read uplifting, feel-good books
- Avoid addictive food, drinks, habits and behaviour
- Detox your body
- Believe in your own ability to deal with all situations
- Believe you are always being supported by spiritual guides or angels; ask for their help

Why are we depressed?

That is a simple question; however there is usually no simple reason. We have a tendency to look for answers in what is occurring or has occurred in our lives. That may provide an obvious reason, or it may be very complex, but it doesn't always suggest a solution. There is therapy, counselling and anti-depressants to assist.

In any case, looking at what is actually occurring within us to *feel* that way, we can often link it to an imbalance in our biochemistry in the brain. Rather than delve into the reason through over-thinking that leads to confusion, another approach is to get the chemistry back in balance before attempting counselling.

That is probably the rationale in using anti-depressants to rectify the condition, which was often something of a trial and error to get right, for me at least, being sensitive to drugs. They can help to bring things back into balance, but can also mask symptoms and become addictive. For me at least, they also had side-effects I found difficult to deal with.

Exercise, movement, herbal medication and meditation are some of the alternatives that worked better for me once I got a reduction in my anxiety, associated with my depression.

I have not suffered from deep or acute depression, so I don't wish to say too much about something I haven't actually experienced. Where do you draw the defining line in such a subjective condition? Some degree of depression for periods of time at various stages of my life did occur, particularly on my return to civilian life from Vietnam. I've talked about that and how I dealt with that in another section.

For much of my life, I had put up with those feelings of suppressed enjoyment and happiness, believing I didn't deserve to feel so good whenever they did emerge. I would quickly push them back down if someone else didn't do it for me.

I put up with times of frustration, sadness, sorrow, anger, rage, aggression, shyness, aloneness, embarrassment, insufficiency, inadequacy, anxiety, and depression. Those emotions and more, fortunately, were not constantly present, but present enough to somehow cause me to feel unworthy of full-on happiness. You may say "that's just life and normal". I don't believe that it needs to be the case beyond brief periods.

Reaching a point of believing I deserved to be happy over these last few years wasn't enough to reach that state. I had to let go of the feelings that created them that was trapped in my physical and energy body. I then had to take pro-active steps to heal my condition. The condition I carried with me was created though a negative transformation, brought about by trauma. It required a positive, healing transformation to take me beyond which has resulted in a consistent joyfulness.

"And the day came when the risk to remain tight in a bud was more painful than the risk it took to blossom."
- Anais Nin (1903-1977)

It took me over 45 of those years to reach the point of awareness that I had a problem I wanted to change and was able to do something about it. That's a large proportion of my life to be robbed of allowing joyfulness to be more present in my life. I blame no one. Not even myself. It has been my journey. It was unlikely I could ever have fully appreciated the wonder and benefits that joy brings, without experiencing the contrast through which the traumatic events of life has taken me. Thankfully, I am now consistently free of depression.

Breathe in/🐾/Breathe out/🐾/Breathe in/🐾/Breathe out/🐾

I Can Think Clearly Now!

Why Couldn't I with PTSD?

My first awareness of having PTSD started with a visit to my doctor about my anxiety which was causing confusion, memory problems, frustration, and anger. There had been no connection in my mind to trauma – until then. What I have since learned -

- The most powerful instinct we have is self-preservation; survival. When we are threatened, the emotion of fear triggers hormones within us to either fight or run to escape the danger.
- If we do neither, but freeze, those hormones get locked in our body. That trapped *energy* must then be released to avoid PTSD. It normally would have been spent if either fight or flight had been taken.
- Trauma in itself is not the problem. It is the failure to release the emotions and *energy* that is the problem which can become PTSD.
- It has been scientifically (neurologically) proven that it is difficult to solve problems while we are in a heightened state of 'fight or flight', triggered by trauma/stress/anxiety.
- At such times, our brain that is triggered by hormones to focus instinctively on survival, rather than solutions to other problems. That can become habitual or addictive, leaving a person in a frequent or constant state of high alert.
- The problem-solving area of our brain/mind functions far more effectively while in a relaxed state. We can reach that place through meditation which clears our mind of thoughts and the body of tension.
- We can then think more clearly, allowing logical thought processes required to solve problems or to focus on activities like reading a book.

- Trying to solve problems while we are caught up in a mental tail-spin or negative thought loop creates more of the same thoughts.
- Initially, anti-depressant medication helped me to slow down the constant thoughts that created my anxiety.
- I had fewer repetitious thoughts, however it dulled and clouded my thinking – so still felt confused at times. I had trouble judging space/time when driving.
- It lowered my energy
- I sought an alternative solution.
- Meditation overcame the clouded head to allow clear thinking and feeling well.

Breathe in/❀❀/Breathe out/❀❀/Breathe in/❀❀/Breathe out/❀❀

ENERGY and WELL-BEING

The following chapters pertain roughly within the category above.

Breathe in/🐾🐾/Breathe out/🐾🐾/Breathe in/🐾🐾/Breathe out/🐾🐾

Energy

A Big Pot of Soup

The enlightened scientist Albert Einstein, brought us into the nuclear age and expanded our consciousness of the world we live in. He said in effect that everything in our universe is made up of energy, which was a huge leap in our concepts of the world.

Yes, we are all in this big pot of soup – together, every one of us and every 'thing', seen or unseen. Even our thoughts and emotions. Imagine the whole universe as we know it being contained in a huge round aquarium. We are inside that, along with every other thing in existence.

We all breathe the same air that circulates around our planet. The water that makes up about 73 percent of our heart and brain, lungs about 83 percent – about 60 percent of our body overall, is constantly being recycled through our bodily processes. Water covers 71 percent of our planet which is constantly being recycled with the climate processes.

We all have a connection to everything else in our world energetically via the make-up of the contents within the space around us. We can't avoid it. It just is - according to Einstein and modern science.

Therefore, we are all connected through the elements which comprise us of earth, water, and air. The mystics and native peoples have been saying that for thousands of years, and more recently it has been proven scientifically. Furthermore, every little particle is charged with a degree of energy we can appropriately call Universal Energy, or Life Force; qi; chi; prana, call it what you will.

"Every living being is an engine geared to
the wheelwork of the universe.
Though seemingly affected only by its immediate surrounding,
the sphere of external influence extends to infinite distance."
- Nikola Tesla (1856-1943)

An acceptance of those findings by Einstein and Tesla, and a basic understanding of that huge subject in just a word, would be helpful in the reading of this book. *Everything is energy,* but of course we can't cover everything in all its many contexts. We are interested here in the fact that in order for anyone to change from disability to wellness, they must obviously change their energy – transform it – manage it, in simple terms.

Trauma impacts, changes, stagnates, disables, and corrupts our energy from the 'normal' behaviour and character. It affects this amazingly complex energy field/factory we call the human body we sometimes take for granted.

We must transform that energy in order bring us back into the form in which we want it to be. Empowered wholeness is an excellent target, attained through a shift of energy within us that brings our heart, mind, and body cells into coherence. You and I both have the capability of doing that regardless of how bad we see ourselves as being mentally, emotionally, or physically. We just have to *know* how and to *do* it.

What we as human beings aren't able to understand, we have a tendency to dismiss, call it *magic*, and avoid. Stepping beyond that avoidance into acceptance can create the possibility of *magical healing* at a *miraculous* level. We don't need to fully understand it beyond knowing the basics.

Energy Imprint Awareness

You are settled comfortably into your saddle on your horse, just going along in an easy walk that the single file string of four horses. You are feeling good, relaxing in the movement and soothing morning sunshine on your back. You are absorbing and appreciating the beauty and tranquillity of the forest and the gurgling rocky stream in the world of nature that surrounds you.

It is very different to the rat race of the city life you'd yearned to escape from for weeks. Forgetting about the city environment and engaging your current one, your mind gently drifts into an easy flow of pleasant thoughts, with occasional gaps of no thoughts. You are an experienced rider and know this horse that you like and trust from previous rides, so you just relax and enjoy the space and time you are in, basically leaving the ride to your mount.

Suddenly your drifting thoughts of your environment are replaced by the instinctive reaction of your body to the unexpected behaviour of your trusted steed. It has started crow-hopping and bucking for some reason, not yet apparent. Your attention is now very much on staying in the saddle and bringing the horse back under control.

The fleeting thoughts of the dangerous consequences of coming off his back onto the rocks alongside the trail intensify the desire to avoid being thrown onto them. Or worse yet, being thrown with one foot still caught in a stirrup and dragged along the ground unable to control the horse.

Wondering thoughts about the cause are second to survival. You know that it is no time to go into fear or panic, but to focus and follow your training and skills until your powerful mount can be brought back under your control. Your body is using all of its innate abilities to preserve itself with the use of your legs to maintain grip and balance with your feet well-placed in the stirrups. You automatically try to gain control with the reigns. You talk gently to your mount.

The other horses on the ride are agitated by your situation, but their riders move away to avoid having a similar problem or interfering to cause further chaos. You are gradually able to restore order - rider and saddle intact, much to your relief and to that of the onlookers. When safe to do so, you dismount slowly and gracefully, to investigate the cause of the commotion. You have a face-to-face talk with your four-legged friend with gentle soothing and stroking. Apparently, your horse has an aversion to snakes, as was seen from the rider behind at the start of the mini rodeo.

The Energy of Trauma

The explosive *energy* of that sudden eruption is restored to one of peace. However the *energetic imprint* of that event certainly changes the cellular memory of *every one* and *every 'thing'* witnessing it at some level in the process - organic or otherwise. Even the surrounding plants and rocks, according to science! Naturally all of our human senses are receptors to everything around us.

The example of an energy imprint of the horse incident probably had little if any trauma associated with it. It could have with a nastier ending. If trauma had occurred, and that powerful *energy imprint* wasn't resolved, it could have potentially become PTSD, whether the event was remembered not. You may have blocked it out of your day-to-day memory with your innate instinct of self-preservation, but it may still there be with its effect on your cells.

When the cause of PTSD is more cumulative over a period of time, it can be harder to pin down the cause(s) or even to identify the condition for what it is, unless it comes to a head and investigated by an expert, which is what happened with me.

When I was diagnosed with PTSD, I was unaware that those life events that created trauma for me, *were* traumatic until I underwent counselling with the Vietnam Veterans Counselling Service. They deeply affected me and I was totally conscious of their occurrence, but I simply didn't understand the concept of trauma with its effects. It was quickly brought to light and to my greater comprehension from that point on. That helped me to come to terms with those emotional effects and eventually the greater connection with my *overall* wellness.

The *energy* of that imprint is what changes our cellular body. Our body then needs to be brought back into alignment, or coherence. In order to overcome that impact and to heal, according to trauma experts, it requires an energetic force *more powerful* than the one which created the undesirable effect. It is our body's *response* to that impact which is the potential problem, rather than the *energy* from the event in itself.

Do we feel traumatised or do we shrug it off somehow like those creatures in the animal world? (They don't have the frontal cortex part of their brain like humans that analyses what took place.) Does it disempower us with a sense of fear? Or withdrawal? Or stagnated thoughts and bodily movement even to the point of virtual paralysis? Or some other form of negativity?

That *energy imprint* needs to be overwhelmed with a positive action in our body. To achieve that reversal of the negative impact of trauma with a cellular level approach, thankfully, trauma experts trained specifically in facilitating that process have become accessible in recent years.

Dr Peter Levine discovered he was able to achieve that with a client about twenty years ago on a sudden inspiration he tried, almost by fluke. He believes that patient went on to be clinically cured of diagnosed trauma, after having been treated for some time with limited success.

That story in his book, *Waking the Tiger,* fuelled the hope within me. In his documented confirmation he states that it is indeed possible to totally overcome not only the symptoms of trauma, but the effects that it is having on our bodies at a cellular level.

YES! So it *is* possible! I have improved from my condition to a great extent, but not completely, so I will keep pursuing that goal. Symptoms, like memory blips or raw emotions, still pop up and affect me at times, but I've learned to manage them. As good as I feel even now in my improved state since being diagnosed, I want to ensure and prove that I no longer have that *energy imprint* affecting my body at *any* level.

In that vein, I have been using very powerful techniques developed by neurologist Dr Joe Dispenza, who takes that principle idea further. He has conducted years of scientific research on thousands of people to determine first-hand evidence of proven positive results in restoring wellness for people by 're-wiring' the neural pathways in the brain. That comes from restoring *energy* coherence between the body and mind in touch with the *Power of the Divine* – a 'team' effort with proven results. The methods are self-managed once trained and understood, thus I can orchestrate my own healing. That is also very beneficial for the fact that I can employ them virtually anywhere, anytime.

Apart from Dr Levine as one of the pioneers in that form of treatment, there are many others now to include Dr Joe Dispenza, Dr Bruce Lipton, and Dr Bessel van der Kolk. They lead a large field of doctors and scientists world-wide, acclaimed as being skilled and effective in their individual techniques. There is now such a wonderful body of knowledge available to us all, not only through practicing directly with them, but through their web-sites, YouTube and books. It is like an answer to my prayers after my early years of searching for ways to manage the effects of trauma and stress.

Breathe in/🐾/Breathe out/🐾/Breathe in/🐾/Breathe out/🐾

Introduction Chapter to Wellness Section

The chapters in this section of the book pertain to a wide range of general *wellness* and healing practices that I have either used or are known to be effective. I use a holistic approach to my health as much as possible (literally the belief that the parts of something are intimately interconnected to the whole), using both conventional medicine and more alternate methods. I like to use natural therapies whenever possible, but of course that isn't always possible or necessarily the best course of action. I see more and more acknowledged authorities on a variety of modalities claiming that we must also treat the whole being, regardless of what specific problem we may have. Consequently I focus a lot on overall wellness. So, what is *wellness*?

Dr. Bill Hettler, co-founder of the National Wellness Institute (NWI), gives this definition of wellness:

- It is an active process through which people become aware of, and make choices toward, a more successful existence
- It is a conscious, self-directed and evolving process of achieving full potential
- It is multi-dimensional and holistic, encompassing lifestyle, mental and spiritual well-being, and the environment
- It is positive and affirming

Recognising Wellness

- In my optimum wellness, I feel *good, alive,* and *vibrant!* Ideally, I want to feel physically energetic, mentally sharp, emotionally relaxed, and spiritually connected. I feel at peace with everything and everyone; basically happy and hopefully joyful as well. That is my idea of wellness. It is my constant objective.

- When I *feel* good, it is an obvious indicator to me that I am getting things right, at least in most areas.
- Conversely, if I don't feel good in one or more of those areas, it is a sign I need to pay attention and take action to correct it. Follow the trail from the symptom back to the source if possible. i.e. Why do am I getting a headache? Tight shoulder muscles? Tension? Sore eyes? Etc.
- Those indicators are vital to the balancing process, so vigilance and self awareness of what is going on (without obsession) are important.
- Do you have self awareness; are you 'in tune' with your self? Does your perception go beyond your emotions and physical body? i.e. to include your mind and spiritual Self?
- Little note – I hear people say that they aren't 'spiritual'; perhaps they believe that because they aren't religious or believe in some form of god. I reckon that anyone (or any 'thing') that draws a breath of air has a spirit. Our spirit comes into our body when we are born and it leaves the physical body at the end of our life, as we all know. Therefore we are spiritual beings by nature, whether we wish to engage in some form of 'spiritual' practice or not, and we nourish it through a variety of means, consciously or not, from music to connections with nature.

Why Do I Want to Work on My Wellness?

My health is my greatest asset. It may seem obvious, but there is a human tendency to not fully appreciate it until we lose it. Does it require effort? Yes.

Is it difficult? That can be up to the individual; hard and easy are a perception, not necessarily reality. But then again, it can certainly be if a person is restricted in some way beyond their means to deal with it.

Is it worth it? Well? Is it? I truly believe so.

Laziness in not working hard enough at it is my biggest hurdle. I know what I know, but I have to sometimes push myself a bit to do what I know is required. The more it is practiced, the more it becomes a habit, so the easier it gets. We really do function better and our bodies enjoy it as the 'feel good' hormones like endorphins kick in.

So what are the benefits and trade-offs for the effort involved in achieving and maintaining good health? Why am I focused on wellness in my life?

- Simply to feel good with the potential of being free of pain
- A better quality of life
- Possibility of a longer life
- Capability of a greater range of mobility and activities I can participate in
- Potentially lower present and future medical costs

Wellness Strategy

- Keep an open attitude; be willing to try anything even if it sounds 'too simple' to be effective
- Accept that wellness or healing may take time; it is a process
- Keep it as simple as possible
- Use a variety of modalities or practices that cumulatively produce overall results and wellness
- Eliminate 'bad' habits detrimental to your good health if possible but don't focus on them
- Focus on establishing 'good' habits into regular practices and routines
- Believe in the long-term strategy of routine
- Visualise the desired result, not the problems you've had or have
- Start easy and build up as your thinking clears and your overall ability improves
- Have realistic expectations and be kind to yourself
- Keep notes or measure to be able to realise and confirm the progress you are making

In the Mix

Over the past few years I have investigated and utilised many forms of treatment or healing, education, and training. Here are some:

- Counselling
- Medication i.e. anti-depressants
- Tapping – Emotional Freedom Technique (EFT)
- Energy Healing, including hands on with Healing Touch Program
- Meditation – many techniques
- Prayer
- Massage – recipient as well as trained in therapeutic massage
- Neurological education, testing and exercises
- Trauma Release Techniques
- Breathing Techniques - many

So, "Which ones are the most effective?" you ask. A simple question with a complex answer, because it has been a mixture of them all at various phases of my condition(s) over a long period of time. The symptoms were more significant in the earlier times with different things being tried than later on, so it is unclear. It's a bit like creating a cake; I can tell you what is in the recipe or you can guess some of the ingredients from the taste of it, but once it got blended together, it is pretty near impossible to tell the eggs from the flour, even before it was baked.

Breathe in/🐾🐾/Breathe out/🐾🐾/Breathe in/🐾🐾/Breathe out/🐾🐾

Wellness

Breaking the Pain Pattern

"I just wanna die!"

Those were the last words I can remember coming from my dear grandmother Miles in July 1971. They were not her last words that day, nearly fifty years ago, but they are the ones that left a strong imprint on my memory. Her voice carried the impact of bodily pain as well as frustration from her unwell condition for several years. Her long and full life no longer had the peace and happiness it once held for her, and she struggled without hope of improvement. She got her wish within days.

I also remember my last visit with my grandfather just before I left for Vietnam four years earlier. He was propped up in bed at the local hospital in a pretty good mood, particularly considering the pain he was suffering from cirrhosis of the liver. He was no doubt on pain-killers. Little did I realise he was in his final days. That news came about with total shock and grief just weeks later in Vietnam.

My mother's parents and extensive family had a strong presence and influence on my life for which I feel so grateful. There were laughs and lessons aplenty for me, laced with a great deal of wisdom they possessed and passed along. They all had very eventful lives, with various degrees of tragedy a common component. In spite of that, they also had a wonderful, but sometimes devilish sense of humour. None were beyond the occasional prank or practical joke. Perhaps that helped to save their sanity in dealing with some of their grief.

My grandparents had to deal with the deaths of three of their children; one still-born; another just days after birth, and later, 'Sonny' a week before turning 13 due to Bright's kidney disease. The drowning of my sister Marguerite occurred in their back yard later in their lives. That and each tragedy must have taken its toll on their health.

Without therapeutic counselling available then, dealing with trauma was largely through a spiritual manner – either pleading for peace of mind through one's appeal to the Divine, or out of a bottle. I think Gramma leaned towards the former, and Grampa to the latter. I would have gladly given up the considerable pocket money I received for taking his empty beer bottles to the bar, in return for his health and happiness, affected by his drinking in later years.

My mother was a very strong woman in many ways, who chose the 'Divine' spiritual approach for much of her life. She once told me that connection saved her from insanity, yet she largely 'existed' the final few years of her time on Earth with dementia or Alzheimer's disease.

How much did the many traumas in her life contribute to her condition? She was a 'work-a-holic' for most of her life – staying up half the night most nights, working at whatever, until she would collapse into bed, to be up early and at it again. We suspect that was her distraction from some of the anguish she must have carried with her through life. Exhausted, she would drop off to sleep in the middle of a sentence if she sat down from her activity to have a conversation; she was famous for it.

- She was just two years younger than 'Sonny', who like her younger siblings, idolised him. The family members naturally were all devastated by his early departure.
- She somehow endured the grief of losing her daughter Marguerite.

I write about them in the theme of wellness for the following reasons:

- The impression I got from watching a loved one leave this life in a state of pain. That may be common in our western lifestyle, but perhaps that can be avoided, as it is in many 'native' cultures around the world.
- How much of their health issues and pain late in life was due to unresolved effects of trauma?
- How can I avoid that pattern?

Inspiring Examples

Recently, two unrelated people I have known for some time died, aged in their early 90's. Marie and Bernie (unrelated), lived well until their final stages of life with bright eyes and sharp minds to the end. They remained as active as possible and participated in life, taking an avid interest in their families and the world. They were really an inspiration to all that knew them. I believe they were excellent examples of people living lifestyles with good, simple, values that gave them long and fulfilling lives, in spite of their struggles along the way. They were the type of person I try to emulate in my pursuit of wellness.

Creating the Wellness Mould in Me

My parents, Joe and Joyce, not only created my being, but also instilled a mindset of wellness within me from my earliest memories. I can remember lying on the living room floor at night in pyjamas before bedtime with my siblings, a stick of wood between my hands, lifting from my waist up over my head with outstretched arms. There were directions on knee bends, touching toes and push-ups.

My parents were very conscious of looking after their health and subsequently that of us children. All their actions testified to their priority to provide the best that they could for our welfare and enrichment of our mind, body and spirit. They knew good nutrition and strived to ensure that our diet was the best possible.

Despite whatever aliments I have encountered in life, which seemed to congregate from 2000-2010, I have applied an approach they taught me, i.e. try to find the source of a problem. They also taught me to take full responsibility for my own health, to listen to the advice of others, consider it, but ultimately decide for myself what is best for me, right or wrong.

My Health

For most of my life until 2000, I had considered myself to be reasonably fit. Then when the anxiety reached a point I couldn't ignore, a number of problems seemed to pop up like dandelions in the spring. Why? The focus of my life went from earning an income to trying to get well again. I didn't twig to the influence *stress* may have caused on virtually all symptoms that presented.

I can remember questioning myself during that time when I was in my early *D-Tour* years: "Is the way that I feel (with this cloudy head, poor memory and erratic thinking) 'normal' for someone my age (early 50's)? Shouldn't I be better than this?" I thought about older people I'd known.

Were my parents like this at this age? No. My father was pretty good until he passed over at 82. My mother was nearly 84 when she died. She had Alzheimer's, probably since she was in her early 60's, in spite of a clear head, full of wisdom, able to recall extensive poetry and memorized Bible verses in earlier years. A lifetime of long days of hard work and lack of sleep probably contributed to her condition.

Her siblings were still sharp at advanced ages. Other people I could recall were 'with it' to a ripe old age, so why was I not like that or like I used to be. Was I heading down the track my mother had gone? What was going on with me? My work ethic was good but I didn't work endlessly like my mother, and yet I would nod off to sleep anywhere, anytime to my embarrassment, much like my mother had done.

Those concerns were enough to give me an incentive to question and pursue the matter further. The overall balance of my health had always been an important consideration, even if I didn't pay it enough attention at times. But it was coming more into my focus as I struggled to find answers to my questions and solutions to my health issues.

- Sometimes I would get confused when I was driving – directions in my memory or my mind map would be confused, even with familiar places. It would *seem* like I was suddenly on an alternative route but I wasn't - and surroundings would 'overlay' more normal or regular images as such, like on a computerized drawing, giving my mind what seemed to be a different way, but it wasn't. Weird. It was like portions of a mind map were suddenly swapped. Sometimes I would briefly forget where I was.

- To the best of my knowledge, I had an excellent pulse and blood pressure all my life until 2000. Heart palpitations and a failed stress test on the walking machine had to be halted when the pulse went ridiculous and caused concern to the doctor. Why? I was put onto blood pressure medication.
- Bladder problems had started to worsen which had been slowly developing over several years. I resisted having a procedure for years through ignorance and a fear of possibly having a scalpel go where I felt it has no business going. I was finally forced to undergo an operation in 2009 to relieve the blockage of the urinary tract caused by my enlarged prostate gland. A TURP operation successfully removed the blockage. No scalpel! Thankfully there was no sign of cancer in spite of a slightly elevated PSA reading prior. What a blessed relief when one and a half litres of toxic excess baggage was drained from my always near-full bladder! I felt so appreciative of the skilled surgeon and so blessed with the results. No problems there since!
- However there seemed to be damage done to my kidneys in the years when I could not urinate properly, which resulted in chronic kidney disease. Consequently that got monitored every six months with blood tests for a couple of years, then stretched to yearly. I still have periodic blood tests but no longer required to have regular visits to my urologist. The test results are consistently good with acceptable levels.

An important note to men here: get regular prostate/bladder check-ups before the age of fifty. Many men are suffering and dying from having problems there that get left until it is a crisis. That is often *too late!*

- I have had colonoscopies to remove polyps from my colon and have since been getting regular check-ups.
- I still have skin rashes. Could that possibly be due to my kidney or liver performance? Could that have been caused by chemical defoliants and pesticides sprayed in Vietnam? Or perhaps hormones associated with fight/flight impeding their function which in turn affects my blood pressure? I'm working on determining the causes and a solutions, preferably without medication.

My Intention of Wellness

I don't want to age any quicker or die any sooner than I have to. I want to enjoy my life, which to me means to have good health, mobility, and an alert mind and senses while I am alive. I believe the effort that I need to put into maintaining my wellness is worth it.

It is common knowledge that *stress* is the pre-curser to disease; literally *dis-ease* in our body. Fairly typical of men in our society, my health issues started appearing as physical and emotional problems around the age of fifty. Although I treated my body reasonably well over most of my life, those underlying stresses of trauma and busy life unconsciously took their toll on me. Naturally, inherited health traits have an impact on my wellness and longevity, but the stress trail linked to my environment and lifestyle choices, are those I can probably influence the most.

Moving On

Over the past few years since my prostate operation, I've been feeling consistently better overall than the ten years prior, so that is a good sign. I feel great! I have probably tended to look after my health and kept reasonably fit better than the majority of men I've known around my age along the way, or at least seemingly more conscious of it. Yet I basically came unstuck enough at the age of about fifty to greatly disrupt my life. Why?

It was undoubtedly the impact of trauma and stress coming to a head. In pursuit of answers to 'why,' I have gained greater awareness of myself and many of Life's secrets in the process. Tests indicate I am in very good health overall, and I am enjoying my life. I feel very fortunate that I have been able to reclaim my wellness before it reached a point which could make it more difficult to do so.

Would I have awoken from those earlier subtle indicators to address the deep down causes without such an abrupt turn in my life, forcing me to make a decision to take action, or not? Perhaps, but I doubt very much that it would have brought the benefits of the greater level of awareness that it has.

Early on in my *D-Tour*, I shifted my desire. '*Normal*' prior to that was probably just '*comfortable*,' which is the state many of us live in. It is often just a bit unbalanced and not ideal, but we tend to put up and don't want to rock the boat. Once I got past the anxiety where I couldn't think straight, I decided '*normal*' wasn't good enough. In order to get past that, I had to change more than just my thinking about it. I had to *do* something about it.

My journey went beyond just struggling to get mentally, emotionally, and physically better. It became spiritually oriented as well. My spiritual aspect had not been nurtured in the manner in which it had wanted to be for some time, so it cried out for attention. I eventually gave in, which changed my overall life considerably. The only way I could truly heal and get back into balance and wholeness of my being, was through finding my personal truth, or my 'self'.

Writing this book has been very much a part of that process. I had to face some challenges –

- Search harder to find *my* truth of *who I am* and *what* I believe - already a life-long process
- Ask 'Is that true, at least in my view?' as much as possible, with every word written
- Realise that many '*truths*' appear differently according to one's perception

- The fears that presented themselves such as talking to others about this project
- Feeling virtually naked before the world to judge me in a sense
- Face and accept my own judgment; *I am that I am.*

Nearly 18 years down the track now since being diagnosed with PTSD, I feel I'm headed in the right direction with my health care with a vast improvement in my wellbeing. I am still working on some aspects of my body, mind, and spirit. It's always a 'Work-in-Progress.'

Breathe in//Breathe out//Breathe in//Breathe out/

The Breath

How important is the breath? Have you ever been with someone when they took their last breath of life? Literally, alive one moment; not the next. Whether it's a peaceful release or somehow more dramatic, in any case, it is something of a wonder how a living thing suddenly is no longer that. The breathing process stops - the body lies motionless and communication ceases. It's a powerful moment to behold. The 'being' is no longer 'be-ing' in the physical body.

Or have you been at the birth of a new life? I had the wonderful experience of being involved with the birth of the last three of my four children. The final was Ben, who was not breathing on his entry to the world. Perhaps a bit shy or couldn't believe his eyes at what he was looking at and wanted to go back? Arrival was the front seat of our car as I drove my wife Kris to the hospital.

Kris didn't want to wait around a delivery room for hours on end for him to appear. Her water broke earlier in the day, but the previous children needed inducement after that point so she continued to weed her beloved garden. She figured she had plenty of time which could be used more effectively. Wrong. After lunch she suddenly realised things were happening *very* quickly.

Some Magic!

Ben decided he was in a hurry to join us. I suggested an ambulance but she insisted on just going - quickly as possible! I helped her into the car as she tried to walk and hold him inside as best she could. The old Ford Falcon V8 roared and we were away, the adrenaline pumping through my body causing my right foot to bounce up and down on the accelerator. Gosford Hospital was less than ten minutes from our home, but it wasn't close enough.

Ben entered the world as we waited at the last set of lights to go green for a right hand turn with a couple of blocks to go. We left home with the two of us on the front seat, then incredibly there was another, no delivery team visible. The newest one wasn't breathing, in contrast to my rapid breathing. His mother gave him the kiss of life – literally, one vital breath – and he started exercising his lungs and voice much to our relief. He still does so very well, some 30 years later.

So, isn't there something quite *magical* about the way that our physical lives start and end in just one breath? Somehow we tend to forget or take for granted, that *energy* which is contained in all those breaths we take every minute of every day between the beginning and the end. What is contained in the breath to create that *magic*, or essence of life?

The Mechanics of the Breath

Ancient wisdom from many cultures teaches of two aspects to the breath – both invisible and usually unnoticed. The physical breath brings oxygen into the lungs and expels carbon-dioxide and moisture without much thought. The other component of the breath is our *life force energy* referred to as *spirit, chi,* or *prana* depending on the culture source. Although separate, they work together and must both be present in order to maintain life. A life support breathing apparatus can keep our body alive, but it does not contain the life force energy.

Why we are concerned with this subject in this book is because it has ***everything*** to do with our wellness. You wouldn't be reading this without it. It is central to virtually all healing practices. We take over 23,000 breaths each day if inactive, most or all of them unconsciously. By becoming conscious of our breath and training it to be an effective tool or servant, rather than a necessary but forgotten slave, we can easily employ that magic that is contained within it. It is a major player in our approach to wellness.

It is the only thing that can bring me the clarity I seek when I'm in a foggy, scattered state or feeling anxious or depressed. It also brings in the energy or calmness. It is the component necessary to our health and healing, regardless of whatever methods are used.

This function (or tool when used consciously), has to be the most important yet simplest device I know for dealing with stress and anxiety. It is so obvious but so overlooked – probably due to its simplicity. Our humanness seems to want to look to someone else to 'fix' us, which often complicates our lives. It is the most fundamental and essentially the easiest to use. It can be done anywhere, any time. I call it my first aid kit – it's the first thing I use to reduce stress or anxiety.

Breathing is crucial to our state of wellness. You can:

- alter your mood and state of mind and body into calmness and relaxation
- shift your awareness and control of your self like nothing or anyone else can
- improve your long term health
- lower your blood pressure

It's quick, amazingly effective, always available, with no side-effects, and of course it costs nothing. Improper breathing leaves us feeling less than being fully alive.

Stress and anxiety automatically alter our breathing pattern into shortened breaths of oxygen as we prepare our body in a fight or flight situation, **whether it is real or simply imagined**. We often, or generally, fall into a pattern of shallow breathing without even being aware of it, leaving us performing at less than optimum levels.

We sometimes blame lack of sleep or something else for feeling tired, while poor breathing could well be the culprit. Prolonged shallow breathing can also extend our anxiety if we are feeling anxious.

There are many breathing techniques one can use for different reasons. We can improve our wellness, from simply relieving tension or energizing the body through to total relaxing. Yoga, tai chi, qigong, martial arts and most such disciplines focus on the breath. There are many breath exercises that can be found online or in books.

The Science of Breath

Pranayama (Sanskrit) = science of breath; prana (life force), yama (the control of)

The prana rides in on the breath and circulates around the body. The out-breath carries out body waste. The power is the breath is in the pause or gap between breaths. It touches our consciousness. Our breath is the meeting of the conscious and unconscious.

Pranayama brings the breath and prana into consciousness.

When you pause at the end of your incoming breath, you have to be aware (or conscious) in order to override the automatic unconscious act of breathing. Therefore you become the conscious observer.

It is a powerful realisation to know this and utilise this tool for –

- greater understanding,
- mental clarity,
- peace of mind and body, and
- good health.

Our energy comes from the prana carried by the air. We can stop breathing for a few minutes and still be getting the life force or energy - if we know how to shut down our thinking or busy mind that is taking up our energy. Yogi's have been practicing that for thousands of years.

At Another Level

When we are in the space or pause between the in and out breath, we are in 'neutral'; we have no identity, which is a powerful place enabling us to change. View http://www.nithyananda.org/

Breathe in/❀❀/Breathe out/❀❀/Breathe in/❀❀/Breathe out/❀❀

Breath Exercises

Our breath plays the most vital role in our overall wellness!

Apart from simply delivering oxygen to our body via our lungs, it is a vehicle for our *Life Force*. Every aspect of our self depends then on the breath. Athletes, actors, singers, speakers, and shooters all depend on controlling it for their performance. For thousands of years, masters of wisdom have used control of the breath to overcome anxiety and stress and to bring inner peace - the focus of this book.

There are many techniques and levels of breathing and on to mastery available through many sources, but it all starts with very simple steps. A few basic ones here can get you started. You can follow up through a number of excellent avenues which can be more powerful with the techniques and procedures.

It's a process like learning to ride a bike or drive a car, but even easier because it is so natural - you've been doing it all of your life. To become effective, it is a matter of becoming mindful of what is going on with the breath we take for granted. We can then train it to do what we want to accomplish.

We all have to breathe anyway - just decide that your mind is the master and your breath is here to serve you. It is mostly keeping your mind on track which gets easier with practice. Your mind will be thinking, "Well that wasn't so hard," and your body will be saying, "*Thank you, thank you, thank you!*" Breathing exercises for a few minutes every day can have amazing results on your health.

Controlled breathing:

- Calms emotions of anger, anxiety and fear
- Strengthens your immune system
- Brings homeostasis to our body

- Massages your internal organs
- Lowers blood pressure
- Increases energy levels
- Brings clarity to mind
- Improves posture
- Releases tension
- Relieves pain

Breath control is a key ingredient in meditation to energise, concentrate, empower, and calm. A few deep breaths can very quickly reduce stress or anxiety, help focus attention, and relax. We all use it unconsciously, but to use it *mindfully* it is much more powerful and effective.

Before you begin any breathing exercises, take note of your breath pattern – frequency and depth. Do the same again when you complete the exercises. Be *aware*. When we breathe in, we should feel our stomach push out first, before drawing the air up into the chest.

The Simplest Breathing Exercise

- Expel every bit of air possible from the lungs
- Hold (pause) for 2 seconds (🐾🐾)
- Breathe deeply as possible. Feel the expansion of the tummy area before drawing into the upper lungs
- 🐾🐾
- Exhale fully
- 🐾🐾
- Repeat that cycle a few times
- Return to normal breathing - feel the difference
- Do that routine whenever you think of it; make it become a healthy habit

I usually do that several times a day whether I feel the need or not. It's just a matter of establishing a habit while sitting at my computer, driving (reducing driver stress), etc. I often find an improvement in the release of any tension held in my body I wasn't even aware of.

My Favourite Breathing Exercise

Anyone can do it regardless of attention span issues. It can lead to the capability to meditate easier if that is a hurdle. It's great for a quick fix for a busy mind or trouble focusing. It's a method which helps me to be present and forget about an issue that may be fighting for my attention. A normal breathing frequency is about 16 times per minute when inactive. The following slows it to about 10-12 times.

- Breathe in to the count of four; hold for 2 seconds (🐾🐾)
- Breathe out to the count of four; 🐾🐾
- Continue the pattern for up to 20 minutes
- The pause after the in and the out breath is important. It allows time to integrate the oxygen and to expel carbon dioxide from the body. It provides space between breaths to be conscious of the presence of self – more and more with each gap or space.
- Keep your mind on the counting so it stays present to that and not on other things – a very useful device that is quick and effective for calming a busy mind (mind chatter or monkey mind).
- After some time as you get accustomed to the frequency, you will probably not bother with the counting, but just say to yourself 'breath in, breath out' etc.

Breath in Energy or Relax

Sit or lay.

- Expel all the air from your lungs

- Take a deep breath. Hold it 2 seconds (🐾🐾)
- Expel it all and do it again
- Close your eyes and focus on your inner vision. Visualise a cloud of energy above your head. As you exhale the air in your lungs from the deep breath, visualise a cloud of energy slowly coming down through your body from your head to your feet and deep into the earth as you reach the end of your air supply
- Push it through deeply, expelling it all
- Repeat three times. I find it to be more effective if I utter 'aaaahhhh ooooo mmmmmm' from start to finish, changing the tone as I visualise the energy proceeding through my body filling every cell with *Energy; Life Force; Chi.* There is both a peace and a power in the vibration of the sound.

Overall, it very calming and also has a grounding effect with the added bonus of lowering my blood pressure. Just three times makes a great deal of difference. It will also generally lower my systolic blood pressure reading by up to 20 points immediately for a period of time. I've monitored this in tests I've done over several years. It's that simple – try it – it may work for you as well!

Breath of Fire

This is a breathing exercise designed to invigorate the body and mind with short, rapid breathing in and out using the stomach muscles to control a panting action.

- Imagine you are man's best friend after a long run. Start with the in-breath through the mouth and out through the mouth for about half a minute
- Rest for a minute
- Next, breathe through the nose and out through the mouth for a similar time
- Return to normal breathing

- You can repeat the procedure several times if you like or extend the timeframe for each session, followed by simply sitting in silence allowing your body and mind to relax.

Breathe in/❁❁/Breathe out/❁❁/Breathe in/❁❁/Breathe out/❁❁

So-*What?*

Psoas!

That word, like so many in our funny language, is not pronounced as it appears. It's "so-az", with a silent 'p' as in many medical words of Greek origin, which means "loin region". Why does it get a mention here? It plays crucial complex roles in our makeup:

- with emotions and trauma
- with bodily movement

I learned about the psoas and other closely related muscles in my training as a massage therapist, but I have only fairly recently become more aware of the intimate connection it has with trauma. I feel it is very important to share this limited exposure with you in order for you to have enough information to encourage you to explore the subject more extensively.

It seems to be a little known fact, outside the realm of muscle-related therapists and some body movement pursuits like yoga, that *the psoas is the core muscle of our body.* Well, so what you say.

- It is buried deep within our body,
- is connected to or in contact with virtually everything that is vital to our being, and
- influences or responds to messages and actions going on *throughout* our body.

Amazingly enough, the extent of the complex role that it plays has only begun to be realised and better understood. For a very long time it concealed the relationship it has with our emotions and trauma.

It is also the only muscle that ties the legs to our body. It is attached to the inside of each upper leg, running up through the pelvis, to attach to and help support, the lower spine. It obviously plays a crucial role in the movement of our legs and most of our bodily actions and posture. Because those muscles are buried deeply within our anatomy, covered by other muscles and organs, most of us are unaware of its existence and the extent of its function.

So what is its function?

- It is not quickly or easily answered here. In simple terms, it plays a very complex multi-faceted role with virtually all the organs of the body to some extent.
- It is the centre of our 'gut awareness' and **intimately involved in the complexity of our bodily response to trauma.**
- Its involvement with our autonomic nervous system gives it a connection to our brain. This system is the primary mechanism in **control of the fight-or-flight response and the freeze-and-dissociate response.**
- If the brain is the system manager, the psoas seems to be a site foreman amongst the body activities we aren't usually consciously aware of; out of sight, out of mind so to speak - until it tightens up causing a problem in the lower back for example. Even then, you would probably blame your back and wouldn't know the psoas was involved without some awareness of such a connection.
- It is involved with other muscles in a range of bodily movements with the body, pelvis, and legs. While that aspect of its function isn't to do with trauma, its involvement there is **crucial in our mobility and stability, so therefore our overall wellness.**
- The Psoas Major muscle works in conjunction with the Iliacus to become the Iliopsoas, also referred to the hip flexor muscles, or simply the Psoas.

Why am I so vitally interested in this particular aspect of my body? What grabbed my attention to it so intently when I heard a bit about it? Several reasons:

- It is obviously such an **intrinsic part of our anatomy affecting so much**, I want to know more

- What I was learning immediately resonated with me at a deep level
- The release techniques I learned had a noticeable, positive response from my body, so . .
- Follow the trail; get to the source, the core of a feeling
- It obviously ties in with our 'gut' feelings (intuition) and nervousness felt in the tummy
- Our core feelings and core awareness are buried in our core muscles; to soothe and heal it really makes sense to me (and feels good, the ultimate focus and determiner of well-being)
- The more I've learned about it, the more I want to learn about it; it feels right and makes sense (have I mentioned that already?)

The more that I've investigated information on the psoas, the more fascinated I have become. It's a bit like entering a beautiful cave that leads on to another and another and another, each beautiful but different.

My motivation is:

- Release all the tension and 'unease' from my body, a key contributor to our dis-ease
- Improve and maintain my (and your) overall wellness
- Improve my mobility through increased ability of movement and flexibility, one of the vital keys to aging 'gracefully'; i.e. slowing the aging process at a number of levels – physically and mentally.
- It all centres on the core area of our body; entire spine and pelvis – keep loose, stand tall and stay hip at the hips, so to speak; KEEP MOVING*!
- If it was effective for me even after all the tension release and healing work I have been doing for years and feeling good overall, then it would might be able to help those also in need.

*When I was deep in the rut of my D-Tour, my way out was not through my mind; it was through *movement.* I was depressed and lethargic. The anti-depressants relieved my anxiety but stifled my motivation. I gained weight I didn't need. I lost my fitness. I was undergoing regular counselling which helped me to learn and understand, but it didn't lift me enough to get me out of the muck; it required *action.* I had to get *moving* . . . get on my feet and drag myself away from that TV, that computer, that book. 'Suggestions' of that nature from my wife were largely ignored. I needed a kick start.

Eventually, I had to virtually force myself – take my beautiful dog Cookie (who was more than willing) – to take those steps out the door, down the street, and beyond; more each day. Sitting and going around and around in my head was not the way out of the rut. It was *movement* that got me going and out of the hole I was in.

One day I got to the corner of the block and I actually felt like jogging. *What*? Where did that come from? So I had a little jog from time to time along my walks. I didn't force it or push myself. I just wanted to; it felt right and felt good. And I got better. I got more interested in other things; I started *doing* things! What?? Yep - I did!

🐾🐾

The following are some of the areas or conditions that can be affected by tension in the psoas:

- bodily energy flow
- lower back tightness and pain
- sacroiliac (joint that connects the sacrum and the pelvis)
- sciatica (pain in the lower back, hip, or thigh that is caused by pressure on the *sciatic* nerve)
- disc problems
- spondylolysis (a specific defect in the connection between vertebrae – usually lowest)
- scoliosis (a sideways curvature of the spine)
- hips
- knees
- sexual function/dysfunction/enjoyment/infertility/menstruation pain

- digestion
- inefficient breathing
- throat

I can't begin to cover this extensive subject here; only emphasise its importance both in the fact that it plays a lead role in our bodily response to traumatic situations, and to our overall well-being. There are a number of expert sources of valuable information via books and the internet (incl. YouTube) that can provide guidance in tension release and good habits to restore vitality and good health. I strongly encourage you to pursue this fascinating and vital aspect of our being to your benefit.

It has been the study and the focus of Liz Koch over the past thirty years to become an acknowledged authority on the subject. Her efforts to cure her scoliosis led her onto a path of great discovery and sharing through her classes around the world and acclaimed 'go to' books, *The Psoas Book* and *Core Awareness,* designed for practitioners and students alike.

According to Koch on her website Core Awareness, "it is part of the fear reflex system preparing one to flee or fight. Sitting for long periods of time with a constricted psoas muscle depletes vital energy, curtails blood circulation, affects organ functioning and signals flee/fight reflex, thus draining the adrenals and immune system. Its health and suppleness affects every level of well being." That statement alone is enough for me to want to take action to determine how I can ensure its good health.

Contraction of that involuntary muscle, along with its companion the iliacus, during trauma at one extreme can send us into the foetal position in an unconscious act of self preservation and protection of those vulnerable vital organs. That is a survival action; fight or flight (or freeze), with adrenaline and cortisol from our adrenal gland activated. Just being startled or being tense also tightens the psoas.

The Effects and Consequences

- Tension from a modern lifestyle has a similar effect in tightening the psoas as if in preparation for fight or flight.
- If action doesn't take place then, and burn up those hormones injected into our cells, the tension gets stored in the psoas and other muscles and various organs.
- The negative effects of tension can be held in the cellular structure without realising it.
- Left unaware and unattended, the tension can and often does impact our behaviour and manifest as disease in various parts of our bodies, particularly the lower organs, so it is very important to release it.
- Since we cannot consciously control or feel the psoas, the care of it is through bodily movements and emotional awareness.

Yoga, Pilates, tai chi, chi gong, exercises, and dance all have movements to enhance the psoas and related muscles. Koch (and others) demonstrates many effective ways to release the tension created by trauma and stress through their books and websites.

Also an excellent source of information for better understanding of its extensive importance in our overall being and graphic care techniques is *The Vital Psoas Muscle* by Jo Ann Staugaard-Jones.

Successful world renowned expert on trauma release, David Berceli, Ph.D, uses a system he calls Tension and Trauma Releasing Exercises (TRE). It helps release the deep chronic tension created in the body during a traumatic experience or that has accumulated from prolonged stress. That, as I mentioned earlier, is held in the virtually untouchable core of our body. His method induces bodily shaking, which is acknowledged as the immediately effective way in which animals in the wild release the effects of trauma they encounter.

There is a self-help technique I use to ease the psoas you can't feel, so more noticeably the lower back. Lay on the floor next to a chair to support the legs - thighs vertical, and shins parallel to the floor on the chair.

It may feel uncomfortable in the small of the back to begin with, but usually within a few minutes, that eases. It is important to simply let go and relax all over. Things settle and often there is an adjustment that takes places along the spine without the pushing, pulling, twisting (or sometimes pain) of a 'tuner-upperer'. And it's free – which can make it all feel even better when you look in your wallet. The time it takes to reach 'the happy zone' varies for me, from five minutes to an hour. I'm told that it has been noticed that I've dozed off, snored and restored.

Every few months I visit a specialist 'body worker' who works me over. The psoas is an area I get him to give some attention if it needs it, which requires someone who knows what they are doing to probe that region. It can be tight from holding in emotional energy acquired through trauma, so be aware that treatment may cause an 'interesting' release. If nothing else, it may improve your posture and sense of well-being.

Breathe in/🐾/Breathe out/🐾/Breathe in/🐾/Breathe out/🐾

A Patchwork Quilt

Random Ramblings of Observations And Occurrences

Like much of my life, this book is a compilation of far-flung events and learning. Much of the subject matter interweaves across broad categories of subjects such as 'body, mind, and spirit' that defy separation. There are more definitive aspects, like 'Wellness', but there is no clear distinction of boundaries or time lines for much of it.

This section of the book contains the strays, mavericks, and misfits that haven't fit comfortably into a category. They form a ragged 'patchwork quilt'. It is often the mongrel that becomes your best pet. I hope you find one amongst them.

Breathe in/🐾/Breathe out/🐾/Breathe in/🐾/Breathe out/🐾

LAUGHTER

"The body heals with play, the mind heals with laughter, and the spirit heals with joy!"
– Proverb

If you would simply laugh until you had tears of joy every day - you would have no need for this book.

Breathe in/🐾/Breathe out/🐾/Breathe in/🐾/Breathe out/🐾

Where Angels - and People - Fear to Tread

The Elephant in the Lift

It's Monday morning; back to work day in the city. You squeeze into the lift on the ground floor that is already virtually full, having come up from the underground car park. You nod to a couple of familiar faces amongst the group but it is not possible to have a conversation amongst the pack, or even a personal greeting unless you were next to that someone. You remember you are supposed to go to a meeting on the top floor at the start of the day so you ask someone to press that button.

It gradually becomes apparent to anyone on board with a nose that someone or something does not smell the freshest. The few short quiet conversations stop. Noses twitch. Eyes water as they sneak quick subtle glances around their limited field of vision to look for a clue to the source; it's instinctive. It's obviously not from armpits. The looks can't conceal the thoughts – who did it and what could they have possibly eaten to create something so powerful to overwhelm the senses of every person on board?

The field of candidates thins as people step off at the floor of their workplace, discreetly watched by all. Noses re-calibrate to see if the odour followed them out. Nearly everyone remaining secretly wishes that they had gotten off as well. You wonder if some may have jumped out to wait for the next up-lift. Bad pun?

By the time you reach the top floor you are alone on your upwards journey. You step out of the lift to an empty room – it's just you now and the bright light down at the end of the conference room. The elephant in the lift is momentarily forgotten to ponder the fact there appears to be no meeting or a message to say otherwise.

You pull the phone out of your pocket to ring the workmate that was also on the lift part of the way. "Isn't there supposed to be a meeting on the top floor this morning?

"It's been cancelled."

"And what was that choice fragrance in the lift – was it you that dropped a rose mate?"

"No! I thought it might have been you after another one of your beer and baked beans camping trips over the weekend. From the looks on everyone's face, they are all wondering - but no one is talking about it . . . yet.

"Yep. Bad timing 'ay. It's all about timing. They say its strongest force in the world - even an elephant can't hold it back!"

(Note: my childhood friend Larry provided me with that riddle over fifty years ago. He often had one or a joke to share each day, no doubt provided by his father and three older brothers.)

Such is our humanness. Like the smell in the lift, we avoid talking about certain topics once we reach school age. A child in that lift may have asked, "Who farted?" Adults tell us that it is inappropriate, even though that thought occupied every head there.

We can think privately or whisper and snicker together at any age when it feels safe to do so, but we don't discuss some things openly in public without disapproval. Fair enough with some subjects like religion and politics, which can cause some unresolved disagreement and conflict.

But the innocent subject of *spirituality* seems to be a victim of such cultural stigmas for many people. Why? If you are alive, you have a *spirit* operating within your body, therefore you are a *spiritual* being. What's the issue? Why is it so? That is a very good question! Why didn't I think of that? Well . . . I have. Maybe you have also.

It is our undeniable, vital life force - the *spirit* within each of us. It is not a religion, or referring to religion, if that is the issue. It is the *spirit–ual* aspect of our whole being. It is a matter of semantics. Some word has to be used to convey the idea regarding that essence of life force within us. Why don't we just accept the use of the word *spirituality*, embrace that invisible elephant in our humanness, and move on.

Spirituality and Religion

Two topics of this book are integral to my life and the story here of my *D-Tour* journey. One is *spirituality* as I just pointed out. The other is *religion* – one of the other subjects that are often avoided in general conversation. However they are part of my story, thus near impossible to avoid here. To me, there is a distinction between them that I feel is important to bring up.

They have been part of the fabric of my life since my birth and interwoven through it. The spiritual aspect is there by default with each of us, but I took it for granted until coming into greater awareness.

Both had a major role for me early on, having attended Sunday school since I was born. I gradually distanced myself from active church participation in my early 20's when the answers to some of the crucial questions I had on religion never arrived.

I did however investigate various churches at times in my search to satisfy my spiritual needs, particularly during those first years away from home. Later in life, I was exposed to the teachings of the major religions after a long absence of direct religious influence. I have observed and appreciated the similarities and differences of those.

Nature

Nature for me is a major connection to my spiritual essence. I have always felt a very close to Nature as a result of the environment I was raised in, and the influence of my parents with their close connection to it throughout their lives. I was surrounded by that wonderful world, with a river flowing past our home as a child and the view from our dining room window of a mountain on the other side, sometimes with deer on it. There was often the presence of a bald eagle and migrating birds such as ducks and geese.

However, in my youth I didn't think of it as a '*spiritual*' connection as such, but I certainly felt and responded to that *energy* I found in it. It was a magical magnet. I loved it and sought to be out in it at every opportunity - walking in the forests and mountains, fishing for trout in the creeks, lakes, and rivers, and hunting for wild game abundant in that region at the time.

Just going for a drive out into the countryside would help to satisfy that pull. I didn't fully realise the extent of the influence of that *energy* until I moved away from home into a city environment for the first time at 18. I ached for it. The excitement of a city experience couldn't satisfy the longing within me to be out in Nature.

Soon after, I was in the army, mixing with men from various environments around the U.S. Generally speaking, those from the cities like Chicago and New York City, said they loved the lifestyle there and wouldn't want to live anywhere else. The idea of going to the wilds of Montana or similar even for a peep didn't appeal to them. Those of us from more 'country' surrounds didn't want to spend any more time in a city than necessary. In any case, we all couldn't wait to get back to the surroundings we felt comfortable with – the *energy* pull beyond just our family and friends.

In my searching, experiencing, introspection, and speaking with many people from around our planet, and life analysis intensity of my D-Tour years in particular, I have come to an interesting conclusion. We are all sponge balls of fluctuating *energy*, giving and taking; some of us being more so of one than the other at times. We constantly need *energy* in one form or another – food, breath. All of that is probably no surprise to you.

What I have noticed, is that most people, as with myself, seem to be drawn throughout their lives to the *energetic* patterns of their upbringing. That is where it appears to me that we feel most comfortable, regardless of whether it is a city or more rural; coastal, mountainous, or plains environment. That is the *energy* that feeds both our cellular and spiritual aspect of ourselves. I need to be close to Nature regardless of the size of the population around me. Likewise, I have been drawn almost beyond my control, back to my roots from time to time.

Some people recognize the need and are drawn to the *spiritual energy* feed in a religious context or framework. I believe the fellowship found in a gathering of like-minded people of any positive nature such as a sports or social club also provides *spiritual* nourishment. The *energy* of human beings interacting with other humans in a giving and receptive way feeds our need.

For me, Nature provides a pure, personal, un-demanding way to feed my soul. That to me is the essence of *spirituality.* There are no expectations of a response which is often the case through the human source, as wonderful, beautiful and powerful as that may be. A mountainous terrain, preferably with forests, valleys and streams can take me to a place of peace and awe within me, with no interference or response other than gratitude. When that hasn't been so possible in my life, I would instinctively try to get away into some form of Nature such as parkland or nature reserve at every opportunity to invigorate me.

Religion - Wikipedia

Religion is a cultural system of behaviours and practices, world views, ethics, and social organisation that relates humanity to an order of existence. About 84% of the world's population is affiliated with one of the five largest religions, namely Christianity, Islam, Hinduism, Buddhism or folk religion.

Spirituality - Wikipedia

Spirituality may refer to almost any kind of meaningful activity, personal growth, or blissful experience. Traditionally, spirituality refers to a process of re-formation of the personality but there is no precise definition of spirituality.

Religion vs Spirituality - ReachOut.com

Religion is a specific set of organised beliefs and practices, usually shared by a community or group. Spirituality is more of an individual practice and has to do with having a sense of peace and purpose. It also relates to the process of developing beliefs around the meaning of life and connection with others.

❧❧

We all have a spirit and are therefore *spiritual beings*, whether we choose to engage in so-called *spiritual* (or religious) practices or not. I believe the trip through any displacement from life's 'normal' track could not come back into alignment without bringing the body, mind, and spirit all into balance, whether that balance existed beforehand or not. A person's religion, if any, is presumably practiced to nurture one's *spirit*, and would be an influence in that re-balance onto healing. I believe that my journey is testimony to those thoughts.

My beliefs have gotten manicured through the process of further discovering of who I am over my lifetime. I try to convey my relationship with the essence of *Divine Spirit,* using inadequate terms such as '*God*', '*Unconditional Love*', '*Universal Love*', '*All That Is*', and '*The Great Mystery*'.

Somehow I have maintained my connection at a deeper inner level even when I have not practiced in a more overt sense. I have challenged my beliefs and investigated various churches, religions and philosophies. It has been a fascinating journey which has taught me much. My *spiritual* essence has always been the common thread through it all – my soul no doubt being the driving force through my curiousity.

Most of the religions I've investigated or observed out of interest seem to have the same foundation as the Ten Commandments of the Christian faith, or ideals to that effect, along with other guidelines. People practice them with different styles according to their culture which varies incredibly of course, but they each appear to believe they have a connection with their perception of '*God*'.

In my travels around the world and mixing with many nationalities and cultures, it seems that people everywhere that practice their good beliefs with good intention appear to be fundamentally good. Many people, whom I would consider to be very *spiritual,* seem to be very connected to Nature. They often do not practice a particular religion, but seem to innately live by those esteemed values.

So, through all of my searching, reading, observation, contemplation, prayer, meditation, practices and just living, it really comes down to my belief that the one *true* religion is . . . *the life that each of us live.* My beliefs are a guide, but they are not specifically what makes me happy or make me feel good '*spiritually*'. It is whether I practice them or not in order to nurture my soul. My ideals and beliefs really don't count for anything if I don't try to live my life accordingly. Enough said. Off my soap box and back to doing the dishes.

Breathe in/ /Breathe out/ /Breathe in/ /Breathe out/

Rodger

I was seven years old when my cousin Rodger became part of my life; a big part; like a brother. His family moved to my home town in Montana from California in the summer of '55. We soon became like brothers. He was just three months older than me, but a year ahead at school. I have many happy and humorous memories of us together until he finished high school in 1965. He departed into the U.S. Marine Corp soon after. He couldn't wait to go.

Rodger had a particular knack for creating adventure and near misadventure, often landing one or both of us, and others in a bit of hot water. It began within days of their arrival at our home, where they stayed until they could get accommodation a few blocks away.

It was noticed by adults that my father's pickup canopy on the ground near our garage was seemingly on fire. On investigation they found Rodger, his sister Linda (a year younger than me) and I smoking cigarettes pinched from his parents supply. The smoke released from under the canopy was not nearly as much as that coming off my backside soon after; thank you Rodger. That was one class I didn't bother returning to.

There were numerous other incidents, some best not disclosed. He always had an activity or project going that usually involved others in practical jokes, a trait honestly come by from his father. Like the day he crammed as many people as we could fit into his father's '59 Chevy at the front of our high school at lunch time. He wanted set a record for entry into the Guinness Book of Records. He organised the same for the nearest phone box. Both attempts failed but we escaped with few injuries and a few laughs.

The war going on in Vietnam was a major issue in our lives in 1965. It was an unavoidable topic; TV, papers, magazine, discussions with others at school, home, amongst friends and family. There was no escaping it. Not for most able bodied young men. Rodger along with his friend Joe, enlisted in the US Marine Corp and departed soon after graduation from high school.

We kept in touch by letter during his tour of Vietnam. He shared an inside picture of the role he played there as a grunt, his thoughts and feelings - the hell of it all. It was not something he enjoyed or I envied. It didn't take long for his perception of war to change.

Before his 12 months tour of duty near Da Nang was completed, he lost his lower right leg and gained shrapnel in parts of his body. He was shipped to a military hospital in San Francisco for months of recovery and adjustment, before being released from service.

I saw him very briefly during my leave prior to going to Vietnam myself, in August of '67. He was living with his father who managed the restaurant at the Stage Coach Inn in West Yellowstone, Montana. He took me for a drive through part of Yellowstone NP and later to the garbage dump that night in his dad's '53 Chevy pickup to watch the grizzly bears forage. It was perhaps a bit too close as one big beast ambled alongside my door; tall enough to peep in while on all fours. Thankfully there was more appealing, or at least easier targets in the leftovers outside our vehicle.

It was a great day - so good to see him again after two years, and to assess how he was going with his injuries and life beyond his military service. He had adjusted to his adopted lower limb which he showed me and told me about sensing his itching toes that he no longer possessed. He could drive a manual vehicle. He was in good spirits and obviously getting on with life, doing most of the things he always had.

That evening we went to dinner together. He introduced me to his girlfriend and announced they planned to marry. They seemed happy.

But things turned sour when Rodger spotted a young Asian man dining at another table. He was became quite upset and abusive and wanted to take him outside. That was not the happy-go-lucky, practical joker that I grew up with and knew so well. We finally convinced him to settle down and forget about the innocent nearby patron. It could have gotten rather ugly, but fortunately we managed to get past it.

I'm telling you about Rodger because he was a casualty of a war that changed him dramatically - physically, mentally and emotionally, like thousands of other young men. He was transformed from an affable young man that got along with every one, into a person who at times then was consumed by hatred of certain people. (Note the contrast of the photo of him above at 17, to the one at the 'In Memory' taken a few months later.) Like millions of other young men, he was indoctrinated to hate and kill another human being that had no issue with him, in order to participate in a conflict on the other side of the world; a war that his government chose to become involved in with questionable justification. The ramifications are still being suffered by many millions of people and our planet some fifty years later.

I was serving in Vietnam less than a year when I got the news that Rodger was killed in a car accident in his little Jaguar XKE he loved. Sadly, his girlfriend, who was driving, was left with serious, lasting injuries as well. I couldn't believe the news until I got home and saw his headstone. He was four months shy of his 21st birthday.

Another virtual 'sibling' taken from my life - another big hole impossible to fill. Thank you Rodger for the wonderful part you played in my life for a brief time and for your service to our country.

Breathe in/🐾/Breathe out/🐾/Breathe in/🐾/Breathe out/🐾

Stan

An Enduring Friendship

After dozens of job applications, interviews, outright rejections and near-misses since arriving in Sydney in January 1972, I finally landed a job in March. It was outside the computer industry, but I took it as a fill-in to get some income, as low as it was.

There I met someone who was to become instrumental in my integration into my new life, and a very good friend. Stan was a likeable, intelligent fellow with a broad understanding of the world we live in, and who still maintained a sense of humour in spite of it all.

He immediately took me under his wing for some reason, helping me in my new job and to adjust to my new way of life. He had valuable advice and explanations of my new culture which I found enjoyable and amusing, but sometimes perplexing.

Stan was a native Tasmanian and also a Vietnam veteran, but with the Australian army. He had been stationed at a small communications outpost with the 506th Signal Troop near Nui Dat. He had mixed with the U.S. troops stationed near there as well, so he understood my language and ways, and was able to effectively interpret things for me. He said he felt he owed a debt of gratitude for the money the American troops graciously contributed to him in poker games which supplemented his measly pay.

On our first pay day in my first job, Stan took me down to the Ship Inn, a famous old pub at nearby Circular Quay near the Opera House in Sydney, where we cemented our long-lasting friendship over several glasses of amber fluid.

A few weeks later, I was able to get a foot in the door of the computer industry. Although I was seeking work as a programmer, I lacked the elusive two years of experience every potential employer wanted. Fortunately, I was able to call on my operator experience I gained while at college which got me a position in operations.

His dear partner Helga, a migrant from Hamburg, Germany, soon became a part of our friendship as well. She often seemed to manage to find enough food in their tiny kitchen to put a meal in front of this 'poor' migrant as well. They were both very kind and generous to me.

I had only worked with Stan a matter of weeks, but our friendship endured through numerous changes in our lives. We always kept in contact and did activities together when it was possible. They moved to Queensland, a day's drive to the north on their retirement, but we remained in contact by communication and visits.

Stan's health was adversely affected from wounds to his lungs during his time in Vietnam, which impaired his quality and length of life. He always had to use an inhaler in the time that I knew him, and had to employ an oxygen apparatus at night in later years. However, he never complained about it or outwardly blamed anyone. He obviously dealt with the wounds and trauma in his own way and didn't get government assistance until it was virtually too late.

Sadly, my dear friend died on my birthday in 2012. He is sorely missed for his friendship, generosity, wisdom, good humour, uplifting spirit, and endless supply of good and bad jokes.

Breathe in/🐾/Breathe out/🐾/Breathe in/🐾/Breathe out/🐾

Steve

It was the 2013 Christmas / New Year holiday season - a time to celebrate Christmas for all that means and the end of another year in our lives. It was also the time of hope as we look forward to what the new year might bring.

As I joined the gathering to celebrate with just one day left in the year, the feeling in the air felt anything but festive. We were meeting for a very definite, but different reason. The family and friends of Stephen Karaberidis had all come together to say 'goodbye' to him; to 'celebrate' his short life, as is the custom that society seems to be adopting when someone in our community dies.

Steve had been a workmate and a friend of mine and I had come along to pay my respects. We shared the same birthday and, as fellow Aquarians, were quite like-minded in many ways. He had a sharp mind and was very knowledgeable on a wide range of subjects. He enjoyed talking and joking during work and breaks or outside of work. He was a very good carpenter and general building tradesman, who was quite particular the quality of his workmanship. He was a seeker and adventurer with a sense of freedom. He had a curiosity about life that perhaps was both a friend, and an adversary, when he over-stepped boundaries.

Days after learning of his demise, I was still in shock. It had taken place over two weeks previously, but it wasn't known immediately after. I sat quietly in the funeral chapel, waiting for the service to begin, contemplating what had taken place, and what he must have been thinking and feeling to take his own life.

My thoughts were broken when Steve's family was ushered into the front row, just prior to commencement. The chapel wasn't overflowing, yet I think he would have been surprised by the number of people present that day - the number of people that cared about him and loved him.

Steve's father and two sisters courageously went up in front of the assembly to pay tribute to him, sharing their stories, filled with love and humour, while struggling to hold back the tears of sorrow and grief. His mother somehow had the composure to present a beautiful slide show of family photos and stories that gave us all a more complete picture of his life. More stories were shared amongst us all after the service over food and drinks in the next door facilities.

🐾🐾

Steve had come by my house shortly before Christmas, perhaps only hours before his death. It was evening, after dark. He stopped in to pick up some of his belongings he had left in my garage. We stood at my front door for awhile, talking about his decision to get out of town for a bit to get some peace of mind; away from the constant voices in his head.

It was something I was aware of through many conversations together, but he seemed okay and pretty normal to me at the time. We wished each other a Merry Christmas and shook hands. I wished him well on his camping trip in the Barrington's, which he had been wanting to do for awhile. Of course I never dreamt that it was our final time together.

Thinking back to those moments many times since, I haven't been able to perceive anything that night that gave me a clue to his intentions. Had he planned to take his life before he left, or was it something that he decided later during his aloneness where he thought, "Enough is enough; this is the only way to escape the voices in my head", or something similar?

His mother, on reflection afterwards, seemed to think that he planned his ending. Even though she didn't pick up on it during her last conversation with him, she later thought of indicators that made her think so. She is not only his mother, who knew him intimately, she is a psychologist and had worked with him in every possible way to help him get beyond the 'demons' that had troubled him over his adult life and most of his teens. Experimentation with drugs as a teenager took him down a dangerous, unforgiving path.

In dying at just 38 years of age, he'd spent more than half his lifetime trying to find his mental, physical and spiritual balance. He self-medicated with alcohol and marijuana when things got rocky or just out of habit. He found most of the prescribed medications unworkable and couldn't convince his counsellors to allow him to use the ones that seemed to help him the most. He had received much support from family, friends, and professional treatment over the years, but ultimately, he was unable to find the peace of mind in life he pursued.

Steve was a gentle and caring soul who turned the other cheek when confronted with verbal or physical abuse and bullying, which seemed to be something of a common occurrence for him. He was an easy target I suppose when under the influence of whatever substances. Steve wasn't a weakling. He was very strong and was fully capable of defending himself, but he chose not to. He was a sensitive Being who couldn't understand why everyone isn't loving and giving. His overly honest, generous, and compassionate nature was at odds with much of our world at times.

I wanted to help and tried, but I feel that perhaps I could have somehow done more. Just prior to his departure, Steve seemed to be going well, turning his back on those addictive substances yet once again, and making a real effort to get his life on track.

He wisely moved away from a bad environment he had been living in. He started running and surfing and took other positive actions towards improved physical and mental fitness that all indicated a renewed hope. His decision to strip down to his barest, sober self, and leap off a cliff to his death, caught me by surprise.

I have been dealing with the deaths of people close to me from a very young age - people of all ages that have died from sickness and accidents to old age. I have attended numerous funerals. There is often a celebration of that person's life, but almost always varying degrees of grief and sadness at the sense of permanent physical separation.

I haven't experienced a suicide within my own family, but I've witnessed the anguish in the family members of people who have taken that course of action. The often unanswered questions, the "why's", the "what if's", the "if only's", and the individual self-blame and guilt, take a huge toll on the mental, physical and emotional health of those close to them.

There often seems to be no answer or conclusion to the pain felt. It is perhaps, *debatably*, the ultimate sense of loss of another human due to its complexity, intensity, and the total ripple effect throughout the connections to the deceased.

With Steve, I can understand why he chose to take that path. I'm sure that it wasn't what he really wanted to do. He simply gave up trying every other method of shutting off the relentless chatter in his head he spoke of. Given more time and the right approach, I felt he could have gotten past that fateful decision which closed the door and connection to all of us. I can only hope that he has found the peace of mind he so desperately sought.

And now Steve, as I celebrate another trip around the sun, I appreciate *your* birth as well. Thank you for having been a part of my life! I'm wishing you were here, but the good memories you brought to my life while you were physically with us will have to suffice. I often think of you on other days also. There is evidence around me with your work done on the house in which I still live, which triggers nice thoughts of you.

Breathe in/🐾🐾/Breathe out/🐾🐾/Breathe in/🐾🐾/Breathe out/🐾🐾

Follow the Trail

What is the magical attraction and indeed grip, which the sight, thought, possession and desire for gold has held on people everywhere throughout history? People kill for it, so it must hold a higher value than human life for some people.

There were a number of great discoveries of that precious metal in a variety of places around our planet about mid-1800. The ensuing stampedes of people to 'strike it rich' altered the course of history and the genetic mix across the continents.

It created a trail of humanity around the world chasing from one place to the next in the hope of potential wealth. While few of those seekers were fortune enough to end up in a more favourable financial position as a result, those that provided services to the miners too busy to provide for their own needs, apparently were in greater numbers than rich miners. Still, some of the dedicated ones got very lucky indeed.

Most of the largest nuggets found anywhere came from Australia. Two miners in Victoria found one in 1869 dubbed the Welcome Stranger, weighing over 78 kg or 173 lb for a pure yield of 71 kg or 2284 troy ounces. Not much chance of keeping that a secret for long was there!

Another of those, distracted with other money-making pursuits was a German migrant to Australia, Bernhardt Holtermann, whom along with a Polish partner, found a gold matrix in quartz at Hill End, NSW in 1872 after several years of promising discoveries and perseverance. It yielded 15,488 troy ounces (or 481 kg) of pure gold and another nearly as large followed not long after! It proved well worth the focus and diligence they demonstrated in following their dreams! What's my point in telling you this story seemingly unrelated to wellness?

Most of those seekers were motivated to take action, to change the course of their lives. They followed the trail often blazed by others in search of something they desperately wanted, often at their physical peril and even their demise. Whether they made the initial discovery or joined the mob in pursuit, they all sought the source of their desire; potential wealth.

As I see it, our greatest wealth is our health and well-being. What rewards would we get if we focused on our health with the same level of interest as they did in their pursuit of gold? What can we take from their techniques and enthusiasm?

- Keep focused on our main intention to attain and maintain optimum wellness
- Obtain knowledge or awareness of good health
- Follow the trail of clues and symptoms of problems affecting our health
- Get to the source or core of a problem to eliminate it
- Pursue until you reach the desired point of understanding, solution, or wellness
- Be happy with your pot of gold of wellness

The trail keeps circling back to the main point in our intention:

- Well-being
- Joyfulness

Breathe in/🐾/Breathe out/🐾/Breathe in/🐾/Breathe out/🐾

My Secret Weapon

There have been times I have reached a point where I have found it difficult to get myself out of feeling down. Positive thinking might get me out, but sometimes that just hasn't been enough. My efforts to get past those emotions through mental efforts can put me into a 'thought-loop' that can just keep bringing up the same thoughts and emotions.

Then, I learned a terrific secret which I will share with you now. Again, it is getting out of the thought process and into the *feeling* or emotion, in order to *feel* better. It can be even quicker than a two-minute breath exercise.

I have used it many times when nothing else seemed to work. I use it even when I am not feeling low, (because I rarely do anymore), just to feel even better, or if I feel I'm heading in that direction. It's good mood maintenance. When I *feel* better in myself, everything around me seems to improve – (funny that isn't it)? If that's our intention, then with practice, it soon becomes our reality. Remember our intention from the Preface? Wellness = *feeling* good!

It goes like this:

- **Gratitude or appreciation creates joy**; it is a fact of our bio-chemistry according to scientists.
- The feelings of *joy* and *appreciation* or *gratitude* are inexplicably intertwined like lovers in a heartfelt embrace.
- Just as *gratitude* generates *joy*, so too, *joy* fosters *appreciation* for whatever it is that made it so.
- One cannot exist without generating the other. Prove it to yourself!
- Furthermore, the combination of *joy* and *gratitude* transmutes into *love*, which can spread throughout every cell in our body, thus **transforming** our state of being with healing.
- Doesn't the feeling of *love* want to express itself with *joy* and *appreciation*?

Go on – just try it. Think of something you are really grateful for and then *feel* it – let the *feeling* flow through you. It could be the love of your pet, or partner, or family, your home . . . whatever. There – you have just produced your own *joy* – the elixir for well-being!

It is simply the easiest and quickest way I know of for getting out of a low spot and reaching the state of *joyfulness* - the top end of happiness. That is where I like to spend my time. You can also incorporate simple breath exercises to greatly enhance your efforts.

Breathe in/🐾/Breathe out/🐾/Breathe in/🐾/Breathe out/🐾

Hope, Love, Peace, Happiness, and Joy

Let's be honest, not everyone reading this is experiencing or perhaps has ever experienced all of those desirable states of being; maybe not any of them. I certainly didn't feel connected to those when I was diagnosed with PTSD in 2000. Had all of those been a part of me at that time, the condition would not have been able to co-exist with them. I had known each of those in varying degrees at various times in my life, but not together as permanent friends of mine, as they are now.

If you are struggling to identify with any of the above, don't let it despair you; I felt fractured and scattered, but I've been able to change that. I believe that you can too.

Let's start with Hope on step 1.

- Once I realised I had a problem and sought help for my anxiety, and I received help, I felt hopeful of being restored to 'normal'. That was all I was consciously seeking at that point. Help gave me hope! I got some understanding and knowledgeable assistance. I felt supported. Please believe that there is a great deal of help available now.
- Love? Fortunately I had the love of my family, and I loved them dearly. But I didn't love myself much, which was even more important, without even realising it. That was not my focus. I just wanted 'normal.'
  Self-love (not to be confused with ego,) eventually improved with some understanding and effort and is progressing. It's an inside job.
- Peace? Not bloody much in that head of mine back then. Have you ever watched a dog chase its tail? That was my thought pattern - no peace in that! Peace? 'Yes please – where are you?' Well . . . there it was, right there inside me; I just had to find it, grow it and maintain it. Peace of mind is the starting point to

greater healing, expansion, good health – and potentially joy! From that clearer space, you can catch your breath and think with clarity, focus, plan, create and action effectively. You've got the monkey off your back and you no longer feel like a cornered rat. You are in control! That is gold!

- Happiness? Sure I'd known happiness at times, but it wasn't a permanent fixture and I wasn't really thinking that was possible to be as such. It was more like a happening than a state of being. Yes, it was there inside me as well – I just had to make a choice; to be or not to be! It really is that simple – not something to be chased outside of me. Then to fully appreciate what I have. Once I accepted the teaching that I had a choice in each moment to be happy or otherwise, it suddenly became much easier, and eventually, my pre-dominate state.
- Joy? Well that was something for other people who were too simple, blind or selfish to care about all the problems in the world like I chose to do. It certainly wasn't on my list of attainable pursuits. The times that joy tried to enter my being, it was treated with embarrassment or like an uncomfortable stranger; those rare appearances were fleeting, arriving unexpectedly rather than the object of my desire.

  Joy was the unexpected icing on the cake that magically appeared after I dealt with the others on the ladder. It was the butterfly that landed on my shoulder without my chasing. 'Thank you!'

I never went back to the same state of 'normal' that I wanted to reach initially. It wasn't possible. I went way beyond that because that was what my soul *really* wanted, but I hadn't consciously realised. What is 'normal'?

- 'Normal' was being comfortable in my way of life that I have grown accustomed to.
- It was fitting into society as one of the crowd
- Stuck in routine

- Not make too much noise, or too many waves
- Trying to please others even when it feels uncomfortable
- Keeping the peace at all cost (which a big cost and always borne by the 'peacekeeper').

We are often oblivious to the impact that trying to fit into the 'norm' is having on our happiness and overall state of being and wellness. But we can make our own 'normal' one of happiness or joyfulness if that is our desire.

When I reached the bottom of my trench, and started climbing up, it was pretty dark along the walls, but I could eventually see the sky up above. I couldn't see a destination above that horizon, but there was no limit – anything was possible once I could get out of that hole and kept looking upwards.

Breathe in/🐾/Breathe out/🐾/Breathe in/🐾/Breathe out/🐾

Waiting For the Other Shoe . . .

Life is a trail of thoughts and emotions forming habits, moods, and patterns of behaviour, expectations and attitudes. (Just ask Lucy) When the view behind us looks like a series of disasters and negative events, we can form a negative outlook for what is to come next. We form an expectation that it is just a matter of time before the next shoe hits the floor - loaded with some disaster.

We reinforce that expectation then with thoughts like "I *knew* that would happen," or 'That is just my luck – *again*!". We may feel disheartened or devastated on one hand, but conversely, we could possibly feel a slight sense of elevation for being right . . . again! "I *told* you so!" The pattern becomes our attitude towards our life.

Most of us can relate I think. I had to break free of that thinking to move on in a positive direction. It took –

- Becoming aware - observing my 'self', my behaviour
- Stepping back from the negative emotions – acknowledging them and determining why I felt that way – learning the lesson and changing
- Learning to change negative thinking to positive thinking and behaviour
- Habits, bad or good are formed through repetition - unintentional or intentional
- Keeping up positive actions long enough to become 'good' habit forming
- Never think of the practice as being difficult. That is just a belief which we can change.

Like any skill from sports to driving, training is required to develop the skill until it becomes almost automatic. The more practiced and skilful, the easier it becomes. Life as a whole gets easier and flows in the direction we focus our attention on. The easiest, most effective healthy habit we can form is breathing mindfully, which helps to create homeostasis in our body – *naturally!*

Breathe in/🐾/Breathe out/🐾/Breathe in/🐾/Breathe out/🐾

Imagination

From Wikipedia, the free encyclopaedia -

'**Imagination**, also called the faculty of **imagining**, is the ability to form new images and sensations in the mind that are not perceived through senses such as sight, hearing, or other senses. Imagination helps make knowledge applicable in solving problems and is fundamental to integrating experience and the learning process. Einstein claimed that it was more important than knowledge.

Memory and imagination have been shown to be affected by one another. "Images made by functional magnetic resonance imaging technology show that remembering and imagining sends blood to identical parts of the brain." The neocortex and thalamus are responsible for controlling the brain's imagination, along with many of the brain's other functions such as consciousness and abstract thought. Since imagination involves many different brain functions, such as emotions, memory, thoughts, etc., portions of the brain where multiple functions occur—such as the thalamus and neocortex—are the main regions where imaginative processing has been documented. The understanding of *how* memory and imagination are linked in the brain, paves the way to better understand one's ability to link significant past experiences with their imagination.

Imagination, because of having freedom from external limitations, can often become a source of real pleasure and unnecessary suffering. Consistent with this idea, imagining pleasurable and fearful events is found to engage emotional circuits involved in emotional perception and experience. Imagination can also produce some symptoms of real illnesses.'

I believe that our imagination is arguably the most powerful tool we possess, if we look at it in that context. We can use it in a positive powerful way to heal us. It's the engine room of our creative talent and should be nurtured. It can be a wild and wonderful Pegasus, taking us on a joy ride to great heights in emotions and possibilities and ideas. It can also be a powerful stallion taking us into our darkest fears if it gets out of our control. It needs to be free to be creative, yet balanced within the boundaries of reason and acceptable behaviour.

It is often our imagination that takes us into fear and negative thinking (if we let it), so it also the vehicle out of negativity into optimism. That is where we can see possibilities, potential, and produce positive outcomes. That is where negative thinking can be curtailed and turned around before it activates. Stop; think – 'how can I change this thinking or situation etc?' - and act. Imagine the situation playing out the way you want it to be. It is often just that simple. Attitude and intention are key factors as well, but those should be well manicured and already in place, ready to respond.

Some people will say they are not imaginative. While it's true some are much more so than others, we all are enough to be creative in positive ways. We can all dream. That's imagination. Our fears are usually imagined images and thoughts that may never happen. Images get formed in our mind. We hear a story with our eyes closed and we see images in our mind's eye. That's imagination. We can all do it. And every person hearing that story would have a different picture in their mind. With some effort and perhaps training, we can all use this powerful tool to our advantage.

Some of the ways are:

- See yourself in the state of being that you desire; peaceful, relaxed, happy or joyful, etc
- See a situation as working out and believing that it will
- See the positive aspects of something
- Dismiss negative thoughts that enter the mind
- Exercise your imagination by telling or writing stories
- Look for the beauty in the world
- See yourself doing something you really enjoy or would like to do; enjoy the feeling it gives you

- See yourself as being younger, healthy, and feeling fantastic
- Think of the endless possibilities of changes you would make to the world if you could
- Think that you can
- Try to think of something positive made by mankind without imagination or creativity

"You know what the issue is with this world?
Everyone wants a magical solution to their problem,
and everyone refuses to believe in magic."

– Alice in Wonderland
Lewis Carroll (Charles Lutwidge Dodgson 1832-1898)

Knowing

Using My Intuition

Another Tool for Wellness

As I gradually developed my healing and wholeness and through my pursuit of wellness, I began to realise that something was developing within me that was an unexpected blessing. It came as a sense of *knowing.* More and more, I seemed to just *know* things without necessarily thinking deeply about it or pursuing that particular thing, but later would often prove to be accurate. Sometimes it was important to me while other times it was just fun.

Was it *instinct* I could sense when I paid attention? Was my intuition developing stronger? I guess I've always been intuitive to some extent, which has benefited me many times throughout my life, but this greater awareness seemed to take it a step further.

At first I began to test it and play with it to see if it was *just* my imagination, which too is important. As I proved its validity to myself, I realised what a powerful tool it was, rather than just a form of amusement.

I believe the power of the 'knowing' comes in trusting it when it appears in the gut, which often comes without warning. That comes with belief and allowing it to go ahead in complete trust that it will all be for my best interest. It's not logic of the mind. It is instinct in my gut.

I mustn't stop to think about it or analyse it or the consequences. I have to trust that voice in my head if it feels right in my gut. That brings about more trust, empowerment. That is trusting my innate gift of intuition. We all have it.

The reason for me sharing this with you? To encourage you to use this powerful tool to enhance your power over PTSD and stress-related issues. Have fun with it and embody it for your greater power and wellbeing.

Do you remember our focus and intention is for wellness? What is our simple formula?

- What is wellness? Feeling well and good, beyond whatever the physical evidence.
- What brings about our wellness? One of the things is our own empowerment!
- What gives us empowerment? Mindfully employing the tools that we know makes us feel better and getting the results we are seeking!
- How does empowerment make us feel? Great!
- Feeling good or great = an indication of *Wellness*!

So let go of the scepticism and just try it – here's some suggestions to try:

- '*Know*' who is ringing you (or even someone else) next time the phone rings
- '*Know*' what someone is going to say even though it may be out of context of what has been said
- '*Know*' who will win a sporting event and by how much (*knowing*, not guessing)
- '*Know*' what is going to happen about something
- '*Know*' what time it is without thinking about it when you wonder, or wake in the night
- '*Know*' where the parking spot is waiting for you – amaze yourself with that!

As I said before, *don't think about it*; just go with whatever pops into your head. When you are able to think about something with a positive outcome without breaking your brain thinking about it, you will also realise what power you have in your *intuition!*

Breathe in/🐾/Breathe out/🐾/Breathe in/🐾/Breathe out/🐾

Past; Present; Future

Visualise standing in front of a production line that moves from your right to your left. There is a mirror behind the line directly in front of you where you can see yourself and the object arriving in front of you on the line. It is the *present.*

There is a veil over the line to your right, which is the *future.* You can't see it coming until it is directly in front of you. It then moves off to your left and drops off into a box, called the *past.* It is no longer visible to you.

You can use all of your senses and take action to alter the object *only* in the *present.* You can close your eyes and imagine what was past and what may be the future, but that is not the *reality*, only available in the *present.*

The line never stops moving, but the amount of time it seems to take to pass through the *present* depends upon your perception rather than the *reality* of it.

Such is my simplified perception of *reality.*

<u>Past</u>	<u>Present</u>	<u>Future</u>
No tangible connection	Now; Tangible; Action	Just a thought or a mental image

Past = memory/recollection

- no longer in 'reality'; no feelings present; feelings about the past are created or re-created or relived in the present from the past thoughts or feelings
- thoughts of past are in the mind; perceptions and memory are changeable and often not accurate
- feelings of the past can be locked in body memory cells

Present (Now) = Real time as we perceive it

- breathing; conscious thinking; creative thinking; problem solving; sensual awareness; conscious awareness; subconscious activity not consciously aware; perceptions of sensual awareness are variable and often unreliable

Mental clarity = present, focused thinking and sharpened awareness

- Feeling good; distractive thoughts of bad feelings and pain mentally are set aside
- Lack of mental clarity = disconnected, incoherent thoughts; erratic thinking; emotional and bodily feelings, often pain present, distract from and/or override clear thinking; inability to stay present and focus thoughts

Problem Solving

- Problems cannot be solved outside the present state of mind, i.e. not in the past or future
- Problems are best solved in a state of mental clarity and the body is relaxed
- Senses are heightened during a state of fight or flight; instincts take over body and mental functions; analytical thinking ability is reduced or even impossible

Future = imagined, projected thoughts

- not yet real; no feelings; feelings about future events are projected or created in the present state of mind; all in the mind
- Problems requiring cognitive thinking cannot be easily considered and solved in a state of fight or flight because the mind doesn't give attention to any problems that aren't survival oriented
- Anxiety and other stress-related issues have similar effects to fight and flight body/mind states in our efforts to solve problems; the analytical mind shuts down

Stress-related problems need to be addressed while we are in a calm, relaxed state of being, free from active anxiety hormones. We can only address them in the *present* state.

> *"If you are depressed, you are living in the past. If you are anxious, you are living in the future. If you are at peace, you are living in the present."*
>
> – Lao Tzu

Breathe in/🐾/Breathe out/🐾/Breathe in/🐾/Breathe out/🐾

Overcoming Some of My Fears

I guess most of us have our 'cupboard of fears' don't we? I had a fear that held me back from enjoying some of the great pleasures in life. It was my fear of deep water, which was with me from my earliest memories. I can still feel the fear I felt at the age of about 4 looking into a neighbour's swimming pool while my sister Marguerite, two and a half years younger, blissfully floated on her back. No amount of coaxing from my parents could get me to copy her example. I don't know where that fear came from, but it was very real and held me back from doing things that could have given me enjoyment.

As I got older I would paddle about or swim under water at the shallow end of our town pool, but would never venture over my head until I was in my teens. I managed to get to a point where I could sort of swim from one side to the other at the deep end of the pool when I was 15 years of age, well behind most of my friends who took it all for granted. There was still an underlying fear in me when I would look into deep water even as I went through much of my adult life. I eventually overcame more of the fear enough to do some sailing which I really enjoyed. However I really wasn't comfortable with the feelings at times.

I am pleased to say that through a strong motive to swim with dolphins I can now swim in deep water with very little apprehension. I can thank the patient assistance from my water baby friend Lyn, who has taught me to snorkel and various water training. Consequently, in 2012, it brought about a very special experience in Hawaii. Overcoming that fear allowed me to swim with the dolphins and manta rays in the wild that could not have taken place without me.

One the first occasion there I was snorkelling with a group of people off the coast where pods of dolphins were swimming past. The dolphins were chattering, frolicking and chasing and having fun including occasional nurseries of young dolphins tended by adults as they passed.

Then something special happened for me personally. A lone adult dolphin came up from the deep to me and virtually danced on its tail eye-to-eye as it circled me 360 degrees before swimming off. It was so close I was having trouble not to touch it as I treaded water and remained in eye-to-eye contact as rotated together. It was a very memorable and moving experience.

The second experience was a couple of days later when Lyn and I swam out alone from the shore into deep water of the bay. We were about fifty meters out when dolphins started appearing, swimming past and up to us, playing tag with leaves from the trees on the shore. We were amazed that they would hook over a fin and pass it on to another that would hook it over its fin. No circus tricks; in the wild.

In 2014 I had another wonderful deep water experience swimming with massive whale sharks, the largest fish on our planet. We were in very deep water well off the coast, but it didn't faze me. I just wanted to jump in and have another special experience. It was quite incredible trying to keep up with the twenty-odd-foot monster while looking it in the eye at point-blank range, being careful not to touch it.

My point of these stories is that I could not have had these wonderful life experiences had I let my fear of water continue to hold me back. So what did I do to reach a point where my fears didn't stop me doing what I wanted to do?

- I had to admit to myself that I had that fear of water (baths and showers not included); deep water in particular. Trout fishing in fast water was not a problem for me, but fishing out on a lake did for some reason.
- I had motivation. I had long held a desire to interact with dolphins.
- I decided to change my thinking and behaviour and took action. I got help. I took steps. I continued and built confidence. I am so pleased that I did. The rewards have made it all worthwhile.

Breathe in/🐾/Breathe out/🐾/Breathe in/🐾/Breathe out/🐾

Put to the Test

9 October 2014

By and large, I believed I had reached a state of being that allowed me to generally maintain a sense of happiness. After years of working towards that goal, it was still a work in progress, but it seemed to get easier with time. It really is about the journey and not a destination. I had been floating along for some time down this lovely stream of my life that it had become - enjoying the experience more in recent times and seemingly resistant to most negative issues that came my way. I'd learned to deal with things quite well - or so I thought.

Out of the blue, I was put to the test of dealing with a family situation that really rocked me. It has had a huge impact on both me and my family. So, let's look at that situation where I was feeling good about myself and life in general, then something unexpectedly happened that generated those old symptoms of stress and anxiety etc. How did I handle it? What have I done to come back into balance?

The revelation took me by surprise and into a state of numbness in mind and emotions. It took hours and days to assess and process the words coming from one of my beloved children regarding a huge decision made and actions taken. I was in a state of shock and disbelief, wrapped in a sense of anguish and other powerful emotions causing a downward spiral in my mental, physical, and emotional state of being. I had to get past that before I could act to try to come to terms with it all and move on.

I just couldn't make sense of it. In the days that followed, my mind lost the plot and was not on the job I was trying to do. I made mistakes. Driven by fearful, frustrated, and erratic thinking and imposing emotions of grief, sadness, helplessness, and anger, I floundered. So much for my joy or peace of mind. My body was in dis-ease through that period, made worse by the lack of good sleep over a few nights. I was in a state of dis-harmony that I thought I had left well and truly behind me. I was surprised at the overall impact it was having on me. Even friends commented to me that I didn't look well over the following days. I was not where I wanted to be in my mind, body or spirit.

Trauma Symptoms

- I had not been shot at by an enemy soldier; I had not been verbally or physically abused by anyone; I was not involved in a car accident; I didn't participate in or witness a horrific event.
- I was simply told something that my mind applied a set of values to through my perceptions; my mind and body thus responded in a way *similar to actually being a victim of trauma.*
- I became aware that my breath quickened, my pulse and blood pressure raised, my attention span shortened, and my physical behaviour and appearance changed. The anxiety within could not be contained or concealed.
- My mind went into a negative thought loop that projected a range of potential scenarios and outcomes, filtered by my belief system, without any of it even being real to my own experience. It was simply my minds' response to something I was told.
- Much of the anxiety I was experiencing was my over-active imagination hard at work.

That is how powerful the mind is. My conscious mind lost control to my emotionally-driven unconscious mind. It took over and my body responded as if in a state of fight or flight mode or trauma. My previously calm, relaxed body with clear thinking, rational mind all went on holidays and refused to return until the mess was tidied up.

- I struggled to maintain a sense of composure and normal function
- I was virtually in fight/flight/survival mode
- My *energies* were scattered
- My gut churned

- My mind kept searching for understanding, but it really couldn't comprehend
- When my conscious mind switched off temporarily with sleep, my unconscious mind continued the search for understanding, giving shortened, fitful sleep
- My conscious mind will not rest until the dots of understanding connect, but irrational behaviour is not logical. There was no logical explanation to satisfy it, so I needed to STOP LOOKING for a logical solution!
- I had to go into the *feelings* and tame them to stop my loss of mental clarity and emotional imbalance that had taken me over; I *knew* that but had lost the plot
- What I was observing in myself, I didn't want to become as my permanent state of my being.
- It was powerful and it was painful
- How could I pull myself out of my merry-go-round of negative thoughts and emotions?

Fortunately I had a companion with a sharp logical mind and awareness of the processes necessary to help me settle my feelings and focus my mind. With her help, I began to think more rationally and put it all into proper perspective. I was reminded to focus on the solution, not the problem. I had to get back to basics. Those things were forgotten in my mental haze. Thank Goodness for the right friend to assist when an objective view point was required.

As I was reminded, I looked into my tool box of applications and solutions for familiar and reliable ways to steady myself to regain my balance. I had to dig deeper than usual. My liable and crucial first aid kit of breath control eased the anxiety to some extent, but I needed something more powerful as well. Some actions I took to consolidate and re-balance my *energies* were:

- *Accept* the circumstances and choices made by the person involved; it is their choice, not mine

- *Allow* them to be who they want to be as I always have in the past
- Remain *loving* and *compassionate* for all those involved without condition
- Breath exercises
- Physical exercise
- Meditation
- Get and stay grounded to regain mental clarity and emotional composure
- Use empowering mantras, affirmations, and prayer
- Think of the beauty of that person and gratitude for them in my life
- Support the other person instead of trying to 'fix' them
- Connect with nature – walk along the lake or beach, in a forest, or barefoot in the garden
- Try to remain positive, believing that it will be the best for all concerned
- Stay busy and have fun
- Get distracted from the issue; watch a movie or TV program; listen to uplifting music
- *Appreciate* the many blessings in my life the lessons I'm learning from this experience
- Have occasional reality checks with my partner, family and friends

During my 'crisis', I decided to share my situation with just two other people outside of my family that I knew I could trust to not tell others, since it was such a private matter. I got some wise advice and support that helped me considerably, and it helped them to understand my unusual change in demeanour during that time. I am fortunate to have such terrific friends who helped me to get back into a better frame of mind. I truly appreciate their valuable non-judgmental wisdom.

I managed to improve within a few days though it has taken me a few weeks to really regain my balance. The negative thoughts would get settled somewhat then occasionally rebound, but it eventually returned to satisfactory balance.

Still, it was not months. Nor have I forever discarded hope as I might have done earlier in my life. The problem is just as real and present as it was when I first became aware of it, but I've handled it better and quicker than I would have years ago. It no longer robs me of the joy of living my life in the way I wish.

I'm not pleased about the situation, but I can accept and move on in an improved state of being. I've regained enough clarity and control of my mind to nip wayward thoughts and emotions in the bud when they arise. I can now discuss the issues in a calmer, clearer state of mind and being.

- From an analytical viewpoint, even though an event wasn't even a direct action by or to me, simply my awareness of it became a matter that deeply affected me in mind, body and spirit.
- My mind reacted which in turn engaged my body through its chemistry, depleted my spirit *energy* and suddenly my emotions were in charge of my behaviour. It took days to regain my senses and start to take charge again.
- In reality, it was a tricky set of circumstances I'd never had to deal with before and never expected in my wildest imagination. It still had the potential to go horribly wrong. Fortunately I had the desire, the determination and the skills I have learned over the past few years in order to do it.
- Unconditional love, trust and acceptance along with my core values were my saviours and the catalyst for me breaking through the loops of negative thoughts and emotions.
- Once I surrendered to that, I could move on. That was paramount in order for me to regain balance.
- In the process of it all, I was brought into the reality that there are always more challenges with lessons I can learn; in acceptance of circumstances, mindfulness, trust, compassion,

and unconditional love. Ultimately, they will hopefully give me more strength, understanding, wisdom and peace of mind.

- If I want to maintain the equanimity I cherish, I must accept both the actions of others and myself for my own sake and well-being. They have the right of choice in their quest for happiness in whatever way they see as right for them just as I do.
- I just need to keep my equilibrium, love them unconditionally, give them space to be themselves, and be there for them if they want my help.

In summary, the situation confirmed for me the validity of my PTSD recovery and management process when I am challenged, which is why I am sharing it with you. I know I am of no value to myself or anyone else if I cannot maintain my mental and emotional balance.

Staying focused on my desired state of being is the key. I start my day using whatever tools are required to try to reach that state and then try to stay there all day by keeping mentally present and monitoring the emotions; being vigilant and mindful.

Update: yes, all is good now – the 'problem' resolved over time without my interference. Everyone is happy again. A big lesson in *allowing* and *acceptance* with impact! There seems to always be another lesson waiting behind the curtain to jump out when I least expect it.

Breathe in/🐾/Breathe out/🐾/Breathe in/🐾/Breathe out/🐾

Surprise Out in the Styx

One of the most interesting and surprising occurrences regarding Post Traumatic Stress Disorder awareness happened 'recently' in a very unexpected place and circumstances. It was already an eventful day as such, with a so-called 'blood red' full moon and total lunar eclipse hours before.

There was a wonderful chance meeting with a Tassie devil on a night walk in the bright moonlight, who was unperturbed by my presence and my dim torchlight on his pathway. He virtually walked over my shoes without altering his course, much to my delight and disbelief.

Interestingly, Christina and I had become separated an hour or so earlier in our photographic endeavours to capture the moonlight magic coming up over Lake St Claire in Tasmania. Searching for each other in the darkness, she had a very similar experience with one. Same one in a different time? Regardless, we both had our one desire granted in very individual and personal experiences.

🐾🐾

We arrived at the World Heritage Styx Valley to view the massive trees in the old growth forest of swamp gum eucalypts, two of which were over 400 years old and nearly ninety meters (300 feet) tall. There were just a couple of other vehicles and no other people in sight. A few kilometres of gravel road and warning signs about logging trucks must be a bit of a deterrent to people from visiting something very special. Strangely, there were few signs indicating directions to these spectacular giants of the plant world.

We went up a short climb above the road through rain forest to view 'Big' and 'Bigger' as they are known and labelled, perhaps 100 metres apart. We marvelled at their magnificence as we took turns snuggling into the base of them for photos and connecting with their palpable energy.

They were just the two biggest members amongst the many other lesser wonderful examples of their species in the vicinity. The solemn serenity was only broken slightly by the wind in the tree tops and the cries of the yellow-tailed black cockatoos nesting out of sight high above. It felt very sacred to me.

We crossed the gravel road walking slowly towards the Styx River along the easy, open path that descended very gently through the beautiful, dense and peaceful old-growth forest. There was much to fill our senses. No other people, just the sounds and sights of Nature. We stopped to admire some vibrant orange fungus growing on a tree downed long ago.

Another couple about my age appeared coming from the direction of the river. They stopped to admire and comment on the object of interest and the beauty of the whole environment we were all absorbed in. They suggested we follow a short trail upstream when we would reach the river at the end of our path for more beauty.

A Fellow Club Member

As they started to walk away towards the road, I felt the urge to ask them if they owned the vehicle in the car park with the Vietnam veteran stickers on it. They smiled and said yes. I said that I was a Viet vet as well. They came back and warmly introduced themselves to us and we engaged in further friendly conversation about our lives, where we/they lived, livelihoods, retirement, and so on. The synchronicity of our meeting was very interesting. Both woman were named Christina and proud of their Danish heritage.

The man smiled and said that he had some of the best times of his life in the U.S. back in the early 70's while studying to be a chiropractor. There was very little discussion about our military experiences; only briefly where we had served in Vietnam. He talked about post war and how he chose that profession which allowed him flexibility in managing his life.

As he talked, it was becoming obvious to me he had been dealing with symptoms of Post-Traumatic Stress Disorder since the war. He had a calm, composed nature that expressed compassion, but his face also had many years of stress etched into it as well. He seemed to be well aware of that stress and appeared to manage it, so I casually mentioned the term PTSD in reference to one of the symptoms we had just discussed.

The serene appearing man in this quiet scene suddenly transformed into someone very different that stunned me. His gentle, placid persona suddenly erupted into a man seemingly possessed by an emotional, wailing energy like a young child with a painful injury. There was tearful blubbering about PTSD which I couldn't understand. He was distraught, his face flushed and his body was responding with movement of hands, arms, and feet.

At first I was astounded, and then quickly drawn emotionally into the energy as well, with tears flowing from both of us. I apologized to him and moved to give him a hug and say it was okay. We eventually disengaged to wipe our tears, though it took some time for him to settle down so I could understand what he was trying to say.

With the release of those emotions, we were then able to talk about some of the effects the war had had on us individually. We discussed how we each chose to deal with the symptoms and our life-long pursuit of ways and means to obtain and maintain peace and happiness as best we could.

There were many similarities to our symptoms and processes in learning about PTSD and associated stresses once we came into the awareness of what it was. We had both chosen to treat it in our own unique but similar ways that worked best for our selves.

- We had both resisted the use of prescribed medication due to the side effects we encountered.
- We both found great solace and value in being in touch with the energy and solitude found in Nature.
- Neither of us felt safe in large cities for any length of time. He chose to live in a mountainous environment that allowed him to make a living and to find peace and activities he enjoyed.
- We both tried and learned to manage our fluctuating physical and emotional energies in an attempt to maintain balance of

body, mind and spirit as best we could through our work, physical and mental activities, and the environments we chose.

- He couldn't work sitting at a desk which was a problem for me as well.
- We both needed movement to manage our energies. I became a qualified computer programmer and system analyst in 1971, but found I couldn't sit still for any length of time. I needed to be physically active as well as mentally, so I worked in computer operations and network communications.
- He started in 1971 to become a chiropractor;
- I had inquired about and nearly enrolled in a chiropractic college in Melbourne about 1981 at the encouragement of my chiropractor, but decided not to when I married soon after.
- I became qualified as a massage therapist few years ago.
- We both chose modalities for healing that move healing energy both in other people's bodies and our own.
- There were more similarities in our stories.

I mentioned that I was writing a book with the intention and hope of helping others through my experiences and findings around PTSD. He said he would look forward to reading it when it becomes available. After perhaps more than half an hour, we went our separate ways . . . with a sense of common connection at many levels, and a great deal of unexpected healing down on the forest floor. Peace was restored. The only crying was that of my beloved black cockatoos in the trees high above.

I can never know what that man has been through in his war experiences that we never mentioned. Nor he mine. We only talked about the issues we dealt with following our time served. The rest of our stories are buried deep within each of us, surrounded by inarticulate emotions that rarely surface. They have no translation into words and are therefore difficult to be shared verbally. No words are necessary.

We can only share the common knowing and compassion for whatever we each experienced. The fire of those experiences burnt out long ago, but the embers linger on with sensory reminders that refuse to die with the flames. The healing processes just go on and on in various ways in our searching for peace and joy.

- What we *can* all do is assist each other in the healing of our mental, emotional and in some instances physical wounds and pain.
- We can share our presence with or without words.
- We can connect in a common energetic and psychological bond that is a healing in a way that often only two people of the same trauma can relate to.
- We can simply be there and hold the energetic space with knowing and compassion, not saying a word.
- We can gradually transform that pain into healing through awareness, acceptance, release, forgiveness, love, and even gratitude. That in turn brings peace, and potentially joy found through those processes. Flowery words perhaps, but each has an incredible power within the context and parameters - so crucial in the healing of our wounds.

Such was that unexpected encounter in the Styx Valley on the first day of February 2018. It was a potent reminder for me to never doubt or underestimate the place and potential for healing and finding peace anytime anywhere.

There were at least two important 'surprises' for me in that event:

- Firstly - the *urging* and the courage that I felt to engage him in conversation about Vietnam and my book. It's something I have normally avoided in the past, but it is recently nudging me more and more when 'situations' like that 'mysteriously' appear. There can be healing in sharing – in connection.
- Secondly - A gentle emotional release would not have surprised me if we had been discussing a particular symptom or issue, but the incredible explosive response at the mere mention of the term PTSD from someone shocked me. It must have been

> building within him and the term simply popped the cork from the bottle.

I know we both walked away feeling better for our healing experience, which showed in his face and his handshake. We can now consciously draw on that experience for further healing. What a blessing in disguise for us both!

Breathe in/🐾/Breathe out/🐾/Breathe in/🐾/Breathe out/🐾

A Blessing in Disguise

Did you ever have an event happen in your life that seemed like a disaster for you, but eventually on hindsight appeared to be more of a blessing in disguise? Such was my case. In the early stages of my *D-Tour*, my situation seemed to be setting me back physically, emotionally and financially. The lack of work put pressure on top of the typical concerns about a mortgage and other living expenditures. Emotional support for my wife and three teenage children was still needed, while I was trying to get myself 'back together' and on track.

We had recently moved to a small rural community in the Hunter region of New South Wales after fifteen years on the Central Coast. We left behind our network of family and friends, over an hour away. We were all trying to adjust to a new lifestyle where we didn't know anyone and our three kids still at home were trying integrate into a different high school.

Being mostly unemployed for long periods, I was given an unexpected gift that was obviously lacking in my life for a while prior to the side track. I was handed an opportunity to re-allocate the way I used my time. I was still focused on ways to support my family, but much of the time that had been used for employment and getting to and from my work had become available to me for other uses.

It was difficult for a while to enjoy that 'extra' time since I still used much of it to look for work and figure out ways to make ends meet or to simply worry about it. Eventually I changed the way I tried to manage it. It was a stressful time, but I had more time to interact with my family, communicate with distant friends and relatives, learn new things on the internet, do woodwork I enjoyed, and to read when I could hold my concentration. I didn't see the true value in all that at the time due to the concerns I let weigh me down, and trying to see through the fog in my head.

That also lead led me to getting involved with Stroud Writers, a lovely group of generally older people with an interest in that area. Most had reached that stage of life where they could devote more time to that passion. My drawing to them was at the urging of Kris when she met a member, Jean Moase. I had a desire to learn how to leave a personal and family history in some form to my children so I agreed to join.

My good neighbour Dennis McCann (Macca) managed to get me past my reluctance to interact with other veterans or other groups. I joined his ex-servicemen's club at Maitland and took part in the parade on ANZAC day each year after that. I learned to enjoy and appreciate their acceptance and assistance which helped to gradually pull me out of my anti-social rut to some extent.

They were all factors in shifting my perspective and direction in my life that I now see largely as favourable. It certainly didn't appear that way to be in the beginning. It took a seemingly sudden event I had actually created over a long period of time, to put me in a situation where I could stop, look, and respond in a different way.

How many people are ever granted that 'opportunity' which may have presented itself as a muddy pit on the path of life? How many people will recognise it as such and appreciate it for that? Most of us live our lives at a stressful pace in order to 'get ahead' or reach some goal, with little time to appreciate the journey along the way. We tend to work hard and save our money for a vacation or holiday that often times iss more hectic than our normal pace of life - then go back to work from holidays to have a rest!

That's all good too, but do we take the time along the way to connect with our Self regardless of what we are doing? Before marriage and family became my focus, I had done so, but I had to re-engage that practice which led me to a new level of awareness of myself and the world around me. Why did it take something so overwhelming in order to get me to wake up that aspect of myself that obviously wanted my attention?

Breathe in/🐾/Breathe out/🐾/Breathe in/🐾/Breathe out/🐾

Down to the Nitty Gritty

For the sake of simplicity, I refer to the whole mix of stress-related conditions as 'the Stress Family', or just 'Stress'. In particular - anxiety, trauma, Post-Traumatic Stress Disorder, and depression.

- Many of the traits of PTSD, anxiety and depression are similar. They can affect our ability to physically read, hold our attention, connect the words into thoughts in the message, to understand, catalogue, and remember – even as we read those very words.
- I have found the remedies we use for pain and depression relief can interfere with our reading and mental processes as well. I may feel relaxed by them, but not mentally clear and sharp.

To be able to pass along the information held in this book within a few brief, easily digestible pages would be great. However, I haven't mastered that. Still, just for people like me that have had trouble holding onto thoughts during reading, I shall attempt to simplify and condense some bits within this brief chapter which might help . . .

🐾🐾

Not everyone can or wants to take the time to read a book to find out some information to which they feel drawn to know about - or to simply be entertained by.

Some people truly have difficulty holding their attention while reading even if they are very interested.

They can't remember what they have read while they are reading it.

Busy mind with too many thoughts that won't obey orders to be quiet while they read.

If you struggle with those issues, you are in good company, and plenty of it.

Oh yes, of course – I nearly forgot - the "I don't have time" issue.

I've suffered with all those at times -

I couldn't keep the carriages of my train of thought on the same track at the same time.

A hindrance to such a convenient method of learning (reading - and listening).

Solutions?

Perhaps get someone else to read it to you.

Or, they can read it and tell you what it is about.

That doesn't work well for me, but we are all different aren't we?

Speaking of which, the perception of each reader is different, so you only get their interpretation of it anyway.

How about the idea used by every student since the creation of books? – To sleep with it under your pillow to absorb the contents by osmosis. It hasn't been overly successful for me thus far.

Just trying to be helpful here - looking for options.

My method of reading: read as much as I can absorb in one thought or idea, consider it, and read on until I hit the 'full' mark, and the mind wanders. Find a brainless activity until it settles. Rerun. Don't hurry - no worry!

I've read just a line or two and sat with that until I got it - then move on and do it again.

🐾

Much of that condition applies to listening as well – again I fully know ;)

What I have *heard,* quite plainly, is that the problem is *very common.* We are not alone!

I've heard people saying they think that they are 'stupid' or 'dumb' - that and 'bad' memory.

That is wrong!

Gone brain dead might be closer to the truth. Ha!

It is really a case of getting the neurons in the brain firing again and re-wiring pathways.

NO – it not a surgical procedure! ;)

It is fixable!

Can you breathe?

If so, the YOU *can do it*!

Breathe in/🐾/Breathe out/🐾/Breathe in/🐾/Breathe out/🐾

Yep – just follow that instruction for 'a while', thinking about each breath in and out as you do it.

BTW - 🐾 indicates having a 2 second 'pause' between in and out – (yes I know – I've been told).

(Just focus on your breath, ignoring my sic puns thank you).

Conscious breathing gives you a triple-whammy –

1. It starts to restore order in the brain, 2. Calms the mind, *and* 3. Calms the body.

You are forcing your mind to focus on what you are doing – retraining it to **follow your command! Being Present.**

Furthermore, fresh regular supply of oxygen makes you start to feel ***alive*** again – what a bonus!

No surgery, no funny little pills, no poking or peering into ears to see if there is a brain inside.

Yep, just -

Breathe in/🐾/Breathe out/🐾/Breathe in/🐾/Breathe out/🐾

There is no right or wrong way. Just breathe and experiment with it and see where it takes you. You will probably be very pleasantly surprised how fun and easy it is once you let go of expectations. Just focus on each breath and keep breathing . . . and *enjoy* it! Too simple, right? You can learn techniques elsewhere to breathe in much more powerful ways which will energize yourself to get your mind, your memory, and your life back!

STRESS

Chronic Unmanaged Stress, is the Greatest Underlying Contributing Factor to Health Problems and Death in Australia and the U.S.!!!

Being able to manage STRESS
is crucial to our well-being!

Well-managed Stress –

- ***Is Powerful!***
- Can be a great source of ***energy*** to achieve your desires in a positive way!
- Is achievable for most people

Thankfully -

- There is much assistance available within both ancient and modern methods
- Moreover, we already have the ***power*** **within us!**
- We innately know what is best for us – we just have to listen to ourselves, and
- Follow the inner wisdom of our heart and mind

Beyond Peace of Mind –

- Step 1 of restoring order in our mental processes is finding 'peace of mind'
- A Mind at ***Peace*** can then be Life's greatest treasure
- Creative; organized; logical; efficient; intuitive; reasoning; focused; fun; funny; happy; energized; mental clarity

- There are formulas within this book . . .

Stress is 'allowing' the world around me to make Chaos of my *'inner'* world – that private world behind my eyes only *'I'* can see. It is entirely up to me whether that happens or not. I can flap my lips and wag my tongue and perhaps fool people into thinking that I am sane, okay. Or, maybe not fool them. Ha! In any case, it is what goes on in my private thoughts that determines whether or not I really have my act together.

- That is where my potential Chaos must be managed – Centre Stage of My Mind.
- That is where dark thoughts hide behind the curtains to jump onto the stage when it gets quiet
- That is where I must be an effective 'stage manager', curtailing impromptu interruptions
- That is where I must keep the peace so I can formulate cohesive thoughts into expressions
- That is where I must be able to find the letters of my Scrabble board to form thoughts and words and spell them out in a cohesive manner in order to communicate effectively.

How do I do that?

Well, you'll just have to find it hidden somewhere in this book.

- But in short, it goes back to what I said earlier – managing my breath in a 'mindful' manner.
- I'll never stop saying – "It's all in the breath" as the core method to overcome all forms of stress and focus on wellness.
- That leads to the 'simple' art of *meditation*!

Meditation Enables Me

- To find peace of mind
- Improves my ability to think clearly

- Relaxes my body
- Greater sense of well-being/feeling *alive*
- Be creative
- Improves my sleep / Reduces the amount of sleep I need
- Connect within the framework of myself
- Connect to the earth
- Connect to Divinity/the Universal Mind

Now – before you tell me you *can't* . . . let me just say that *we **all** meditate* – everyday!
We either do it unconsciously or consciously (mindfully).
We do a form of it without realising it as we sit –

- Staring into space thinking about being in a situation different to the one we are in
- Mesmerised by the TV ad in front of us while we think of something totally different
- Driving our car as if it is on autopilot while we think about something totally different
- Being non-present in a conversation with someone
- Riding on the train or bus, staring out the window in a 'dream-like state'
- We are virtually oblivious to the world around us while we focus on our 'inner vision'

Effective meditation is using that 'dream-like state' in a more '*mindful*' way.
We can *consciously* enter that state -

- Through guided meditations in groups or alone
- Through music, sounds, silence, connecting to Earth and Divine Energy
- Through practice - to eventually arrive in that *peace* virtually instantly anywhere, anytime
- Observing thoughts and emotions - allowing them to pass *through* - and to

- Pay attention to those that *seem/feel beneficial* to focus upon
- A quiet place can be helpful, but can't you tune out someone talking to you while focus on a TV program or ??? Eventually you can meditate under any conditions

You can find out more on the enormous benefits of meditation for our mental, physical, and spiritual well-being and as a more empowering healing tool in another part of the book. There are many avenues available outside the scope of this book to pursue that as well.

Meditation in a More Powerful Way

It is the key to unlocking the doorway which places us in the point between the *energies* of the *'Earthly' divine* sense, and those *energies* of a more *'Heavenly' divine* sense, if we choose to do so.

In order to turn that key, we must open up both our heart and our mind so they can dance to the orchestration that takes place. That combined energy is different each and every time I do it, regardless of how identical to another time I might have gone about it, because all three factors are constantly in motion.

It is up to the mind to ask the partner to dance, then step back from active thinking to let the music and movement take over with an open heart. You have an awareness happening, but 'overthinking' inhibits the music, diminishing the potential magic of the moment. Just observe the thoughts/feelings and let them flow.

- Our *awareness* and *intuition* are switched on more fully in our mind's eye
- Our energy/thoughts/feelings receptors and transmitters become more powerful
- All things become possible in that *creative* state of being, sensing Oneness with All
- We can reach a greater point of *healing* for our mind, our body, and our spirit

- Spontaneous healing is a possibility by raising the vibration of *Love* to a state of *Wholeness* when the magic of *belief* and *passion* are in the mix!

🐾🐾

Some *D-Tour* Random Radical Readjustments (that have helped me) –

- Accepting myself for who I am
- Feeling appreciation for - my life, well-being, family, friends, abundance, love, grace
- Imagining myself in the ***joy***ful times of my childhood; relived it, mentally and/or physically
- Letting go – of perfectionism; fear of ideas of what others think of me; fear of 'death'
- Letting go – of feeling unworthy of the goodness and love of family, friends, or anyone
- Being the Boundary Rider of my mind – saying 'STOP' to unwelcome strays trying to enter
- Looking at and *appreciating the beauty* of the world we live in
- Focusing on what I *want* my world to *look* like and *feel* like, rather than the problems
- Surrounding myself with the people and the ways of achieving that
- Focusing on my *well-ness* and *whole-ness* rather than 'problems'
- Assisting others with 'problems'
- *Appreciating* the power in discipline, habits, structure and rituals
- *Appreciating* the vitality and joy that freedom of spirit and creativity bring
- Realising that *EVERYTHING is ENERGY* and the infinite implications
- Seeing and *appreciating* a greater sense of the divinity in our humanness

- Seeing the thread of *Spirit* running through every thing, thus making every thing Sacred, which affects my perception and appreciation of life – a game of Life changer
- If I believe *everything is Sacred*, then my attitude is different to all of life and our world
- Surrendering to my perception of a ***Greater Power*** that has my back - and everything else!
- *NEVER GIVING UP* on my 'self' or our world!

In a Nutshell

The Purpose of this Book is to Help Others with What I Have Learned -

- My objective was and is to find my optimum potential for ***well-being***
- Everything is ***Energy*** = ***Energy*** is Everything (Einstein and Tesla edicts)
- ***Power*** = ***Energy***
- ***Pure Energy*** = ***Power*** = ***Love***
- ***Vitality*** = ***Power***
- ***Wellness*** = ***Vitality***
- Un-wellness/Disease = Stagnant/Low *Energy*
- ***Healing Power*** = ***Movement*** **of** ***Energy (Love)*** = ***Vitality*** = ***Wholeness***
- ***Rapid/Spontaneous Healing*** = ***Powerful Movement of Energy (Love)***
- ***SUPER POWER Healing*** = ***Divine Connection*** = ***HOLY SPIRIT***
- Our **well-being** revolves creating a ***coherent flow of energy*** through our body, our mind, and our spirit (heart and mind) in a balanced way = ***Power (Love)***
- Peace of Mind, Self-empowerment, and Joyfulness result from that creative process
- Peace of Mind comes with Unconditional Love and Acceptance of All That Is

- Unconditional Love includes loving and accepting one's self
- The focus of my beliefs, intentions and desires, fuelled by an expression of gratitude for my abundance, are the keys to my well-being and happiness
- The fastest, most effective way of finding that point and holding on to it is through a co-creative, self-empowered process of *energy* management
- I needed assistance to learn those lessons and processes
- I had to let go of crap and allow/accept that help from some sources of wisdom
- I learned to self-manage while being nurtured with more assistance and knowing
- I feed my *energy* daily through effective energy practices and continued learning
- That *energy* flow still involves 'letting go' as well as the incoming
- There are many paths to our **d**esired **d**estination
- There is no right or wrong path, but happiness is a good guide
- My Soul took me on a *D-Tour* path to achieve my needs – you may not need to??
- Look for the Ones with wisdom (head) and an *energy* that resonates with your heart
- The answer will lay in your gut . . .

Solution Oriented Focus

Most of us, by nature or by training, focus our attention on ways to solve a problem based on past experience rather than on creative new ways. As Einstein suggested, we have to change our level of thinking in order to solve a problem. Think outside the box as they say. Try this:

- Focus on the solution, not the problem.
- Think about what you want. Now think about how you want it to *feel* like when you get what you want. See and *feel* it as already done.
- Have total faith or confidence that it will be done or solved. *Believe* it! *Feel* it!

I have learned a very important truth in my pursuit of happiness: the best method to solve many of our issues is actually through our feelings rather than our thoughts. It sounds illogical and it is; but it has proven it can be the most effective for several reasons.

- It has been scientifically proven (neurologically) that we can not solve problems while we are in a heightened state of 'fight or flight'. If you have PTSD (and other states of stress/anxiety) you are in that state somewhere between occasionally and virtually always to a lesser extent.
- We are functioning from an area of the brain that is triggered by our biochemistry, where the senses receptors are focused on survival and not solutions to problems.
- Consequently we find it hard to focus our thinking abilities when we are distracted by the chemistry going on in our brain for survival instincts.
- The problem-solving area of our brain mind functions far more effectively while in a relaxed state. That comes with a feeling, not a thought.

- We can reach that place through meditation which clears the mind of thoughts and the body of tension.
- We can then think more clearly when we choose to resume our have logical thought processes.
- We cannot solve problems while we are caught up in a mental tail-spin or negative thought loop. We can clear that by creating the space through our feelings, which I'll cover in more detail in another part of the book.
- Consider the problem; if the answer doesn't come, step back from it and allow the solution to come to you when you are in a future relaxed, receptive mode.
- That could be when you are asleep or in a semi-conscious state.
- Have you ever woken in the night or next morning with the answer to a problem you'd been thinking about the day before? Or out of the blue, you remembered a name or where you put something long after you'd given up wondering or looking?
- That is allowing the answer to come to you in a clear mind space, rather than in busy mental pursuit; an effective, energy-saving tool.

Breathe in/🐾/Breathe out/🐾/Breathe in/🐾/Breathe out/🐾

Who What Why Where

"The best teachers are those who show you where to look, but don't tell you what to see".
— Alexandra K. Trenfor

Further Information

I cannot and do not claim to be an authority or expert on the subject of this book. I've written an account of what I have learned in my own experience and wish to pass on to others in the hope of helping. Further to that, I suggest pursuing the now vast amount of advice and information of experts in order to gain greater understanding and results in your quest to heal.

There is an incredible amount of information available in various forms and places that can further assist in your search for a better understanding and treatment of the topics in this book. The internet of course is quick and vast for a wealth of articles, studies, discussion groups or blogs, and e-books in addition to the usual source in bookshops and libraries.

There are so many wonderful and beneficial books available at this time with great new ones almost daily. Naturally I can't list them all so I will leave the search to you apart from a few I highly value. You will find the right ones for you once you start your search for an understanding and remedy at an appropriate level at the time. Be led by your intuition.

My experience was that I could only comprehend in a limited way in my early stages of PTSD, which improved as the anxiety reduced and my mind started to clear. Simplicity was important when I was stressed and my attention span was short.

You can feel your way or you can jump in the deep end and drift back to what you find you able to assimilate. The following is a compilation of books that I have found to be beneficial, uplifting or have a profound effect on me, or that I know to have had on others.

I've numbered these books for the sake of keeping things clearly defined rather than as a value of importance. I recommend them all as effective aids in understanding and tools for healing.

1. *Becoming Supernatural: How Common People Are Doing the Uncommon,*
2. *Breaking the Habit of Being Yourself*
3. *You Are the PLACEBO.* by Dr Joe Dispenza. Published by Hay House Inc.
   www.drjoedispenza.com

   The cutting edge work Dr Dispenza is doing in the field of neurology clinically tests, records and shows what is happening in our brain and body under varying circumstances. It is fascinating, expansive, and healing through transformation from our old behaviour patterns to what we individually want to become.

   He explains better than anyone I have ever heard, how conscious thinking alone won't get us there. We need to consciously re-program our thoughts and feelings that are trapped in our sub-conscious that have been showing up as undesired habits and other behaviour.

   He provides the successful formula through his books, workshops, cd, and YouTube videos that has brought about remarkable improvement and recovery from a variety of disease symptoms and conditions. I believe the remarkable achievements are due to his great understanding of human anatomy and behaviour and applying that first-hand to himself and those attending his gatherings. He leads by example with full participation on a constantly evolving level of awareness and methods of practice.

   I can attest to a greater sense of well-being, improved energy, mental clarity and memory in a short space of time through three of his workshop/retreats. Each was effective and healing.

4. *Earthing* by Clinton Ober, Stephen T. Sinatra, M.D., and Martin Zucker. Published by Basic Health Publications, Inc.
   This scientific study shows the incredible connection to free empowering at our feet: the Earth. It tells how that natural energy can quickly stabilize our bodily energy into homeostasis, often correcting long-time health ailments and a sense of well-being. A very worthwhile read. I feel the benefits by following the advice therein.

5. *In An Unspoken Voice* by Peter A. Levine, Phd. Published by North Atlantic Books (www.northatlanticbooks.com).
6. *Waking the Tiger: Healing Trauma* by Peter A. Levine with Ann Frederick published by North Atlantic Books (www.northatlanticbooks.com).

   These two books on trauma by the man considered to be one of the best authorities on PTSD. He gives an excellent understandable explanation of the condition - what creates it and how to deal with it, including some exercises to help. *Perhaps even more importantly,* ***it offers hope with evidence that the condition is curable***, which differs in opinion to much of the medical establishment.
   Dr Levine's follow up book *In an Unspoken Voice* is likewise excellent. I recommend both.
7. *Mind Over Medicine: Scientific Proof You Can Heal Yourself* by Dr. Lissa Rankin.
   An excellent read about the power of belief and your mind in order to heal.
8. *Tapping the Healer Within* by Roger J. Callahan, Ph. D. Published by McGraw-Hill.

   A very good book on the incredible power of tapping by an authority on it.

9. *The Biology of Belief* by Bruce H. Lipton, Ph. D. Published by Hay House Inc.
   A powerful summary of diligent research showing the spiritual/scientific connection between consciousness and our human biology through quantum physics. He explains how and why we can effectively engineer our lives and wellness through our thinking.

10. *The Divine Matrix* by Gregg Braden. Published by Hay House, Inc. Another powerful book to looks at the bringing together the wisdom of the ages with the science of quantum physics – a greater expansion and understanding of consciousness.

11. *The Miracle of the Breath* by Andy Caponigro, published by New World Library.

    This book takes the topic through several levels I've found beneficial. There are many sources available for teaching breathing techniques. I suggest you simply find some that suit you, as people vary so much in preference of style in what they intend to achieve. I have also provided some simple exercises to start with that can be expanded. Initially some guidance can be beneficial through video, cd, internet, books or personal help from someone for quicker and expanded knowledge.

12. *The Power of Eight: Harnessing the Miraculous Energies of a Small Group to Heal Others, Your Life, and the World* by Lynne McTaggart. Published by Simon and Schuster, Inc.

    A fascinating scientific study of the incredible power of intention – groups of people sending positive thoughts through prayer and meditation to heal others. Lynne experimented with carefully organized protocols using varying numbers in the groups. The amazing unexpected find was the benefits received by the healers sending their intention for healing. A great read!

13. *The Tapping Solution (The Revolution Starts Within)* by Nick Ortner.

    A great guide to tapping by a recognized expert on the methods and benefits.

Breathe in/🐾/Breathe out/🐾/Breathe in/🐾/Breathe out/🐾

My Tool Kit

Acceptance

- Shortcut to Peace of Mind
- Cuts friction and unhappiness with differences between yourself and all else
- Accept Life for what it is – that eliminates much pain, suffering and 'correction'
- Accept others for who/what they are – their life is their own to manage
- Accept my self – eliminates much pain and suffering
- Change only things which are for the betterment of myself and all

Bath

- Time to relax, meditate, contemplate

Brain exercises; crosswords, Sudoku, card games, computer games, games of all types

- Helps keep brain/mind active and healthy, Use it or lose it

Breathing

- Fundamental - first and foremost tool in the kit
- Powerful aid to energizing, relaxing, healing, meditation
- Can quickly ease anxiety and restore emotional balance, clear mind and calm body
- Gives sense of well-being, improves health

Change

- Do something different – be creative in whatever that can mean

Communication

- Connect with family, friends, groups, community, leaders, pets

- Helps to feel a sense of connection, heals differences, 're-wires' the brain
- Talking with someone can be very healing for one or both
- Writing, like talking, is a very effective healer

Compassion

- Opens the heart for powerful healing of pain and suffering for others and myself

Contemplate

- Hmmm – consider, dwell, ponder, chew it over, dream, sleep on it, THINK (ha)!

Dance

- Moves energy, is uplifting, fun

Discernment

- Every thought and feelings impacts my well-being so I've learned to be selective
- What thoughts and feelings will I allow to occupy my head and body?
- What is important to me and deserves my energy of attention, vs what isn't which takes my energy
- Decide what I allow to invade my attention – i.e. various media, information

Distractions

- Do an activity to take my mind away from a current problem or thought loop

Games

- Makes life fun, challenges/tests abilities, improves skills, relaxes

Forgiveness

- Such a blessed relief to release issues attached to anger and other emotions that hold us back from moving forward with our lives
- Frees the energy for focus of our attention towards constructive issues and well-being
- Feels good to let go (feeling good is healing energy)

Exercise in all forms –

- Walking and running, hiking, swimming, tennis and other sports
- Strengthens; invigorates; calms; balances mind and body energies; fun and enjoyable
- Use it or lose it

Intuition

- One of my 'best friends'
- Trust my 'gut' instinct
- Use all my avenues of perception, but read between the lines of the obvious

Laughter

- Relaxes, relieves tension, gives sense of joy, be spontaneous, improves my health

Massage

- Relieves tension and relaxes the body and mind, healing

Meditation

- Brings peace within, emotional balance, clarity of mind, relaxes the body
- Can connect to 'God', the' Universal Mind/Energy'
- Can alter states of consciousness – going from depression up to bliss
- Decreases anxiety, stress and depression

Mindfulness practice

- Getting and staying present and consciously aware

Movement

- Keeps the body moving and the mind active for feeling good and longevity
- Walking to whatever moves you

Music

- Singing, playing instrument or listening to
- Alters moods and emotions; soothes, calms, uplifts spirits, relaxes, inspires, energizes, improves brain connectivity/ function

Nature

- My friend for 'life' – pun intended; always there for me to heal and nurture me
- The 'natur-al' soother and energizer of life – the rapid refresher
- Connects to beauty and the life force energy of Earth

Pain

- Yes – surprise, surprise!
- Gets our attention
- 'Befriended' this unlikely 'teacher' to guide me to connect to my Inner Self
- Follow the pain path and ask the right questions

Play

- Makes life fun, adds vitality to mind and body
- With children, friends, pets
- With groups, individuals, on my own

Power

- Our life force –feed it, nurture it, use it wisely
- Balance it – don't avoid it, abuse it, or give it away

- Integrate knowledge into effective action for my well-being and the greater good of all
- All of my power is in this present moment

Prayer

- A daily or more frequent conversation with the Divine
- Connects to 'God' / 'Universal Mind/Energy', brings peace, access to divine assistance, send love/support to others

Reading

- Educates, informs, takes thoughts away from problems, entertains, brings enjoyment

Release

- Let go – feel the freedom after letting go of attachment to pain, suffering, excesses

Sauna

- Relaxes, cleanses/detoxes/purifies the body – sweat it out

Sleep and rest

- Quality sleep and rest to re-energize the body and mind
- Vital to overall well-being

Stretches

- Tones and balances body energies; improves flexibility, strength, digestion, well-being

Tapping (Emotional Freedom Technique, Thought Field Therapy)

- A simple yet very powerful tool to release trapped emotions of fear, anxiety and depression. Quicker, easier, less confronting than counselling.

Visualisation

- Create positive images (imag-in-ation), shift perceptions
- 'See' your desires, 'dreams', and intentions to reach your goals

Voice

- Speak my truth with balance from my heart and my mind
- Listen to my Inner Voice

Yoga

- The ultimate exercise; stretches and tones the body; balances body, mind and spirit

Zumba

- Never tried it but sounds like FUN! Gets energy MOVING!

Breathe in/🐾/Breathe out/🐾/Breathe in/🐾/Breathe out/🐾

Summary

The Circle

Native cultures have always measured time as a series of circles, naturally enough - seasons, years, life-times - from earth back to earth. As I come to the end of this year and the end of this book, it is the end of some cycles in the circle of my life, and the emergence of others.

Since I started writing this book in 2011, I have circled the sun seven of my overall seventy times. My *D-Tour* journey has been a sometimes difficult, but ultimately a fulfilling search for finding my wellness. In the process, beyond physical and emotional healing, I have found a greater sense of awareness of myself and some of the wonders our world. The unexpected re-discovery of the *joy* I once knew as a young child has been a wonderful bonus - another circle.

There has been circles within circles. I have visited my birth land several times during that period. Each occasion, helping me to heal more from the pain of separation and missing aspects of myself, as I re-connected more fully with my family, friends, and the land that I love.

There has much travel to other interesting lands with many enriching activities which has expanded my awareness of life on our beautiful planet. There has been a gradual convergence of my scattered 'self' in the process that brings me more into alignment and wholeness. My circle has been a spiraling vortex which has lifted me to a new level of wellness, awareness and enjoyment of life. I continue to fill that space with my family, friends and adventure.

Another circle of the sun was completed today, 1 January 2019 – a day characterised by resolutions and hope for improvement in our lives and our world. The closure of an amazing year was celebrated, and the New Year welcomed at midnight with a fireworks display from Sydney, first across the planet on TV. Incredibly, that much anticipated spectacle seems to out-do itself each year for the millions waiting for hours around Sydney Harbour.

Earlier yesterday, I gave up the 'hope' of completing this book by the end of the year, then just hours away. Closeness to the goal doesn't really count. It was the excitement of anticipation of the closure of a seven year circle while looking at details for the manuscript submission forms.

Missing yet another self-imposed deadline for completion was just another acceptance of timing and patience for me. But by still working on it, something else may have been of benefit in what I am about to share.

As I stood in the shower this first morning birthing a new year, I thought about the imminent birth of my book. While I adjusted the water, I couldn't help but notice the various irritating and sometimes embarrassing growths that have appeared on my body throughout much of my lifetime and continue to do so. Why? Will they ever stop? I have been searching for solutions for most of my life. The emotions I've suppressed from an early age is the simple answer to the reason, but clearing those energies within me is the challenge.

It is said that they are irritations wanting out of my body in whatever form they have taken – pimples, acne, blisters, warts, moles, cysts, basal cell melanomas, or boils. It can be difficult to distinguish between some of them.

As I pondered the question, a thought about the message of my book popped into my head –

- That in my search for overcoming the effects of trauma and stress, I ultimately found *joy* and a greater sense of *well-being* than I had ever had.
- That they had not been my objectives
- They were bonuses beyond my efforts to 'get my life back'
- Isn't finding our '*happiness*' the ultimate, elusive, intangible quest for humanity?
- If I had already found that in my search, what did anything like skin issues *really* matter?
- Why should I waste my valuable *energy* on 'skin problems'

- The realisation was a light bulb moment of things I knew, but hadn't connected until then

I know that –

- *Everything is Energy* vibrating at virtually infinite variations – including my skin and irritation
- Where I hold my attention and intention is where my *energy* is
- My *energy* management is the key to my well-being
- Healing comes through focusing my attention on how *I want to be* – not the problem
- Feeling '*good*' or '*joyful*' and *appreciative* is the key to unlocking the *power* to heal
- Therefore I cannot heal effectively if I am focusing on my skin 'problems'
- I must focus on my wholeness in a state of *Joy* (which I have already achieved!)
- The highest measured vibration of *energy* is *Love*
- The ultimate healing energy is *Unconditional Love*
- So, my new year aim is to focus my *energy* on my daily practices and being *Unconditional Love and Joy*

My daily practices of good habits – healthy food, plenty of water, sleep, movement, loving relationships, meditation, and prayer – crucial for me to balance my well-being. Happy New Year!

Breathe in/🐾/Breathe out/🐾/Breathe in/🐾/Breathe out/🐾

In Recent Times

One of the Australian singers that entertained Australian troops in Vietnam, along with Col Joye, was 'Little Pattie' Amphlett, at just 17 years of age and 58 inches tall. They had been entertaining all afternoon at Long Tan on August 18, 1966 when their show was interrupted by what was to be the biggest, most significant battle of the war for Australian troops. Sadly, 18 soldiers were killed and 24 wounded in the following hours. She was taken from danger by helicopter as things erupted, but events of those days in Vietnam were deeply felt by her.

Pattie has dedicated a great deal of her time to supporting troops and veterans, as well other causes over her lifetime, and continues to do so. Although I didn't see her perform while I was in Vietnam, I was fortunate to hear her sing *'It's a Wonderful World'* (*beautifully*) at the Vietnam Veteran's Day ceremony in Sydney this year. In spite of the fact the commemoration was in honour of the Australian Forces, I felt deeply moved by the ceremony.

Carol Ward, a long-time friend of mine and retired Warrant Officer in the Australian Army, was the dedicated and diligent organiser and MC for the event, as she had been for five years.

Little Patti singing Place Veitnams Veteran's Day

Vietnam Veteran's Day Sydney 2018 photo kindly supplied by Kaelee Aboud

with Carol Ward at Martin cenotaph 18 Aug 2018

Where Has my *D-Tour* Taken Me?

I've shared how I've shifted my feelings and state of being over the course of my ***D-Tour***.

- How do I face our challenging world now without simply suppressing those feelings?
- Or pretend my war involvement never happened and deal with the thoughts and feelings I held around that matter?
- Or that the current conflicts across our planet don't exist or matter to me?
- I am still aware; I do care, and I am pro-active in seeking positive change in our world community.
- In spite of a feeling of optimism for our world, I still feel a lot of pain for humanity and our planet. I still have fears and tears.
- I handle the emotions I feel caused by the impact of events very differently now.
- I've learned to manage the feelings like fear or passion or anger in a better way – to be aware of what I feel, but then to observe what it is that creates that emotion within me.
- What are those emotions telling me?
- Can I do something about it in an effective positive way?
- Those are ***powerful*** energies - not to be wasted in a negative way or suppressed within me to boil.
- Am I being biased; judgmental; foolish; or objective; realistic; honest; discerning; justified; fair; balanced; caring; forgiving; compassionate; loving?
- Can I do something positive about the situation? Take positive action? Negotiate? Communicate?
- Can I send love? Can I say a prayer, convinced of its power? Can I let go of unwanted debilitating emotions? Can I restore/

maintain peace within me, using meditation, connection to nature and the Divine, or re-balancing my heart and mind?

Being able to balance the *energy* of my thoughts and emotions now makes my life so much easier and enjoyable, with so much more *effective energy* than when I started my ***D-Tour***. I'm sure it makes it much more pleasant for those I interact with as well.

It took a shift in my consciousness and behaviour over a few years.

- Ironically, that probably would not have happened without me having to grapple with PTSD.
- Having that situation in my life effectively forced me to stop and recover.
- It gave me the time and space to analyse *who* I am, *where* I am headed, where I *want* to be headed and what options are available, if any, beyond just asking myself '*why*?'
- Such was my ***D-Tour.***
- It took me along a path of **d**iscovery to move beyond the mental and physical **d**ebilitating **d**ysfunction and **d**isempowering **d**isability in which I unexpectedly found myself.
- At times I felt trapped; cornered; uncertain; frustrated; angry; hopeless.
- I could not let the **d**estructive **d**emons of PTSD **d**estroy me, as it **d**ragged me through a period of **d**ark night of my soul.
- I **d**ecided to turn those **d's** around into an empowering ability to take my life back, through a **d**eliberate **d**esign and **d**iscernment to a **d**ifferent **d**estiny.
- I had to let go of those parts of me I no longer wished to carry.
- I had to find and put back together the aspects of my being that had become **d**ispersed over much of my lifetime.
- In spite of my wellness now, I continue to search for ways and means to move on to the greatest possible wholeness of my being in body, mind and spirit.
- Ultimately my ***D-Tour*** has been a *blessing* in **d**isguise.

- It became my re-connection to the ***Divine*** – meandering around on a sometimes difficult but determined effort to find my way to good health.
- Unexpectedly I found my ***joy*** in the process.

Over the course of my ***D-Tour*** years, I had to deal with a number of physical conditions which were largely attributable to trauma and stress. I can now say that medical and scientific evidence shows that I am in very good health - physically and mentally. Feeling any pain in my body is a rare phenomenon.

Beyond any conventional medical care, I believe my efforts to attain wellness was greatly enhanced through alternative approach medicine. Those include various modalities like meditation, massage, and healing practices such as sweat lodge, and *energy* 'healing' – both 'hands off' and 'hands on' – along with a heaping helping of God's Good Grace.

At the point of being diagnosed with the condition, I was simply trying to cope – typical for people who have experienced trauma. My life has altered dramatically, going from a state of unable to function effectively in many respects, to reach a point where I feel I truly have my life back – well beyond what it was prior.

I have an outlook of joyfulness and optimism. Whenever any of those companions leave me now, I am quick to sense that. I can employ my tools and address the problem. Largely through ***simple daily practices***, I have developed a pattern that keeps me peaceful, positive and healthy.

Overall, it has been a journey of '*Self*'-ish-ness. I had to focus on my '*Self*'. Pre-flight instructions on every commercial aircraft tell us to use the oxygen mask that drops down for each passenger in the event of a loss of oxygen in the cabin – to care for your '*self*' first before trying to help others.

I had to save my '*Self*' first and foremost . . . from my '*Self*' - my limiting and sometimes destructive behaviour. I surrendered to the price of whatever that took to achieve – ultimately an acceptance of Divine help.

I can now appreciate my '*Self*' more, and consequently others, as a result. My *D-Tour* has taken down that path. I have to be most grateful for my journey. *I am that I am*.

❧❧

I feel so fortunate that I born into this incredible age of growing consciousness. There is an expansion of knowledge and wisdom that is becoming so freely available to me through a wide range of sources. My growth in awareness and well-being is only limited by my imagination, desire, choices, and the time to partake of the knowledge and actively participate. It is always a work-in-progress . . . albeit a *joyful* one!

I have

- many wonderful friends
- access to – a fantastic medical system
- effective energy healers
- to education and guidance from dozens of teachers, both personal and distant.

That enriches me mentally, emotionally, physically and spiritually.

The ultimate of those has been my family - my parents, siblings, children and my partners in relationships through my life.

I feel truly *blessed.*

As I embrace and *enjoy* the essence of such in my personal life, I can focus more and more on trying to be a benefit to others – a pay back in service to humanity in various ways for my period of 'self'-ishness.

On the broader landscape, we are now flooded with choices as the expansion continues to lift up our personal, family, community and global awareness, and hopefully, the peace within us and our world. I encourage you to seek and embrace what calls to your heart – your inner wisdom.

"First there must be order and harmony within your own mind. Then this order will spread to your family, then to the community and finally to your entire kingdom. Only then can you have peace and harmony."
— Confucius 551–479 BC

We are currently living in a world that seems to have so many problems, but history shows that has always been the case on various scales and levels. I believe we are just more aware of those problems through the networks of information now available to every part of the globe. We know more – but there is much 'good' beyond the 'bad' that is often more eagerly reported by the media.

Where to Now?

Stress is undoubtedly a global epidemic - causing disconnection and disease within and between individuals, families, communities, and countries.

So what is the solution in dealing with life's stresses and traumas? As a result of nearing twenty years of diligently searching for answers for myself, I believe there are several effective ways we can help as individuals and at every level of society.

Education and Awareness –

- learn to identify, prevent and manage stress and trauma from an early age
- Understand our overall energy and the part that stress plays in managing that

Prevention – stop **conflict and war**;

- Work at becoming a more peaceful world – resolve issues through peaceful means
- Peace in our world starts with being at peace within our 'self' – we must find that first
- Be community active – work with others to reduce trauma and stress
- Join a like-minded group – you support others; they support you
- Communicate your views/concerns with community and government leaders

The ramifications of warfare penetrates right through the layers our world, not just the combatants. The bloodlines of the whole human race are flowing through nearly every other country, so effectively, we are all connected and affected directly or indirectly.

There is a huge cost for '**stress**' at every level, from personal to global. Trauma and PTSD are common issues.

- Relationships of all types are effected.
- Stress leave, unheard of a few years ago, is rampant. The economic cost beyond individuals is billions of dollars to U.S. and Australian businesses and government every year in work time lost and health issues with employees.
- People with valuable skills are 'burning out' long before retirement age. They are leaving in droves from critical services like health, teaching and law enforcement which have become very demanding and stressful.

It appears that something has to change for our world to go on. Is it not up to all of us to create a better world for our children and future generations? We are responsible for their welfare. They deserve better than what they are currently getting, don't they? Something to consider -

"We do not inherit the Earth from our Ancestors,
we borrow it from our Children"

My World of Growing Hope for Greater Awareness and Peace

In spite of those views of our current global situation, it is my shifted belief to focus on seeing the incredible beauty of our world and how we want it to be. That includes our wondrous bodies and minds.

In doing so, my energy is channelled towards solutions rather than the problems in a better frame of mind, (which in turn switches on life-enriching hormones).

The challenges humanity now faces may seem overwhelming at times. However, I believe that will pass as more and more people around the world decide it is time to dynamically, yet peacefully, change the situation. I can see evidence that the shift is happening, which gives me hope and optimism. People I know are changing and empowering their lives in positive ways.

Along with our greater awareness, I also believe, comes greater responsibility to do our part as individuals. Should we expect and demand greater responsibility and positive action from our community, government and corporate leaders?

Cracks are appearing in the facade of deceit in both business and governments, with the truth of motives and intentions seeping through to become more obvious. Our more extensive sophisticated communications systems and incredible technology are revealing the flaws with the truth, but also the many *great* things many people are doing. It has also enabled us to see the incredible wonders and beauty in our world of Nature not possible before. The amazing communication, the *Intelligence*, the *Oneness* of it all is being revealed – more and more!

- I believe that *truth* and *love* will ultimately prevail over the misery and mayhem, caused largely by the greed of a small but very powerful minority that control the majority of the wealth on this planet. We all deserve better.
- I believe it calls for awareness and a fearless proactive voice for the sake of humanity to not only endure, but to live in the security and rightful entitlement of peace.
- I believe that there is *always* **hope**! It is the core of our wellness, which is the focus of this book. It is my story of **hope** - **hope** started and achieved by finding peace within my *Self.*
- In turn it is my **hope** that this book will be beneficial for you and others - for servicemen, past or present, their families, and loved ones, or anyone in any walk of life that is dealing with the effects of stress, trauma and wellness issues of any kind.

It is mostly about letting others know that *it is indeed possible to attain that peace and even joy*, and that there are many paths to it. *You and I and everyone everywhere deserve that as a birthright into this Earthly environment!*

Never believe that a few caring people can't change the world.
For, indeed, that's all who ever have.

Margaret Mead (1901 –1978)

My wish for you –
May you find the peace, joy and empowerment which you desire -
May blessings of vibrant wellness rain upon you and through you!

In Unconditional Love,
Greg (and Lucy)

Breathe in/ /Breathe out/ /Breathe in/ /Breathe out/

Acknowledgements

My 'Circle of Life' might sum up this often ignored, yet I feel important, inclusion to most published books. Where does an author begin and end to give credit for contributions, without missing out on some significant, or more likely, some *seemingly* insignificant piece of the circle.

There are so many components at so many levels to this book, which like a mixed salad from a community garden that gets tossed into the bowl, making much of the individual responsibility for what, nearly impossible to identify.

So it is with many of the contributors to this book. Some are memorable for me. Others contributed to my life in ways that have found their way into this manuscript without my conscious awareness. How then do I pay deserving tribute to all that are a part of it?

I want to pay my dues. This apology will precede my attempts to do so, knowing full well I can't remember or list everyone. Interestingly, when I tell someone I want to mention their help, they tend to say they don't expect any for their efforts in assistance with editing, listening, or candidly commenting on content. So, to those that fit into that category, if I haven't already said 'thank you' to you directly, I hope to, and will say it here in case I can't or don't. My sister Rita Colburn, friends Lyn Parks, Janneia Searle, Liana Green, and Christine Gregg come to mind, outside my writers group.

There are some people whom I want to express my gratitude to who were instrumental in seeing this project go beyond idle talk. There should be an obvious starting point to every trail, but of course, as in the circle or the web of life, it can be more difficult to identify.

There were many who influenced me in my lifetime. Naturally, all the members of my family, past and present in so many ways, including Aunt Margaret, but the one who actually got me on the road that led me to writing this book, was my Swedish wife of the time, Kris (Sigrid Kristina Brunnqvist). She had encouraged me for years to follow that interest of mine in a more constructive way beyond my letters, stories, and poems. Thank you Kris for your 'pushing'.

Once I had children, I wanted to leave them a family history they could read or pursue at some stage of their lives if they so desired. At a 'chance' conversation she had with a member of Stroud Writers at a Rainbow Lodge gathering about 2003, Jean Moase, happily connected me to that wonderfully talented and congenial group. They were members of the Fellowship of Australian Writers New South Wales who met for three hours on a bi-weekly basis. The platform was to encourage and assess all forms of writing in a friendly, non-judgmental space in that little town of Stroud. I was warmly welcomed and so it began for me. It was a half-hour drive in the country then, and now an hour, having moved to Newcastle, but I still feel the pull to attend.

So, I wish to express my gratitude to that group for their shared support, encouragement, expertise, and friendship beyond our meetings for over fifteen years, but especially for this project. There have been many members from its inception, and during my attendance, who have contributed to my writing development and enjoyment, and to my social life. Some have passed on, leaving great memories and a legacy of their writing. There are too many to name and feel it would be unfair to name some and not all, so I will leave that appreciation unwritten. I am indebted to you all, past and present.

However, I cannot leave it unsaid, that without our intrepid president, Sue Filson, this book would never have happened. She has dedicated herself to our group all these years through thick and thin with her own life 'distractions'. Her husband Rex, although not a member of the group, has also worked very diligently with us through several successful book publications, and on this one, in editing and sharing his knowledge gained through many other publications. Together, their expert advice and encouragement goes beyond words.

In 2010 I had moved away, but Sue asked me if I would be willing to write about my military experiences for the group's book Battlefields & Homefires: untold stories, (which was published the following year.) When I agreed to do so after some thought, it was the beginning of the cracking open of the door to my heart/mind vault - which led to more healing.

It was difficult to share to our group, first through writing, and then talking about those times in my life I had concealed from others. Emotions surfaced, and I often choked on my words, but it was transforming.

Until then, I hadn't realised the extent of the pain I was carrying around within me, and the degree of resistance towards releasing it publicly. But it was a safe space in which to gradually step into outside of one-on-one counselling or energy healing. It was at the point of submitting my stories for that book that I *knew* I *had* to write my own book.

Thank you Sue, and all of our members, for your gentle, compassionate way of helping me to slip out of the toxic confinement I had formed around me. That helped me to move on to further healing beyond the counselling path and the tears and fears of the telling.

A special 'thank you' to: author friend, Pauline Hosie Robinson in Newcastle, Australia and Susan Barrera, counsellor to veterans with PTSD in Albuquerque, New Mexico - both for sharing their stories of marriages to veterans with PTSD - generously giving their time for reading, commenting, and assisting; to author friend Christina Nealson, who also encouraged, pushed and suggested ways last year to help get me across the line with this project; and to artist Rachael M. Wells for transforming my words into the book cover image with such ease.

I want to say a huge 'thank you' to The Hay House and Balboa Press people like Leon Nacson in Australia, calling for authors at the Sydney Hay House event in 2010, with numerous successful authors and speakers present - and again at the Writer's Workshop in Brisbane in 2015 with Reid Tracy and authors offering valuable advice, encouragement, and inspiration to get on with it.

Also a very special thank you to the spirit of Louise Hay for the creation of such a wonderful organisation concept I truly admire – the reason I chose to go with Balboa Press. I have loved the many inspirational books from so many authors over many years. And of course a special thank you to Gemma Ramos, my current guide through the publishing process at Balboa Press at this crucial stage of manifesting my intention to assist others in this form. I truly appreciate your patient assistance!

Lastly, I have to acknowledge every one of my school teachers for many reasons, but especially my long-suffering English teacher through my four years of high school, Mr Virgil Walle. In the context of this book, he must be looking down in amazement from his well-deserved rest high Above.

I was not his star performer in writing or reading, but somehow he did instil a love in me for some of the American classic writers. At the time, I didn't share his passion for the likes of Shakespeare in their 'funny' expression of English. Many years later I embraced, and have tried to follow, his immortal words I noticed on my desk calendar – to thine own self be true, thus inevitably to others. God help me! May that Supreme Being bless each and every one of you along your path, and all those that I have missed in this acknowledgement. Thank You Divine Ones for your guidance on this incredible journey I could not have possibly orchestrated myself.

Printed in the United States
By Bookmasters